Medimont Reflections

Also by Chris Carlson
Cecil Andrus: Idaho's Greatest Governor (Caxton Press, 2011)
The Intercession of St. Dismas (Privately Published, 2006)
A Brief History of the Gallatin Group (Privately Published, 2010)

MEDIMONT REFLECTIONS

Forty Years of
Issues and Idahoans

Chris Carlson

Foreword by Governor Cecil D. Andrus
Chapter photographs by Barry Kough

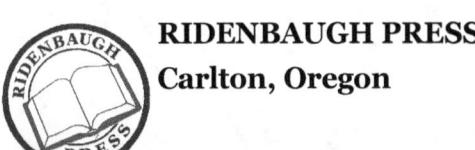

RIDENBAUGH PRESS
Carlton, Oregon

Copyright © 2013 Chris Carlson
All Rights Reserved.
No part of this book may be reproduced, stored in a retrieval system, or transmitted in any form by any means, without prior permission of the publisher.

Composition and editing by Ridenbaugh Press, Carlton, Oregon.
Cover design by Randy Stapilus.

Library of Congress Cataloging-in-Publication Data:

Carlson, Chris
    Medimont Reflections
    ISBN 978-0-945648-05-5 (softbound)
    1. Idaho. 2. Politics 3. Geography 4. Business. I. Title.

Printed in the United States of America.
May 2013
10 9 8 7 6 5 4 3 2 1

    Cover photo by Marcia Carlson
    Chapter page photos by Barry Kough, unless otherwise noted.

To my beloved spouse and partner for so many years, Marcia; and for our children, Alisa, Marissa, Serena and Scott, and their loved ones; and, for our grandchildren, Nathan and Marin as well as those still to come.

Table of contents

Foreword by Governor Cecil D. Andrus	1
Introduction	5
1: Protecting Hell	8
2: The Missing Ballot Box	26
3: The Pantry	52
4: Idaho's 800 Pound Gorilla	68
5: Who Is the Lioness of Idaho?	91
6: Thirty Pieces of Silver?	103
7: Betwist and Between	111
8: The Toothless Tiger	131
9: Give A Boy A Gun Revisited	151
10: Nobody Calls me Senator	161
11: The Sensible Monkey Wrench	189
12: "They Also Serve. . ."	203
13: "I could not stop for Death. . . ."	224
Appendix A: Northwest Power Council Members	242
Appendix B: 1972 and 1974 Elections Abstract	245
Acknowledgement	257
The Author	261

Foreword by Cecil D. Andrus

Any successful politician will confirm that indispensable to his or her success is a good press secretary. I have been blessed with several – such as John Hough and Marc Johnson – over the years. However, the great French commander, Napoleon Bonaparte, once said, "I have six or seven good, competent generals. All I really need, though, is one *lucky* general."

My lucky but also competent press secretary was (some say, still is) Chris Carlson, who ended up working directly for me the longest. Good at feeding the news media sharks whether in Boise or Washington, D.C., he was also lucky. He had a great feel for what the news media would be focusing on, knew how to play the game, and was good about getting back to reporters. The couple of times in nine years I questioned his judgment or was about to come down on him, be damned if what he did invariably turned out to be correct.

Talent is an element obviously needed. A press secretary has to be bright, able to digest reams of information, and then articulate to the newsperson his principal's key message points. An ability to charm a skeptical reporter is also a desired attribute. All that said, there is simply no substitute for luck. Chris possessed luck in abundance.

His instinct for knowing how I would respond to a question or an issue was second to none. Smart people in the state of Idaho's government and at the U.S. Department of the Interior recognized the alter-ego aspect and would often try out their ideas on him to get a gauge on my reaction.

He and Marc Johnson were the only two people I ever allowed the freedom to speak for me, if circumstances demanded, without first checking with me. This is, of course, a form of power, but neither of them ever abused it. Nor did they ever forget that it was my name on the ballot; they worked for me, not the other way around. More importantly, we all worked for the people of Idaho.

After working for me for almost nine years, Chris spent nine months (1981) as one of Idaho's original members of the Northwest Power Planning Council (see Chapter 8) before accepting a job in Seattle establishing the government affairs section of Seattle's largest independent public relations firm, The Rockey Company.

Chris was lured back to Spokane (where he had attended high school) in 1984 by a couple of savvy Kaiser Aluminum executives, Jesse Erikson and Ralph Cheek. They recognized the probable answer to Kaiser's soaring power bills was the fashioning of a political solution rather than pray for a favorable court ruling.

They enlisted my assistance for television and radio commercials as well as print advertising to plead their case to the general public across the Pacific Northwest.

Chris helped fashion the correct solution, a variable power rate that tied the price of power to the price of the metal, but it was too late to save Kaiser from bankruptcy and eventual takeover by the Houston corporate raider, Charles Hurwitz. As a point of honor, Chris left Kaiser.

In late 1987, Chris put together a group of friends from across the region at a lawyer friend's cabin on Lake Coeur d'Alene. All would become founding partners of the northwest's most successful regional public affairs firm, The Gallatin Group.

Forced by two sizable health challenges, Parkinson's disease and a rare form of cancer, Chris took early retirement. It was critical for him to reduce the stress in his life, and by so doing, prolong it.

I'm not surprised though to see him take up writing columns and books in his retirement. While I took exception to the title of his first book for being too boastful (*Cecil Andrus: Idaho's Greatest Governor*), the book sold well for essentially a semi-biography on me. I tell people it is the story of "a fading politician in the twilight of his mediocre career."

In writing *Medimont Reflections*, Chris captures that indefinable something which makes Idahoans so unique while also capturing the essence of the individuals and their issues. Chris has returned to his roots – journalism and column writing.

We are all the better for this and even the least politically engaged Idahoan among us will enjoy the profiles of the men and women that helped to shape politics during the last half of the 20th century. Likewise, his analysis of the issues they focus on leave one feeling he or she has just undergone a thorough academic seminar on matters that dominated Idaho thinking for so many years.

His goal is to provide insight and perspective, based upon 40 years of laboring in the vineyards, which he trusts readers will find informative. He wants his readers to say, "I never thought of that," or "I never knew that." He candidly concedes he likes to quote H.L. Mencken, a legendary *Baltimore Sun* editor at the turn of the last century, whose purpose was "to comfort the afflicted and afflict the comfortable."

He especially loves giving the Republicans in Idaho hell for their systematic dismantling of the legacy he helped me to build. He quotes Harry Truman: "I tell the truth about their stupidity and they think it is hell."

He pleads guilty to being biased if not outright self-righteous at times. He often goes a step too far by either questioning opponents' motives or exaggerating what they have actually written or said. Sometimes, too, he wanders off into the weeds and gets lost in some contorted thinking.

He is always thinking, though.

You will enjoy his reflections as much as I did. Like me, though, you will also wonder from time to time just what's in the water he's drinking. From essays on folks that need to be remembered periodically for their great contributions to the state, like Frank Church, Louise Shadduck, and John Evans, to issues like abortion, additional wilderness, gun controls, and how Idaho is going to deal once and for all time with the need to remove nuclear waste above the Snake Plain Aquifer, you will appreciate his thought-provoking tour down memory lane as well as up the yellow brick road to the future.

Enjoy the read!

Cecil D. Andrus
Boise, Idaho
December 31, 2012

Introduction

In early November of 2011, I was sitting on a stage with Governor Cecil D. Andrus in front of an audience at the City Club of Boise to discuss my just published remembrances of the many fine years I spent with him as press secretary.

He had generously agreed to make some promotional appearances to generate sales and to co-sign some books.

Moderator Marty Peterson, then government affairs coordinator for the University of Idaho, is a true Idaho history buff. Andrus had tapped him years before to be the executive director of the Idaho Centennial celebration.

Marty turned to me and asked, "Chris, just where the hell is Medimont?" I answered too quickly, giving him the literal answer and describing accurately where it is geographically.

I did not get a word in edgewise after that. (That was fine with me. I knew who folks were coming to see and hear). Andrus was off and running with a one hour-monologue that rivals anything one has ever heard. My home was the only question tossed directly to me.

I could have and should have answered the question in a metaphorical sense. Perhaps something like this:

"Marty, Medimont, while an actual old post office stop in southern Kootenai County, can more accurately be described as a state of mind one comes to terms with as they move through life. It literally means "middle mountain," but it also conveys a sense of being at the half-time of life's journey, the mid-point, if you will, between idealism tempered with harsh reality."

As we grow older, we acquire knowledge bumps, going through the process of trial and error, and hopefully learning from our mistakes. We should reach a point of equilibrium. At this balancing point, this *medimont*, we are at last at peace with our own mortality. We come to recognize salvation lies in service to others, sublimating our ego and squashing our selfishness in the interests of others.

The genesis of this book grew out of a conversation with Randy Stapilus, owner of Ridenbaugh Press and publisher of this work. I was telling him about having gone through the clips of columns I did from Washington, D.C., for the *Lewiston Tribune*, the *Idaho State Journal* and several other Idaho clients during my sojourn there in 1971 and 1972.

I could not help noticing many of the issues I covered from D.C. were still alive and well 40 years later, still being debated, still controversial. Some of the players, ancient though most of them may be, still are influential in the game.

I thought to call the book "Then and Now," but the title did not resonate. Initially, the plan was to run the old columns, do notes on what had and had not changed, and in the instances where I had written columns recently, simply republish them.

"Too formulaic," Stapilus said. "Readers would be more interested in your stories as told by you. People like to read about another person which is why biographies in one form or another will always be read. It's the perspectives one brings from 40 years of being involved that will help readers understand why some issues take years to resolve and require several ball carriers."

Indeed, one of the themes running through many of these essays is that bringing about change, especially if it requires Congressional action, is one long slog. Those desiring to protect special areas, for example, better be in it for the long haul and better be prepared to invest a considerable amount of time. It is also my modest hope readers will learn more about some of the less remembered but still important figures of the past who helped make Idaho the great state it is.

As conservative and Republican as my native state currently is, I hope my undying love for its citizens shines through. I feel incredibly lucky and blessed to have played a small part in the various events that have shaped this state in the last 40 years.

Medimont, Idaho
March, 2013

1 ■ Protecting Hell

Hells Canyon. Photo courtesy Steve Lee.

For 25 years, our family's first spring outing into the wonderful wilds of Idaho has been a trip into the Hells Canyon National Recreation Area. Even in 2006 and 2007, at the height of my battle against a stage IV cancer, I jet boated up to the Jordan Ranch and camped overnight in the old horse pasture beside Kirkwood Creek.

We always tried to get there early enough in the day that we could claim the campsite on top of the bench, closest to the creek, because it always had a picnic table we could set our food and packs on, or by lantern-light sit and play cards at night with a fire roaring in the nearby grate. Additionally, the over-hanging limbs from tall hackberry bushes were perfect for spreading and tying down a light tarp to keep us dry when rain showers would come.

Most importantly, though, it was the campsite closest to the biffy and that was no small item for the women in our contingent. Over the 25 years we watched the Forest Service install several iterations of toilets, from the early basic old backwoods outhouse, to a solar-driven waste recycler that ended up smelling pretty bad, to a modern two-bathroom model one might find at any Idaho rest area.

I thought each of the last couple years would be the last I would see the rays of the evening sun crawl up "Old Shark Tooth" – the large overhanging hillock that looms above the homestead to its south. Each year since 2006 I gave thanks for another opportunity to revel in the stark beauty of the place, listen to the chukars clucking nearby, to watch for elk on the ridges high above the river and catch some bass while just listening to the quiet flow and occasional gurgling of the Snake steadily flowing north towards its merger with the Salmon and then with the Clearwater.

When younger and in better health, we sometimes did 10 backpacking trips a season. Almost always, though, the season began at Upper Pittsburgh Landing and we would hike the six miles along the river trail to the Jordan Ranch at Kirkwood Bar and set up a base camp. After signing the register in the old museum that had once been a bunkhouse, we would take day hikes north or south along the river or up the draw a mile to the Carter Mansion, once the home of the canyon's best bootlegger.

Bootleggers cabin. Photo by Marcia Carlson.

Other times we would charter a jet boat to come down from the Hells Canyon Dam, pick us up at Upper Pittsburgh Landing and take us 33 miles back upstream where we would put off just below Granite Creek. Then we would take three or four days to hike back down to the trailhead, camping along the way with the last stop for the night always being the Jordan Ranch.

"We" usually included our youngest son and daughter, Scott and Serena, as well as some of the family from our old neighbors from Bainbridge Island, Rick Richards and one or two of his children. It has been a wonderful way to connect and have quality time with our children.

Since it was early in the hiking season, it was often cool in the canyon, though some days would be quite warm, especially if the wind was not blowing. At that time of the season, we didn't have to worry about rattlesnakes yet, but we did have to keep our eyes out for poison ivy, which is hard to recognize when there are no leaves yet on the plant. To this point, unfortunately, I can bear painful witness.

Rick Richards and Father Dublinski. Photo courtesy Marcia Carlson.

I knew Len and Grace Jordan before I knew about Hells Canyon. Indeed, it was my keen interest in the Jordan's that first led me to understand what a special place it is and how important it is to protect and preserve its uniqueness.

When I arrived in Washington, D.C., in January of 1971, I met all the members of the Idaho Congressional Delegation. Frank Church was the senior senator (having first taken his seat in 1957), though at 47 he still looked like a kid who had just graduated from college.

A well known liberal, his hero was the iconoclastic William E. Borah whose oratory was second to none and who was Idaho's dominant political figure for much of the first half of the 20th century.

Jordan was the junior senator (having taken his seat in 1962), but Church always showed great deference to Jordan and the former governor, likewise, held him in high regard in spite of different political persuasions. Such was the respect each had for the other that while they would always "endorse" their party's nominee against the other, neither would actively campaign against the other.

Tall, silver haired, sun wrinkled of brow and face, Jordan looked every inch the former rancher who ran sheep in Hells Canyon for eight years during the Depression.

Having heard that Grace Jordan, the senator's talented, well educated spouse, had written a slightly fictionalized account of their years in the canyon, entitled *Home Below Hells Canyon*, I acquired and quickly read it. The book is fun, informative and interesting.

Little did I know how much of my time in later years would be taken up with writing about and tangentially participating in efforts to suitably protect much of Hells Canyon.

In 2010, I wrote two columns about Hells Canyon, one on May 5 about the annual pilgrimage into the canyon and the other on May 12 about then Interior Secretary Walter J. Hickel's 1974 float trip through Hells Canyon as part of a sophisticated lobbying effort put together by two of the Northwest's early conservation leaders, Boyd Norton, from *Friends of the Earth*, and Brock Evans of *the Sierra Club*.

Working with Governor Andrus' natural resource aide, John Hough, the group enticed CBS television personality Arthur Godfrey and folksinger Burl Ives to be the celebrity "hooks" that succeeded in landing the Interior Secretary's participation. It was a true publicity coup and helped other efforts to advertise the importance of protecting the area from future development. The primary audience, of course, was the United States Congress.

I called the May 12th column "Hickel's Trip Through Hell," which was done to attract attention to the historical retelling rather than characterize the trip which the then Interior Secretary thoroughly enjoyed. Hickel emerged from the trip a solid convert for federal protection, but just what form that protection would be was not yet clear.

Since the area is difficult to get to by car, some people may wonder today why the canyon needed protection. The answer in part is something Andrus identified early in his consideration of protective status for Hells Canyon, and also the Sawtooth Mountains of Central Idaho. Many in the conservation movement immediately thought the Sawtooths and Hells Canyon needed the highest degree of protection possible and so sought to add them to the nation's National Park System.

Andrus knew better. He told all who would listen that a "national park" designation would result in the areas being "loved to death." Early in his first term as governor, he favored a lesser but sufficient form of protection called a "National Recreation Area." Such a designation would allow continued compatible uses and would not lock up the area like National Park status would have.

Andrus knew folks would still want to hunt in areas within a proposed NRA. Park status in the lower 48 states did not allow hunting. He also knew that carefully buying up grazing leases over time and phasing out sheep herding was the only way to secure the cooperation of the state's influential ranching and sheep raising industry. Andrus knew how important it was to get people together on the ground level and listen to each other in a give-and-take process that hopefully would lead to consensus.

In Hells Canyon, he knew there would be conflict with those who favored floating through the canyon as opposed to those who favored jet boats. Both interests had to be accommodated, even on whatever portion of the Snake River below Hells Canyon Dam received the highest degree of protection under the federal Wild and Scenic River Act.

The biggest threat to Hells Canyon preservation was the effort by private hydropower interests to build one more "high" dam in the canyon near the confluence of the Snake and Salmon rivers.

This dam, to be called High Mountain Sheep, would have created a reservoir extending upstream to the base of the Hells Canyon Dam and would have flooded some of the most spectacular places along the river, including the Jordan ranch at Kirkwood Bar.

Incredibly, one of the biggest advocates of the dam was Idaho's junior senator and former governor, Len Jordan. I have never understood how Jordan, who I greatly admired, could support flooding over the old homestead.

One can only speculate that it was a form of "familiarity can breed contempt" – that is when one lives in a place for many years he can discount its unique qualities and cease to recognize how special it may be.

As with all subjects controversial, luck plays a role. In this case, the continuing controversy swirling through the Pacific Northwest in the 1950s and 1960s, the conflict between public and private power, caused a fortunate delay in commencing construction.

Public power, as represented by the Bonneville Power Administration, which markets the output of federal dams along the Columbia and Lower Snake rivers, finally had been checked by Idaho Power and its allies. They succeeded in getting a federal license to build the Oxbow, Brownlee, and Hells Canyon dams on the upper part of what was called the Middle Snake River Reach.

Helping to delay the proposed High Mountain Sheep Dam was the need for completed studies necessary to obtain a Federal Power Commission license. The nascent environmental movement had enough allies in Congress to fashion moratoriums of either five or seven years.

Not only would this allow the studies to be completed, it also bought time for the environmental community to continue to muster support for the Hells Canyon NRA designation that would provide wild and scenic status for 20 miles of the river through the canyon. Most importantly, it prohibited any further dam building.

Both Idaho senators supported a seven-year moratorium on dam building while the studies were completed, hearings held, and the public educated about the stakes and options.

Personalities almost always play a part in these legislative dances and it was clear that Oregon Senator Bob Packwood rubbed not only Idaho's senators the wrong way, but also Oregon's senior senator, Mark Hatfield. Thus, when Packwood introduced a preservation bill in the spring of 1971, it was evident it would be going nowhere for a long time, especially after he threatened to substitute his bill for the seven-year moratorium proposal of Idaho's two senators.

As a "compromise" and a courtesy, the Senate Interior committee chairman, Washington Senator Henry M. Jackson, had the subcommittee chair, Nevada Senator Allan Bible, announce he would hold a hearing on Packwood's bill in the fall. Packwood then withdrew his substitute and the Senate passed the Church/Jordan moratorium almost unanimously.

That fall I was one of the few reporters attending the hearing, having been retained by the *Lewiston Morning Tribune* to provide spot coverage. Green as I was, I knew that in response to a direct question from Jordan about including language guaranteeing primacy of upstream water rights, which Packwood refused to include, the Oregon senator, effectively, had just killed his own bill.

The net effect isolated Packwood, insuring he would be nothing but a bit player in the passage of any bill. This proved to be the case. The combined clout of Jackson, Jordan, Hatfield and Church was too much for Packwood and he faded slowly from the scene.

In the meantime, Idaho's then First District congressman, Jim McClure (the front-runner to succeed Len Jordan who had announced his retirement plans in August of 1971) continued to vacillate on whether to support any moratorium on the Middle Snake. Strongly supported by Idaho Power and other hydroelectric interests, McClure was sympathetic to the business side of the equation and somewhat unfriendly to those espousing the Senate moratorium.

What turned the future senator around was his own mail-in survey. While not truly scientific, McClure put great stock in these self-identifying surveys. Much to his surprise, a solid majority of the respondents indicated support for a dam building moratorium and creation of a Wild and Scenic river. In September, the first district congressman started singing a different tune.

About this time, Idaho's senior senator was attacked by the environmental community for his support of the moratorium on the Middle Snake. Boyd Norton, a former Idahoan then living in Colorado, sharply criticized Church in *Not Man Apart*, the newspaper of *Friends of the Earth*. Calling the moratorium a "sell out," Norton also criticized Church for "almost vindictively" not supporting Senator Packwood's Hells Canyon NRA bill.

Church turned the other cheek, refused to respond to the personal attack on his integrity and brushed it off by saying he still felt they were working towards the same objective. As 1971 wound to a close the state's environmental community looked like they were losing badly on three issues:

1. Legislation creating a Hells Canyon NRA was going nowhere because of Packwood's stupidity and the moratorium issue.

2. Legislation creating a Sawtooth NRA, likewise, was going nowhere, let alone a Sawtooth National Park bill, because of questions surrounding, in part, whether the White Clouds and Boulder Mountains should be added and given wilderness protection. Part of this debate, whether the White Clouds should be part of a new wilderness bill, is going on today.

3. Despite a delay in the opening of bids, the Interior Department's Bureau of Reclamation was proceeding with its plans for the Teton Dam to be built on a prime fly fishing stream in southeastern Idaho. The project was strongly supported in Idaho and by the entire Congressional delegation as well as by Governor Andrus.

As 1972 opened, Church let it be known that the first priority was going to be getting the Sawtooth NRA established by legislation with the issue of additional wilderness acreage added, including resolution of the White Clouds and the Boulders. The senator wanted a Sawtooth-White Clouds NRA. In addition, Church said there would be language withdrawing the proposed NRA from any further mineral entries under the 1872 Mining Law.

In late January of 1972, the House passed a Sawtooth bill, 369 to 9. Despite the lopsided margin, Church immediately said it would have to be modified significantly. In particular, Church said the Sawtooth peaks had to be in the NRA, not a separate wilderness area, because a wilderness designation for the White Clouds and Boulder Mountains at that time would have allowed possible additional mineral entries until 1983 under amendments that took precedence that were included in the 1964 Wilderness Act.

Among the nine members of Congress voting against was John Saylor of Pennsylvania, a card-carrying member of the Sierra Club who believed the Sawtooths warranted national park status. He also claimed his view was shared by major environmental groups in Idaho and by Governor Andrus.

On the latter point, he was flat wrong. Andrus consistently had supported an NRA designation over a national park designation, much to the chagrin of his friend, Paul Fritz, the supervisor of the only park service holding in Idaho, Craters of the Moon National Monument.

Despite this back-and-forth, unlike the debate today over the ten-years-in-the-making compromise bill fashioned by Second District Congressman Mike Simpson, at no time did it occur to anyone to think about utilizing the Antiquities Act (which creates National Monuments) as leverage to force Congress to act.

In the past the Antiquities Act, passed in the early 1900s, gives a president the ability to unilaterally withdraw public land and place it in a "national monument" status that is far more restrictive in regard to permitted activities. The theory is that national monument status is so restrictive it galvanizes Congress to undo the monument designation by passing into law a less restrictive designation, such as a national recreation area or a national park which is still protective of the area's attributes.

The reason was quite simple: Anyone who knew President Richard Nixon knew it was unlikely he would have signed an executive withdrawal even had it been recommended by his second Interior secretary, Rogers C. B. Morton (Hickel having earlier been fired for questioning the wisdom of Nixon's Vietnam policy.)

Much of the political maneuvering throughout 1972 was driven by the forthcoming election of a new senator from Idaho. Conventional wisdom favored Congressman McClure in the GOP primary, and the first district congressman, and his political director, Jim Goller, a savvy and crafty political practitioner, were not about to give a more conservative primary opponent, former Second District Congressman George Hansen, an opening to come after McClure.

McClure skillfully played to those who wanted a dam-building moratorium on the Snake by crafting a compromise with the then Second District Congressman, Orval Hansen (no relation to George), which went nowhere in the Senate but gave McClure cover. In the meantime, his staff began preparing to work with Senator Church and Governor Andrus on crafting an acceptable Hells Canyon bill if McClure won the race to succeed Len Jordan.

On August 8, the state's Democrats chose popular Idaho State University President William E. "Bud" Davis as their nominee. Davis bested the three Ada County Democrats in the race, Attorney General Tony Park, Boise attorney (and later Andrus-appointed Supreme Court Judge) Byron Johnson, and Boise feminist Rose Bowman. Vote totals were: Davis 23,953; Park 17,636; Johnson 15,526; and Bowman 9,327.

On the Republican side McClure brushed aside his three challengers, former Congressman George Hansen, former Governor Robert Smylie and Glen Wegner, an Ivy League educated holder of degrees in law and medicine from Kendrick. The results: McClure 46,522; Hansen 35,412; Wegner 24,582; and, Smylie 22,497.

Despite the heavy Republican tilt starting to manifest itself in Idaho, Davis mounted a surprisingly strong challenge to McClure, even though McClure's campaign outspent Davis' by a 4 to 1 margin. (*See Chapter 10 on the Davis/McClure Senate race*)

As 1973 began, all three major environmental issues remained at play on the Idaho political scene. Additionally, my wife, Marcia, our young daughter, Alisa, and I had moved back to our native Idaho as I had accepted an offer to become press secretary to Governor Andrus. Two years in D.C. was enough. We had seen most of the historic sights to be seen, visited all the museums and had taken in as much history as one could absorb.

My absence, however, insured much less reporting on the give and take in the nation's capital. Not until five years later, when owner A. Robert Smith sold the News Bureau to Steve Forrester, son of Bud Forrester, who published the *East Oregonian* in Pendleton and the *Daily Astorian* in Astoria, and Steve hired Larry Swisher, the son of Pocatello's Perry Swisher, did the level of such in-depth reporting on Idaho issues return.

Meanwhile, in a fine example of bi-partisanship and compromise, newly elected Senator Jim McClure worked constructively with Andrus, Church, and their staffs to hammer out a bill acceptable to most parties, including even the publicity hound, Bob Packwood.

One of my favorite memories from Andrus' first go-around as governor was watching him and McClure on their hands and knees in the Governor's Office poring over a big map of the Hells Canyon area, drawing boundaries that represented hydrological divides, areas where domestic sheep could roam and areas where they could not; and, stretches of the Snake River below Hells Canyon Dam to be protected under different designations.

Both men had hiked, fished, and/or hunted in the area. They knew what they were talking about and could visualize the topography. By no stretch of the imagination were they drawing arbitrary lines on a map. It remains indelibly imprinted in my mind as a fine example of two of Idaho's leading political figures working in tandem for the public good, while preserving historic and scenic recreation values.

In a similar manner, compromise carried the day with the Sawtooth NRA with the exception that a wilderness designation for the Boulders and White Clouds had to be postponed to a later date. The Sawtooth National Forest was charged with continuing to manage under the multiple-use doctrine, but in a manner that would preserve the area's scenic and historic values.

Who would have thought that 40 years later the wilderness designation, especially for the high mountain peak areas, would still not be achieved?

Of the major players still alive today only Andrus and Frank Church's widow, Bethine, remain active, and though retired are stalwart members of the Sawtooth Society, which they helped found. Senator Church died in 1984, Senator McClure died in 2012.

Surprisingly, picking up the mantle of congressional leadership on this issue has been the Republican congressman from Idaho's Second District, former Idaho House Speaker and Blackfoot dentist Mike Simpson. In an almost unholy alliance, "Driller," as Andrus affectionately calls him, has worked closely with Idaho Conservation League Executive Director Rick Johnson, to secure passage of a new wilderness bill affording protection for the high mountain peak areas of the Boulders and the White Clouds.

For over a decade, Simpson has negotiated with the various interest groups from cattlemen to miners, backpackers to ATV riders and appeared to be on the verge of ultimate success in 2011. However, his effort was torpedoed in the Senate by newly-elected Senator James Risch, who toadied up to the coalition of ATV riders and snowmobilers opposed to any set-asides.

In several recent columns, I expounded on the only approach left to bring the parties back to the table and force binding negotiations: invocation, by President Barack Obama, of the Antiquities Act. Andrus has quietly urged the administration to prepare the paperwork necessary for the presidential pen. However, recently departed Interior Secretary Ken Salazar made the mistake of saying before he would support further use of the Act he had to see significant local support.

Andrus intends to renew his request with the President's second term selection as Interior executive, former REI (the outdoor gear and apparel company) executive Sally Jewell.

Use of the Act was the key to breaking the deadlock in Alaska when Andrus was President Jimmy Carter's Interior secretary. Forcing Congress to pass a bill removing the more restrictive monument designation is the only way to get the job done with the White Clouds and the Boulders. President Obama has nothing to lose in Idaho, a state which he did not carry in either the election of 2008 or 2012. In fact, he could have gained some ground with the nation's environmental community had he acted before the 2012 election.

It was no surprise to see Andrus become more outspoken in his support for using the Act to force action. He and Congressman Simpson spoke to the Idaho Conservation League's 2012 gathering in May at Redfish Lake. Without utilization of the Act, Andrus said, Risch will continue to exercise his senatorial privilege "hold" on the legislation; and Governor Butch Otter will continue his opposition also.

Congressman Simpson publicly expressed confidence that Congress would finally act without the Antiquities Act having to be used, but privately told individuals at the gathering that it might become necessary.

Only the Antiquities Act will break this logjam and bring resolution to this last remaining piece of a 40-year-old wilderness fight. Significantly, Simpson's major ally in developing the compromise legislation, Rick Johnson, the executive director of the Idaho Conservation League, now believes as Andrus does that President Obama has to utilize his power under the Antiquities Act to designate the Boulder-White Clouds as a National Monument..

A little noted side issue that emerged during the 1970s debate on the fate of the Sawtooths, the White Clouds, and Hells Canyon was the relentless march to the construction of the Teton Dam. Most environmentalists in Idaho opposed the project, but with the exception of activists around Idaho Falls, like Pete Henault and Russ Brown, few made it their priority.

Shortly after the dam was completed and the reservoir behind filled, the dam collapsed on June 5, 1976, with a loss of eleven lives and damages to property and crops climbing into hundreds of millions of dollars.

The day the dam collapsed Governor Andrus had set aside time to fly into the Idaho backcountry with his good friend, Rex Lanham, who owned and operated a fly-in lodge on Cabin Creek called the Flying W just off of Big Creek about ten miles above where Big Creek flows into the Middle Fork of the Salmon. He planned on getting some restful fly fishing accomplished while restoring the batteries for a few days. Needless to say, he canceled the trip upon hearing the news of the collapse and immediately flew over to the site of the collapse.

Thirty-six years later, some farmers in the impacted area want to reauthorize and construct a better built dam. Incredibly, they seem to have forgotten what happened the first time.

There are enough people in the area, though, with long enough memories to oppose reauthorization. A 2011 poll indicated there was sufficient opposition that members of the congressional delegation, as well as Governor Otter, ought to feel some risk if they support a renewed project.

Such is the knee jerk-pull of the "Committee of Nine" water masters of the Upper Snake projects that Otter nonetheless felt feasibility of a new project should be studied and, unlike Andrus, would not rule out a new dam. Otter clearly does not understand the reach and pull of today's environmental community. Even in Idaho, they quickly can develop and distribute messages, generate massive e-mails and phone calls to congressional offices, and create a sense of tide to the ocean.

By any measure and all accounts, Governor Andrus skillfully handled the most challenging aspects of the dam failure, quickly organizing and personally supervising the state's response to this tragedy by coordinating efforts with the federal government and the LDS Relief Society. Then LDS Church President Spencer Kimball literally laid his hands on Andrus at a post collapse observance held in Rexburg on the campus of BYU-Idaho.

The most important, but little noted, consequence of the dam's failure was the tendency of Andrus to more sharply scrutinize cost-benefit claims made by proponents of such projects. While he always believed some dams fulfill a legitimate and immediate need for hydropower or high head irrigation, he knew many projects had numbers that were "mickey-moused" to create better justifications.

Thus, when he became Interior Secretary, he had little problem participating in a dam project review led by an ardent environmentalist, Kathy Fletcher, the deputy domestic policy advisor who worked with President Carter's lead domestic advisor, Stu Eizenstat.

If Fletcher had an agenda when she went to work in the Office of Domestic Policy, it was axing a large number of mostly western water projects which did not meet hard-core cost benefit analysis. Andrus and Vice President Walter Mondale recognized that some within the administration wanted to kill as many as a couple hundred projects. They were savvy enough to realize this large of a number would in fact create a large enough coalition of angered congressmen sufficient to defeat any effort at paring any project.

Thus, in a series of White House meetings, Andrus and Mondale systematically started whittling down the list. As they zeroed in on a number, 18 in all, that were the worst of the worst, and they thought they could build a coalition of fiscally conservative Democrats who would join with fiscally conservative Republicans to successfully kill these worst dogs, Fletcher allegedly leaked the entire list of "hits" to Congress and the news media.

Instant uproar could be heard everywhere. Knowing what she had done, Fletcher went on to further burnish her environmental credentials during the Carter years through her ability to influence her immediate boss, the president's chief domestic policy advisor. Her efforts to curtail dam construction eventually led to at most the cancellation of four projects..

Because of the Teton Dam experience, Andrus was forever after able to exercise a critical and credible review of the proposed projects and of those projects that had been built. In particular, he started increasing his criticism of the four lower Snake River dams, the last of which was completed in 1973 with Andrus present for the ribbon cutting. In speaking at the final dam dedication the *Lewiston Tribune* reported his publicly questioning whether the Corps (U.S. Army Corps of Engineers) really understood the adverse impact the Lower Snake dams would have on downstream salmon and steelhead smolt migration.

Few folks recalled that earlier in 1973 Andrus, with a look of pure joy captured by *Lewiston Tribune* photographer Barry Kough, had dynamited a small regulating dam near Lewiston owned by what was then called Washington Water Power Co. Its removal restored the

Clearwater to the exclusive list of those rare U.S. rivers without a single dam.

In later years, Andrus also bemoaned in his political biography, *Politics Western Style*, and in "historical look-backs," his regrets at supporting the four lower Snake River dams and the Dworshak Dam on the North Fork of the Clearwater. He recognized well after the fact how much excellent elk habitat and quality cutthroat streams had been sacrificed on the altar of the Bonneville Power Administration and the Army Corps of Engineers.

As the evidence mounted of the devastating impacts of the four Lower Snake projects on Idaho's prized and valuable salmon and steelhead runs, it became clear to Andrus that a "bad trade off" had been made. Upon his return to the governorship in 1987 he started formulating the elements of a fish flush plan on the Snake that would emulate nature's spring flow critical to quickly carrying the salmon and steelhead smolt to the sea.

This, too, became controversial, but Andrus was a formidable debater on these matters and emerged as the natural leader on the subject of dams and fish.

The large jet boat from Beamer's Hells Canyon Excursions powered its way up the Snake River against the largest cubic feet per second flow ever measured in one day on the Snake-127,000 CFS. The river, swollen by the spring runoff and an incredible amount of spring rains, was awash with more debris than long-time river watchers had ever seen.

The date was April 28, 2012 and I was taking members of my extended family into Hells Canyon on our annual spring trek.

April 30th would be grandson Nathan's 8th birthday and I wanted to introduce our grandchildren to the canyon while I was still physically able. I wanted him and his sister, Marin, to visit the old Jordan Ranch bunkhouse, now a museum.

I wanted them to see the pictures of the Jordan's and hear the story about how the long-time occupant of the ranch, who as a United States senator, tried to entice "Gramps" to be his press secretary many years back.

More than anything I wanted them to share my sense of the wild and scenic values I had helped in a small way to preserve, to listen to the wind coming down the river, to see the wildlife along the river – the deer, the mountain sheep, the river otters – as we worked our way upstream.

They listened to the boat driver tell the story of petro glyphs etched in the rocks at Buffalo Eddy, more than 6,000 years old, and to the story of the sinking of the old Imnaha *sternwheeler bringing supplies to the now gone mining village of Eureka. I wanted them to hear and react with horror at the murder of 37 Chinese miners by outlaws looking for gold near Deep Creek in 1887.

I wanted them to visualize Chief Joseph and his fleeing band of Nez Perce warriors, women, children, dogs, cattle, and horses, fording the Snake River at Dug Bar to stay ahead of the pursuing cavalry led by the one-armed former Union general, Oliver Howard. That no lives were lost in that fording still seems a miracle.

On this particular day there was a fly-in at the narrow dirt strip on Dug Bar. A dozen Cessna 182s, smaller Pipers, and other planes lined up along the dirt strip. I made a point of explaining that one of the features of the Wilderness Act of 1964, and imbedded in the act creating the Hells Canyon National Recreation Area, was language permitting continued access by airplanes and motorized crafts like jet boats, into these wilderness areas.

I explained this was done so children like them and health challenged adults like "Gramps" could still visit and enjoy these areas. I told them there were people in this world who felt access should only go to those who were hale and hearty enough to hike or backpack into the wilderness; that they should not be subjected even to the sound of aircraft flying into the various backcountry landing strips.

I told them about another United States senator from Idaho, Frank Church, who authored the Wilderness Act of 1964 and for whom one of Idaho's great wilderness areas is now named. I pointed out that he specifically had people like grandpa in mind when he wrote language guaranteeing the various backcountry air strips would be preserved also.

I mentioned how often I had flown into isolated air strips with my friend, Jim McDevitt, an extraordinary backcountry pilot who would invite Gramps to go along on fishing trips to places like Moose Creek, Shearer, the Flying B, Big Creek, and the Selway Lodge.

Despite legislative language protecting these places for entering the wilderness, I also told them about how the U.S. Forest Service, the unit of government which manages these wilderness areas, had folks hell bent on closing most of these back country air strips; that they had come up with absurd ideas like conducting Limited Acceptable Change (LAC's) studies that measured the amount of dust a plane landing might generate and then speculate that the small amount of dust because of "cumulative" impacts might hurt the fish in the nearby streams.

One story I did not tell them, but of which they might read or hear about someday, was that the day also marked the 39th anniversary of the drowning of a friend of mine, Eddie Williams, Andrus' first chief of staff, along with his friend, Jack Bowman. They drowned when the boat in which they were traveling swamped in the Imnaha rapids.

If I live long enough to instill in them a love for the wild and free, they will learn soon enough a need to respect the wilderness and the wilds, to be properly cautious, to be prepared to deal with the unexpected, to take responsibility for themselves and their actions, to know life can be unforgiving of some mistakes, and where one does survive a mistake to learn from it and move forward.

Soon enough they will learn there is a yin and a yang, the flip side of life, but that a life worth living is one worth taking calculated risks, that wilderness, like life itself, contains great joy and great sorrow. They will come to learn that there truly is a culture of life as well as death, a secular and selfish world along side a spiritual and a sharing one.

I hope they will be graced by The Almighty to appreciate the gifts they have, the talents they have been blessed with, the love they are surrounded by. Once in a while, I also want them to give a thought of thanks to all those preceding them who had enough foresight to preserve and protect special places where one can experience the presence of The Almighty and observe the face of God.

2 ■ The Missing Ballot Box

Church campaigning. Photo by Barry Kough.

At first glance there could not be two more different people than Frank Church and former President Lyndon Baines Johnson. Surprisingly, though, there were more similarities than one would think.

Both men were terrifically ambitious; both had talented wives who played crucial roles in their success; both could be excellent "stump" speakers; both loved publicity as much as they loved being senators; both relished the give and take of politics; both authored legislation that has touched for the better the lives of millions of Americans past, present, and in the future.

Most interesting though is that both first came to the Senate courtesy of a missing ballot box in a key county controlled by friends of theirs.

Robert Caro, in his massive yet-to-be-completed five-volume biography on Johnson, documents with a story teller's flair how LBJ finally made it to the U.S. Senate by an 87-vote margin over former Texas Governor Coke Stevenson. The key to that "victory" was ballot box 13 in Duval County, controlled by one man, George Parr, a Johnson supporter and a true loyalist who was well rewarded for his loyalty.

There's even a picture of the wayward ballot box sitting on top of the hood of a car with several deputy sheriffs, as well as cronies of Parr's, one with his foot on the bumper, posing for posterity before the box went into the mists of history.

Less well known is Idaho's remarkably similar story. Seven years after Johnson took his Senate seat courtesy of the missing ballot box, in August of 1956, young Frank Church defeated former U.S. Senator Glen Taylor in the Democratic primary by 200 votes.

The winner would be up against the already dying and somewhat disgraced Senator Herman Welker, one of the few supporters for the red-baiting activities of Wisconsin Senator Joe McCarthy.

Idaho's usually Republican-leaning business establishment, including the state's dominant paper, *The Idaho Statesman,* began recognizing the damage being done by "Little Joe from Idaho's" support for McCarthy. Behind the scenes, Church's friend and campaign manager, Carl Burke, was thought to have enlisted key establishment support for Church's bid.

The vote from Elmore County was late in being reported and Taylor cried "fraud" right away. Though no fan of Welker's, even Republican Governor Robert E. Smylie said he was pursuing a state investigation into the vote from Elmore County.

For years afterwards Taylor maintained the nomination had been stolen, and wouldn't you know it, a key ballot box could no longer be found. The finger of blame has long pointed at veteran State Senator Bob Wetherell, the "Duke" of Elmore County and the counterpart to George Parr, the Duke of Duval County. By all accounts, Wetherell's influence included dominating the courthouse.

Stories are mixed and facts are few, but the consensus is there were more Democratic votes in a key precinct than there were registered voters. When Taylor drilled down on the vote in the key precinct it did indeed appear to have delivered an excessive number of votes for the young Boise attorney. The ballot box that should have been part of any mandatory recount, however, had "disappeared."

Rumor had the box being tossed into the Anderson Ranch Reservoir, where it lies to this day, by the county sheriff on orders of "Duke" Wetherell.

Taylor filed a complaint with the Senate which conducted a cursory investigation. During his single term in the Senate (1944-1950) he had not endeared himself to his colleagues. Thus, there was little interest in seeing the flamboyant Taylor, who had run for the vice presidency on the Progressive ticket with Henry Wallace in 1948, resume his old seat.

Taylor, at his own expense, went door-to-door in the key precinct in Mountain Home getting affidavits from voters saying who they had voted for, and buttressing his circumstantial case that Church could not possibly have gotten the margin initially reported out of the precinct.

Of course with the key box missing for any recount, Taylor could not prove his case and the complaint was dismissed. The cloud over Church taking the seat he won that November was removed.

No one has ever speculated, alleged, or charged that Church had knowledge of this "favor" done for him by the Duke of Elmore though Taylor surely must have wondered. If any one might know it would be Carl Burke, but if there is a secret here, he took it to the grave. Garry Wenske, guardian of the Church legacy as curator of the Church papers at Boise State, dismisses the speculation out-of-hand as baseless.

Perhaps, but the missing ballot box has a long and infamous history in many states, not just Texas, and maybe even in Idaho. The real conclusion should be that while politics can bring tainted births there can still be much good for society despite the origins of the politician.

When one looks at the voting abstract for that 1956 primary, it is easy to see why Taylor zeroed in on Elmore County. The official statewide tally had Church garnering 27, 942 votes to Taylor's 27,742. On the GOP side the incumbent, Senator Welker, totaled 31,399 votes. There were nine names on that primary ballot: five Republicans and four Democrats. The combined Republican statewide vote was 73,864 votes and the Democrat's combined vote was 64,018.

One would think the vote in rural Elmore would mirror that of its neighbors to the east, Gooding County and Twin Falls County, both of which voted heavily Republican. To the contrary, Elmore was heavily Democratic. In Gooding, the total Republican vote was 1,576, almost doubling the Democrat vote of 889.

In Twin Falls County the same pattern occurred: the Republican total was 5,582 to the Democrat's 3,035. In Elmore County it was a stunning 4 to 1 advantage for the Democrats, 1,584 votes to 403 votes. Welker took 247 of the Republican total while Church took 862 votes to Taylor's 500 votes, or more than half of the suspiciously large Democratic vote. That Taylor decided to focus on Elmore County should not surprise anyone. Additionally, looking at this anomalous vote pattern justifies additional research and a reasonable degree of suspicion.

Church's key support in the fall election, in terms of dollars and workers, was provided by the nation's labor movement, in particular, the United Steelworkers. The USW was intent on replacing the Mine, Mill and Smelter Worker's union in north Idaho's mining intensive Silver Valley (Shoshone County). They sent their top political operative, Joe Miller, to Boise shortly after the August primary to help Church and his neophyte campaign manager, Carl Burke, organize the fall campaign.

In his wonderfully entertaining memoir, *The Wicked Wine of Democracy*, Miller tells an interesting story about Bethine Church, the politically savvy wife of the aspiring senator.

Miller was for 40 years a top lobbyist in Washington, D.C., but early in his career he was paid a then princely sum of $25,000 a year by the United Steelworkers of America to organize and run campaigns for the

U.S. Senate. In his first outing, 1956, one of his winning "horses" was the young Boise attorney Frank Church.

What Miller did not know at the time was that the Senate and Idaho were getting two for the price of one. Had Miller known that, he might not have crossed Bethine the first time he met her.

In his book, Miller tells about the first fall campaign organizational meeting in Boise shortly after Church had won a narrow victory in the August 6th primary over former U.S. Senator Glen Taylor, the singing cowboy. He recounts meeting in U.S. District Judge Chase Clark's home. Judge Clark was Bethine's father, Frank's father-in-law, a former governor of Idaho and as Miller puts it "a shrewd old hand in Idaho politics."

Also present was the Democratic national committeeman, Harry Wall, a movie theater owner from Lewiston; the state party chairman, George Greenfield; attorney Carl Burke, Church's boyhood chum who managed all of his campaigns; and Bethine.

Miller admits he was not happy to have the candidate's wife sitting in the strategy session. His fear was self-fulfilling. In presenting the media strategy Miller emphasized the then somewhat unusual marketing of a candidate through large billboards across the state. Miller recalls Bethine firmly saying, "Democrats do not use billboards in Idaho," adding "they are absolutely out."

Miller shot back he had not come from Seattle at his expense to take part in amateur night. The battle lines were drawn and it was about to get nasty, but Judge Clark salvaged the evening by suggesting to Bethine that her mother needed her help in the kitchen. Glaring at Miller, Bethine obeyed her father's suggestion and departed.

As Miller put it, "the billboards stayed in the budget, and Bethine stayed in the kitchen." Not for long, though. Mrs. Church soon proved to be Church's equal if not better on the campaign trail.

What Miller was providing the Church campaign would by today's campaign rules be illegal. It was clearly a substantial in-kind and unreported valuable contribution.

Another peculiarity of the 1956 primary and general election race was the placement and financing of small print ads in weekly newspapers around the state. The ads all had a tag line at the bottom which said "This ad placed by the Custer County Church for Senate Committee – John Boyd, Chairman."

The ads urged the reader to "unite behind and nominate Frank Church," and with four men vying for the nomination in 1956, as well as a recent history of divisiveness within the Democratic Party, it was understandable why even a primary message would be, "He can unify our party."

Another line that jumps out from the ads, though is, "A man of Vigor and Clear Vision." The ads had a photo of a young but very resolute looking Frank Church. The emphasis on "vigor" is striking inasmuch as that particular word was associated with young Jack Kennedy and his 1960 campaign for the Presidency.

One wonders if Church did not pass along the phrase to JFK as the two became good friends. With 20/20 hindsight one also wonders if Bill Hall, the astute editorial page editor of the *Lewiston Tribune* for many years, who served as the senator's press secretary for 16 months following Cleve Corlett's defection to Senator Joe Biden's staff in 1975, would not have had a hand in designing such a tag-line had he been the press secretary in 1956.

In his book *Frank Church, D.C. & Me* (1995), Hall went into great detail explaining his role in having the upcoming presidential candidate go public and "front-end" the fact that his cancer in 1949 had resulted in Church losing one testicle. Hence, one just knows he would have loved the tag-line: A Man of Vigor!

Unfortunately, Frank Church is little remembered today, even in Idaho, despite an incredibly productive 24 years in the Senate that saw him author and/or oversee a number of bills whose impact will forever be felt and appreciated.

In what would constitute a chapter of its own in any revised issuance of John Kennedy's famous book, *Profiles in Courage*: Church in 1978 carried the legislation that secured the future peace and safety of the critical and vital Panama Canal through a treaty and a renewed, revised management agreement.

Ratification of the treaty was one of the few foreign policy achievements during the presidency of Jimmy Carter. Despite Church's reservations about "the good old boys" from Georgia who surrounded the President, and the man himself, Church led the floor fight for ratification.

There is little doubt his narrow Senate success with treaty ratification contributed significantly to his defeat in 1980. Many political pundits and historians further contend Carter cost Church a shot at re-election in another way.

Some Idaho Democrats still recall hearing that Carter had conceded before the polls closed in northern Idaho which lead to a significant number of Church Democratic voters walking away from the voting places. Happy-go-lucky Steve Symms, the apple farmer who's most endearing legacy after his service in the House and Senate will be nothing more than his first campaign commercial in which he promised to take a bite out of government, dramatized it by a bite from an apple, and won by a little more than 3,000 votes.

At the same time, Idaho went head over heels for Ronald Reagan who had made the give back of the Panama Canal one of the major speech points of attack against Carter. His classic rhetoric – "We built it, we paid for it, it's ours, and we're going to keep it!" – was an easy applause line.

The Republican Party made sure Idahoans were aware that the floor manager of the treaty was the chairman of the Senate Foreign Relations committee – Frank Church.

Some historians believe the initial seeds of the senator's ultimate defeat were sown by Church's sensational hearings into the excesses of America's Central Intelligence Agency in 1976. The hearings highlighted the excesses of a rogue agency, for example, pointing out the CIA's role in fomenting the 1972 overthrow of Salvador Allende, the democratically elected Marxist president of Chile. The complicity of the mega-giant multi-national corporation, IT&T, was also highlighted.

Many members of America's intelligence community sincerely felt the Church hearings compromised national security and in some respects seriously set back agency programs, unnecessarily placed at risk on-going covert operations, and endangered covert personnel. These folks felt Church was placing the national welfare at risk and sacrificing it on the altar of his presidential ambitions.

No credible evidence has ever emerged to substantiate these serious charges, but "facts" have never bothered true believers and ideologues.

Their hatred for Church was visceral and deep. This spleen was vented and voiced to many sympathetic conservatives, such as Richard Viguerie, one of the early Republican masters of targeted direct mailing. Working with other like-minded conservatives, they formed a political action committee known by its acronym, "NicPAC," whose sole purpose was to raise funds for negative ads to be run in targeted states well before the election year.

These ads hopefully would pre-condition the political environment and predispose a state's electorate to vote against incumbent liberals, such "left-leaning" senators as Church and Indiana Senator Birch Bayh. In a state like Idaho, with its relatively small population, and only three major media markets, they discovered how easy it is to buy significant blocs of television time. Compared to other states, Idaho was a cheap date.

Long before First District Congressman Steve Symms emerged as the senator's likely opponent, Idaho voters were being inundated with ads lambasting Church for his near "traitorous" activities in conducting the CIA hearings. In Symms, the Republicans also found the polar opposite of Church.

Symms was personable and charming; Church often came across as aloof and stuffy; Symms was clearly down to earth, while Church was an intellectual; Symms was the master of the quick quip; Church was given more to long-winded oratory. Symms was known as a rogue and a skirt-chaser; Church, considered prudish, was noted for his probity and his fidelity to his spouse, Bethine; Symms portrayed himself as an outsider independent of the inside-the-beltway mentality (though when he left the Senate, he stayed in D.C. as a well-paid lobbyist) whereas Church had clearly become a creature of the "capital culture."

Indeed, a strange metamorphosis took place during the 1980 campaign. People could not help noting that Symms more often wore three piece suits so that he would appear more senatorial. On the other hand, Church began wearing cowboy boots, a sport coat, and shirt with open collar to come across more like the common folks. Neither was being truly authentic to their core personae. (One former staffer termed Church "going cowboy" an every six-year occurrence.)

Cecil Andrus also felt the CIA hearings were the beginning of the end of Frank Church's political career, but for a different reason. Andrus thought the hearings from a purely functional political standpoint fatally delayed the senator's entry into the 1976 primary race for the Democratic nomination.

Frank Church (left) and Cecil Andrus. Courtesy David Frazier.

In a private conversation with Church in early 1976, Andrus urged Church to turn the hearings over to another senator and get out on the trail to campaign in the early primaries. Concentrate, he said, on fundraising and corner the title of the liberal candidate because the former governor of Georgia, Jimmy Carter, was going to capture the conservative and moderate Democrats.

Church and his top advisors, spouse Bethine, former chief-of-staff Verda Barnes, campaign manager Carl Burke, former press secretary Cleve Corlett, staff legislative director Peter Fenn, current chief-of-staff Mike Wetherell, press secretary Bill Hall, research coordinator Garry Wenske, and finance chairman Henry Kimelman all felt that the CIA hearings would provide Church with a national stage where he could shine for months while other candidates sliced and diced each other in the primaries.

They seemed confident no early consensus would emerge, the field would remain fractured, and a late entry would result in a stampede for his candidacy. They were counting heavily on publicity in the *New York Times* and the *Washington Post* which would also inevitably make the senator the unspoken favorite of the news media.

All were wrong. Only Andrus pegged it correctly.

It is easy to speculate that Andrus' advice might have been unfairly viewed with suspicion because of the governor's known fondness for Jimmy Carter, who, when serving his one term, worked closely with Andrus at National Governors Conference meetings and Democratic Governors Conference sessions. They had a deep and abiding respect for each other.

Before Carter formally declared his candidacy and following his departure from the Georgia governorship, he traveled the country in a trumped up capacity underwritten by the Democratic National Committee. His travels brought him to Idaho. Carter had spent time in Idaho in the late 1950s as a member of Navy Admiral Hyman Rickover's nuclear submarine group which had a training facility in the Arco desert west of Idaho Falls.

The Naval Academy graduate thus had a nostalgic and a political reason to visit Idaho. Andrus rolled out the red carpet, greeting and holding a press conference at the Pocatello Airport when Carter landed. Idaho's governor also took Carter to a meeting of key Democrats from Bannock, Bingham, and Bonneville counties, introduced him in the MiniDome at the half time of an Idaho State University football game, and then following his tour of the INL Naval site, saw him off at the Idaho Falls airport.

Throughout the visit, Carter had an aide taking the names of all the members of the news media at the press conferences, as well as those attending the Democratic event. Everyone soon received a thank you follow up note from the Georgia peanut farmer.

Sometime during this visit, Andrus probably explained to Carter he ultimately would be supportive of the Georgia governor's candidacy but home state politics and personal gratitude to Church for his strong support of his 1970 bid for the governorship dictated his backing for Church as long as he was in the race.

Andrus also had another good friend in the primary race. Arizona congressman Mo Udall, was a talented, witty legislator, a problem solver with a truly great sense of humor. Like Church, Udall was a true liberal and like Church he had also spoken at Andrus' hugely successful Boise fund-raiser in March of 1974.

No one likes to choose among friends, but Andrus had reviewed the field, knew who ultimately was going to be the nominee, and walked a delicate tightrope until Carter had vanquished his opposition.

When Church finally formally declared his candidacy on March 18, 1976, in Idaho City, Andrus dutifully appeared and spoke supportively of the senator's bid, though he knew in his heart it was going to be futile. For a brief time, there was a mini-boom let as Democrats in Oregon, Nebraska, Montana, Idaho, the Virgin Islands, and Guam delivered primary wins to Church.

Carter's lead, however, was too big. Plus, the Democratic Party had adopted a rule awarding candidates on a proportional basis (instead of winner-take-all as it was in previous years), which insured Carter additional delegates even as he lost some of the late primaries. Just as the Georgian successfully dispatched Scoop Jackson, then Mo Udall, he went on to force out Church and finally California Governor Jerry Brown.

In 1972, I interviewed Church while there was much news media speculation that he might be selected by the party's presidential nominee, South Dakota Senator George McGovern, as a vice president replacement for the initial selection, Missouri Senator Thomas Eagleton. The Missouri senator had been forced by reporters looking into his background to admit he had been hospitalized for depression and had undergone electro-shock therapy. In that interview Church made it clear he might be interested in the post if the job description were redone.

He had done some homework and concluded most vice presidents were totally ignored by their president or had become mere hucksters traveling the nation trying to sell the public on the president's policies. Church said he would be interested only if the job were to become a true executive assistant to the president, a deputy president.

Always a realist, Church noted he and McGovern were too much alike in too many ways. He said the only qualification that should count, an ability to step in and do the job of president if necessary, was the fundamental requirement. Other considerations such as geographical diversity also were factors. Church said he had urged McGovern to look closely at Maine Senator Edmund Muskie.

I ended the interview with the obvious question and found the response odd. Here are the exact words from that August 20, 1972 interview:

"Asked if he would like to be president someday, Church stumbled, laughed, paused and muttered that he had never given it much thought. Asked if he wouldn't mind being president, he replied 'any man who has been in public life as long as I have wouldn't deny that it is the most coveted and exalted office to aspire to.'"

The response with its double negative no less does not conform to the senator's reputation for candor. Indeed, it is disingenuous at best and self-servingly misleading at worst.

One suspects that by 1972 Church was one of those senators who saw a president in the mirror while shaving in the morning. No less an authority on reading men's ambitions than Majority Leader Lyndon Baines Johnson had as early as 1957 read the senator's ambitions.

Johnson famously said at one time: "Tell me a man's mother's hopes for him and his father's failings and I can measure the man." Johnson has been described by many as almost a psychotic genius at bending people to his will because of this ability to divine their weaknesses, vulnerabilities, and ambitions. Spotting the freshman Idaho senator as a comer, Johnson initially took him under his wing and provided him with a key amending role in securing passage of the weak Civil Rights Act of 1957 (the first such bill to pass since the end of the Civil War).

The real plum for Church, however, came when Johnson vaulted Church over a half dozen senators to a seat on the Committee on Foreign Relations. Johnson's mistake was conveying the plum too soon before he had tied down the Senator's support in the 1960 Democratic presidential primary contest. Johnson thought Church would recognize the extraordinary move and respond with loyal support for the majority leader's presidential ambitions, but he failed to ask Church directly. It was a rare mistake.

Johnson biographer Robert Caro tells a wonderful vignette about Church. Campaigning in the west, Johnson stopped in Idaho Falls to be greeted at the airport by the then 35-year-old Church. Caro writes:

"Having assessed Church's ambition, (Johnson) had once scribbled a note to him at a committee meeting to assure him he would help him realize it: He had, the note said, asked Drew Pearson "to help me give you a buildup over the years" so that one day "you can ... be our President."

Caro goes on to explain, however, that the Kennedys had offered Church a faster buildup, the position of keynote speaker at the opening of the 1960 Democratic Convention in Los Angeles. Church had already garnered the best thing Johnson could bestow. Caro goes on:

"Johnson had heard rumors that this was the case, and, reading the young senator's eyes over the toothy smile he gave him at the airport, he saw it was true. Walking toward the terminal, he told Horace Busby: "The little sonofabitch has already sold out. They bought him."

With almost 30 years having gone by since the senator died in 1984, a fair question to ask is: Would Frank Church have been a good president? Scholars could debate this for years.

Andrus provided a nuanced view. Much as he admired Church, Andrus thought the senator would not have made a good president.

Andrus believes governors make better presidents because of their executive experience in putting together state budgets and having to manage state agencies. He also believes it is fair to judge officeholders by their staff and by how well their campaign team performs. On the former standard, Church does well. He always had excellent staff and surrounded himself with talented people not afraid to challenge him. On the latter point, though, he does not get a passing mark.

Former *Lewiston Tribune* editorial page editor Bill Hall's book on Church painfully documents what a poorly run campaign Church's 1976 presidential was; rife with power factions, backbiting, intrigue and plain incompetence. Church selected Carl Burke, a boyhood friend and talented attorney who ran all of his Senate campaigns, to run his presidential campaign. It was a mistake.

Despite a herculean effort, Burke was in over his head. In particular, he was not prepared to put the Church deputy campaign chairman and national finance director, Henry L. Kimelman, in his place. Church won six primaries in spite of his national campaign team, not because of them. With the exception of Oregon, where the effort was led by two future members of Congress, Larry LaRocco and Mike Kopetski, Church was ill-served by many of the team members.

Andrus was not surprised by this, seeing it as another reason why, if he had to make a choice between the two friends based on who he thought would perform best, he would have given the nod to Jimmy Carter. That Carter also turned out not to be a skilled executive came as a surprise to his Secretary of the Interior.

My earliest memory of Senator Church was watching part of his nationally televised keynote address to the Democratic National Convention at Los Angeles in 1960. I was 13, living in Spokane and just beginning to be interested in politics.

I remember thinking that, while he had a great sounding voice, was obviously young and handsome; the speech seemed pompous and pretentious. That I did not finish watching it speaks volumes to me 50 years later. My view was shared by far more politically sophisticated viewers.

Being proud of my native state, I asked my mother what she knew about Church. She said he was a fine senator representing Idaho well, but then she added a coda with a bite: "To my dying day, though, I'll always know that I beat him in the statewide American Legion Oratorical contest my junior year (1941) in high school, though the judges gave him first place."

That was the first I knew there was a bit of family history with Church. Mother, the class of 1942 valedictorian at Pocatello High School, had been in the finals against Church – a star debater, orator, and student body president at Boise High School. Church went on to the nationals in Washington, D.C., where he won a significant scholarship that enabled him to enroll at Stanford.

I met Church when I went to D.C. to cover politics in 1971. Though I had the political and education beat at the *Idaho State Journal* during 1969 and half of 1970, I don't recall the senator coming through Pocatello. I was surprised he did not accompany New York Senator Robert Kennedy during his much publicized visit to the Fort Hall Indian Reservation.

Church's extraordinarily good press secretary, Cleve Corlett, introduced me to the senator during my first day making the rounds on Capitol Hill, snooping for news the wires wouldn't cover but my client newspapers would devour.

Cleve Corlett is the son of the late John Corlett, who for many years was one of the leading Idaho political correspondents by virtue of his position at Idaho's largest newspaper, *The Idaho Statesman* in Boise. Cleve Corlett always had his camera ready to take pictures of any Idahoan who visited the senator's office. Often, their picture, signed by the senator, would arrive in the mail before the visitor had returned home.

Corlett also produced frequent "D.C. Newsletters" sent to voters throughout Idaho on a regular basis. A prolific writer, he could grind out 10 press releases in an hour. Corlett also astutely introduced me to chief of staff, Verda Barnes, who oversaw one of the capital's finest constituent services operations. Her rolodex was legendary. She knew anyone who was anybody in D.C. and in Idaho.

The legend was she never slept. Staff and reporters could receive phone calls any time of the day or night. Many believe she is the primary reason Church was re-elected three times and he is still the only Democrat U.S. senator from Idaho ever to be re-elected. That she had to retire because of ill health in 1975 and died in June of 1980 may be the primary reason Church lost his re-election bid to Steve Symms.

A prize photo of ours is one Corlett took of my mother, sister, and wife sitting on a couch in the senator's office, with Church casually sitting on the arm of a chair. The photo was taken during an August, 1971, visit to the capital. Despite my suggestion to mother not to mention the oratorical contest some 30 years earlier, she, of course, did. Ever the politician, Church smiled and told her he had no doubt she had beat him.

The continuing fine performance of the senator's staff in the delivery of constituent services helped him win re-election and muted criticism of his deep interest in foreign affairs. Because the staff performed so well, Church could pursue matters dealing with the nation's standing around the world. He traveled extensively overseas during his 24-year career, but seldom did one see any criticism in the Idaho media for foreign travel coming at the expense of maintaining the home fires.

Washington reporter Chris Carlson takes Margaret, Linnea and Marcia to visit with Frank Church, summer 1971. Photo by Cleve Corlett.

(It is interesting to note having an Idaho senator display interest in foreign affairs and undertake service on the Senate Foreign Relations committee, has a long and distinguished history. It was first established by Senator William E. Borah, carried on by Church, and has now been taken up by Idaho's Republican junior senator, Jim Risch. Elected in 2008, Risch is already the second ranking minority member of the committee and is receiving criticism in the home-state press for his numerous overseas "junkets.")

Church's interest in foreign affairs can be traced in part to his service in China as an intelligence officer in the Army during World War II. Few know that the senator received a Bronze Star for his performance while in that theater. He watched, learned, and absorbed the lessons the war had to teach one curious enough to study the causes of the conflict between east and west. Church recognized the vast cultural differences that existed between the ancient civilizations of the orient and western culture.

He appears instinctively to have understood that the U.S. was a superpower on the world stage whose national interests would more than ever have an international component. While fighting the cancer that almost killed him upon his return after the war to Stanford University, he had plenty of time to think and analyze. From these times and lessons, Church developed his strong support for the United Nations and its role to provide a framework for world peace. He additionally recognized the importance of fair trade as a vehicle for spreading wealth among countries with emerging economies. He understood the powerful historical forces driving the leadership in these post-war countries.

While recovering from his near-death experience with cancer he also developed his sense of "living on borrowed time." The future senator felt the Almighty had granted him a second chance at life and he dedicated himself to making the most of whatever time he might have. It enabled him to have a long-term perspective and avoid the passions of the short-term.

During my two years in D.C., Church took several overseas trips, including one to Russia in the summer of 1971 as a delegate to the Sixth Dartmouth Conference which held bi-lateral discussions with counterparts from the Soviet Union. He took trips to East Pakistan (now Bangladesh) and to Canada, leading a delegation to the Ottawa Conference in 1972.

I interviewed him on his return from these trips. Reading the columns today only serves to reinforce how much he knew, how well he perceived and analyzed the international scene, and how ahead of times he was.

On the 10-day visit to Russia in the early summer of 1971 were other notables including Oregon Republican Senator Mark Hatfield, Chase Manhattan Bank Chairman David Rockefeller, former U.S. ambassador to the U.N. Charles Yost, Milton Eisenhower ,and retired Army General James Gavin.

The Cold War was still in full bloom and relations with the Soviet Union were tense. America was deeply involved in Vietnam. Nonetheless, the American delegation was well received. The delegates were able to spend extraordinary amounts of time meeting with the

Soviet Premier, Alexei Kosygin. Casting a cloud over their visit, though, was the announcement by President Richard Nixon that he would be visiting China.

The proposed Nixon visit was the beginning of the end of America's "two China" policy. It also was immediately recognized by the Soviets as a move by the United States to drive a wedge between the world's two largest communist states. The American delegation was instructed by the U.S. Embassy not to raise the subject of the Nixon gambit in their meeting with Kosygin unless the Soviet premier first raised it. Much to the senator's frustration, Kosygin did not mention the Nixon trip.

In the interview, Church said he returned somewhat depressed by the continuing repression of the Soviet state, the emphasis on conformity of thought with communist ideology, and the drabness evident in a centralized state planning process.

Having first visited the Soviet Union in 1959, he noted some changes for the better – more consumer goods available, more autos on the streets, and a modern subway system in Moscow, Kiev, and Leningrad.

In an example of the kind of over-the-horizon look Church was so good at, the senator said he and Kosygin had a candid discussion about whether either society was honestly addressing the environmental issues that come with modernizing growth. Kosygin claimed the Soviets were focused on environmental issues, but cited an "internal contradiction" in the American system that he believed prevented America from addressing its challenges. Kosygin, of course, was implying the profit motive in the capitalistic system worked counter to investing in environmental aspects of development as well as being calculated as part of a project's cost.

Church admired, though, Kosygin's candor in saying the Soviet Union was 10 years behind where they should be in addressing environmental pollution issues and taking corrective steps. He also noted Kosygin's candor was not shared by the Soviet delegates to the conference who continued to claim everything was fine. Church was pleased that all delegates recognized the need for international cooperation in addressing environmental challenges of air and water pollution which respect no arbitrary boundaries.

During the meetings with Kosygin, the delegation also discussed the necessity of achieving a nuclear arms control agreement with the

Soviets. Each side recognized it was a difficult and complex challenge, but it was necessary to continue a one-step-at-a-time effort to reach agreements in the mutual interest of both nations.

Church also displayed an unusual degree of sensitivity to U.S.-Canadian issues. He intuitively understood Canadian unease at being next door to a superpower with ten times the population and a profound impact on a country's culture because of proximity (90 percent of all Canadians live within 100 miles of the American border). As chair of the Foreign Relations subcommittee on Western Hemisphere Affairs, Church followed closely Canadian issues. Unlike the vast majority of American politicians, he could speak knowledgeably on most Canadian matters.

Church was likely aware of the disrespectful manner President Lyndon Johnson had treated Canadian Prime Minister Lester Pearson during a visit to Camp David in the escalating days of the Vietnam War. Just prior to his visit, Pearson had publicly criticized a Johnson move escalating the bombing of North Vietnam.

Pearson reportedly was already at his Camp David cabin when Johnson arrived. Johnson came storming across the compound screaming, "Where is the little sonofabitch?" Marching up onto the Pearson cabin's deck, he grabbed Pearson by the lapels of his suit coat and literally picked him up as he shouted, "How dare you shit in my nest?"

That had to be the nadir of relations between the two nations.

Church was also aware of the importance of the U.S./Canadian agreement on the cooperative management of the Columbia River system with power and flood control dams on both sides of the border. Likewise, he was aware Idaho's junior senator, Len Jordan, had been an Eisenhower appointee to the International Joint U.S./Canadian Border Commission (IJC), a body specifically created to address cross-border issues. No doubt, too, Church was aware of the commerce between Idaho and western Canadian provinces because of a 90-mile shared border and U.S. Highway 95.

Church was careful to place his interest in foreign affairs in the context of future markets for Idaho products. Whether it was urging the dropping of trade sanctions imposed on Cuba, or granting Communist China "most favored nation" trading status as a trade partner, or dropping the "two China" policy, Church saw increased trade as inevitably beneficial to the nation's interests and Idaho's economic interests.

In early 1972, the senator lent a strong voice of approval to the Shang-hai communiqué announced jointly by President Richard Nixon and Chinese Premier Chou En-Lai. At the time Church said, *"For 20 years our fixation that China was a demon over which the United States must stand guard for Asia has been the root cause for our marathon involvement in land wars on the Asian mainland. President Nixon deserves great credit for acting to dispel that fixation. His trip to China was indispensable to the formulation of a new American policy that can write an end to further American involvement in wars of endless attrition on the continent of Asia."*

The communiqué called for a phased withdrawal of American troops from Taiwan and the settlement of Taiwan's future by the two Chinas without outside interference. Implicit in it was the ending of the Two Chinas policy which to Church was a no-brainer. A market with almost a billion people awaited more opening and inevitably greater trade with the United States.

Church had already taken the lead in repealing the Formosa Resolutions in 1971 which he viewed as akin to the infamous Tonkin Gulf Resolution, President Lyndon Johnson's blank check excuse for escalating the Vietnam War. Church always regretted his vote for the Tonkin Gulf resolution. Only Alaska Senator Ernest Gruening and Oregon Senator Wayne Morse, displaying great foresight, had voted against giving Johnson the blank check.

Ever the pragmatist, Church no doubt saw better relations with China as another way to bring pressure on the North Vietnamese to accept a negotiated settlement to end the conflict and allow America to exit from a growing debacle which he had turned strongly against.

By 1971, the Idaho senator had already co-authored legislation with Senator John Sherman Cooper of Kentucky, curtailing funding for the Vietnam conflict. In 1973, Church and Senator Clifford Case of New Jersey passed an even more restrictive amendment restricting funding for the conflict he had come to deplore. His effort on this front alone deserves another chapter in any new updating of JFK's *Profiles in Courage*.

In the international affairs arena, Church left a legacy of far-sightedness – that uncanny ability to look over the horizon and see the way the future would unfold – that stands the test of time. His moral courage in standing up for what he believed to be right will be long remembered especially by many foreign affairs experts.

Many believe, though, that his most enduring legacy lays in what he did for those who want to travel beyond the noise of civilization and tramp through wilderness akin to what it was 500 years ago. Others say what he did for the nation's elderly will be his greatest legacy.

Most Americans and most Idahoans, however, today have no idea how much they owe the senior senator from Idaho.

He is a legitimate hero to the many involved in the nation's continuing expansion of the environmental movement. He was present at the beginning. He authored or co-authored such far-reaching legislation as the nation's original 1964 Wilderness Act, the 1968 Wild and Scenic Rivers Act, and the 1980 Central Idaho Wilderness Act – the latter creating a 2.3 million-acre wilderness – the largest in the lower 48 states.

In 1984, when senatorial colleague Jim McClure learned Church was near death from the pancreatic cancer that shortly would take him, McClure moved quickly, while Church was still alive, to have the wilderness portion of the roadless area south of the Magruder Corridor and the Salmon River renamed the *Frank Church River of No Return Wilderness*. While flattered by the recognition, Church told former aide Fred Hutchison that the name was a mouthful.

Hutchison told the senator not to worry, that folks would quickly reduce it down to "the Frank," much as folks in Montana quickly started calling the Bob Marshall Wilderness "the Bob." Hutchison was correct. The result though today is few folks even in Idaho know who "the Frank" is named for or why.

The senator went to his grave knowing he was instrumental in making it possible for hundreds of thousands of Americans and generations yet to come to be able to enjoy the splendor and the solitude of Idaho's magnificent backcountry. Whether floating the Snake River through Hells Canyon, backpacking in Idaho's Sawtooths, fly fishing on the St. Joe River, or flying into Moose Creek in the Selway/Bitterroot Wilderness, Frank Church is the one most responsible for making it possible.

Church was not exactly the outdoors type. Most perceived him as a city boy. He developed his appreciation for the invaluable intangibles of wilderness largely because Bethine had inherited the family interest in the Robinson Bar Ranch located on the edge of the central Idaho wilderness area, south of the Salmon River between Challis and Stanley.

In the early years in the Senate, the ranch was his special get-away. He, Bethine, and their two boys, Forrest and Chase, loved it. A stickler for avoiding even the appearance of an impropriety, he and Bethine sold the ranch before the Senate took up the 1964 Wilderness Act. The senator did not want anyone thinking his support for the bill might accrue benefit for him by enhancing the value of the property.

While it is a shame he felt that way, the ranch accomplished its purpose in his life by instilling in him a deep love for wild Idaho. The ranch has since changed hands several times and is today owned by singer and song-writer Carole King.

In late July of 1980, in a room in the Old Executive Office Building next to the White House, President Jimmy Carter signed into law the Central Idaho Wilderness Act. Standing behind the President on the stage witnessing the signing were three Idahoans who played critical roles in the passage of the legislation: Senator Church; Idaho Governor John V. Evans; and Interior Secretary Cecil D. Andrus. The latter two had been steadfast supporters of the legislation and each had spoken forcefully at hearings in support of creating the wilderness areas – not always a popular position politically within Idaho.

Perhaps Andrus' greatest contribution had been convincing the President and Rosalynn to join him and Carol on a Middle Fork of the Salmon float trip during the summer of 1978. After signing the bill and passing out ceremonial pens, President Carter began regaling the assembly with several stories of floating the Middle Fork, fly fishing for the wily cutthroat trout along the way. The President needed no convincing to sign the legislation. He had seen and experienced "the Frank" first hand.

Verda Barnes, the senator's canny chief-of-staff, recognized long before the 1974 re-election effort got underway that not only could Governor Andrus be helpful to Church's 1974 effort, but also that Andrus was a remarkable political commodity.

The decision had already been made by the governor and the senator that as much as possible the two campaigns would operate out of the same offices around the state and there would be considerable coordination regarding schedules. Each would give the other a strong endorsement wherever they spoke on the campaign trail.

The Senator, Bethine, Barnes and most of the senator's staff knew who was riding whose coat-tails, but their smarts in clinging closely to Andrus were vindicated when on election night Andrus won with 72 percent of the vote. Church easily dispatched the former chief of staff to Congressman Steve Symms, Bob Smith, by a 58 percent to 42 percent margin.

Andrus won 43 of Idaho's 44 counties, the exception being Lemhi, a county that in five runs for governor he never did win. Church won in 34 of the state's 44 counties. Like Andrus, he too lost in Lemhi County. The other nine were: Canyon, Cassia, Custer, Franklin, Gooding, Jefferson, Jerome, Lincoln and Twin Falls counties.

In looking at the voter's abstract for 1974, two things are clear. The difference between Andrus' vote total of 184,142 and Church's 145,140 is that a lot of Idaho Republicans split their ballots. After voting for Bob Smith, they crossed party lines to vote for Andrus.

The other item that becomes clear is the political smarts Andrus displayed in pulling almost all of his television ads two weeks before Election Day and turning the time slots over to Malad State Senator John V. Evans, who was campaigning to be Andrus' Lt. Governor. Former Democrat State Rep. Vern Ravenscroft from Tuttle, had switched parties after losing to Andrus in the 1970 Democratic gubernatorial primary, and was thought to be narrowly ahead of Evans.

Andrus, already looking down the road, knew that if a Democrat captured the White House in 1976, which in the bitterness of the post-Watergate environment seemed likely, there was no way he could consider taking a cabinet post if it meant turning the state over to any Republican, let alone Ravenscroft.

One of Evans three ads was a joint one with Andrus. The extensive buy surely helped Evans win with 133,307 votes to Ravenscroft's 115,184 votes.

Could Senator Church have won without having combined his campaign with the Andrus effort? Yes, but the margin probably would have been closer.

Besides holding Church in high esteem and having great respect for his integrity, Andrus also admired the work the senator accomplished with his chairmanship of the Special Committee on Aging. I, too, found the time Church and his staff devoted to trying to better the lives of the nation's seniors most commendable.

In an August 27, 1971, I began my column:

"Senator Frank Church, D-Idaho, feels slightly belligerent about the problems of aging. As chairman of the Special Committee on Aging, he is tired about mere talk in the problems of elderly Americans without any meaningful action. Older people in America have typically received the least priority. It's a disgrace that a country such as ours has done so little to care for its elderly," Church bluntly charges."

I noted where Church would focus his clout from additional funding for senior programs to bird-dogging an upcoming White House Conference on the Aging. In the meantime, he used the bully pulpit of his chairmanship to hold hearings on subjects ranging from the plight of elderly Native Americans to the so-called "Death with Dignity" issue which led him into his eight-year pursuit to obtain Medicare support for the hospice program.

Several fine books have been written about Senator Church and his life including the poignant *Father and Son* by F. Forrester Church IV, the Senator's oldest son. Of all the books, this came closest to providing insights into what drove the senator. It was published in 1985, a year after the senator's premature death at the age of 59.

The most inclusive and best biography produced so far is *Fighting the Odds*, by LeRoy Ashby and Rod Gramer. While faithfully recounting the senator's life and legislative accomplishments, it fails to delve into the senator's background to find what drove him other than to suggest his near death experience in 1948 from his first bout with cancer was his "driver."

Like almost all high achievers, the senator was full of complexities, contradictions, and ambiguities not to mention a person quite capable of paradox.

One is left with a series of questions to suggest to a first-rate biographer, a Robert Caro or a Bob Dallek, to deal with when someone of that caliber realizes there's a great biography to be written about a truly great United States Senator.

Some modest suggestions of questions to be pursued would be:

1. What was the senator's early life like? We know little about his family life. Remember the LBJ statement: How did that apply to Frank Church? What were the mother's hopes? Were there failings on the father's part? How did his interest in oratory develop? Did he read the Ancient Greek and Roman orators' speeches?

2. Was the senator a man of faith? His biographies listed his religion as Presbyterian. Did faith in part prompt his precocious interest in the welfare and plight of so many of the elderly?

3. What exactly did he do during World War II? Little if anything has been written about what was obviously one of his life's transformative experiences. Nor did the senator reference his Bronze Star often. Why?

4. Just how influential was Bethine? Many called her Idaho's third senator, but was she really that powerful an influence? And what happened if Verda Barnes's advice was different than Bethine's?

5. Who were the Senator's close friends besides his high school buddy, Carl Burke, who ran all his campaigns? Did he have any close senatorial colleagues? If so, who?

6. Did he know anything about the "Duke of Elmore" county's efforts on his behalf?

7. After failing in his first bid for office, a seat in the state legislature, what made him think he had a chance of winning the U.S. Senate seat of Herman Welker's in 1956?

8. Did he keep a diary that no one has seen?

9. What did he think and say about Cecil Andrus, George Hansen, Orval Hansen, John Evans, Len Jordan, Jim McClure and other of his political contemporaries in Idaho?

10. What did he consider his legacy to be?

Frank Church was a man of considerable accomplishment – great in many senses of the word. Nonetheless, as many answers as there are, there still remain many unanswered questions. Much is known about his public life, though few Idahoans today can recall little if anything about his accomplishments; but little seems known about his private life. He may remain an enigmatic figure forever unless a first rate biographer takes on the task of profiling greatness.

I admired and respected him. He and Andrus will always be in my mind the greatest political figures ever to tread across Idaho's political landscape. He did so much for his fellow man with his "second chance."

3 ■ The Pantry

Andrus and the birds. Photo by Barry Kough.

They warily eye each other, not sure the other is trustworthy. One photo was taken in the winter; the other in summer, but the look in the eyes is identical. On the left side is Andrus, a young governor starting what will become a record fourteen years of sitting in the chair over the next twenty-four years.

On the right side is "Otis," a restored-to-health golden eagle, one of many "birds of prey" nurtured by Morley Nelson, the driving force behind what will become Idaho's world renowned Birds of Prey National Conservation Area.

Andrus met Nelson while serving in the state Senate in the mid-60s. He doesn't remember where, but Nelson, who had retired from the Bureau of Land Management, was well into his program of restoring to health wounded birds of prey.

Andrus, who loves to hunt ducks and geese, was impressed enough he soon found himself bringing the usually discarded parts of his prey by Nelson's home as supplemental food. Nelson used these visits to introduce the future governor to the issue of raptor protection and Idaho's unique status as a rare place where many species of birds of prey – bald eagles, golden eagles, peregrine falcons, prairie falcons, red-tail hawks, and goshawks are concentrated.

This is due to an area along and above a stretch of the Snake River which harbors an abundant supply of ground squirrels – a prime source of sustenance for these birds of prey. Andrus would later dub this the "pantry."

Nelson had been fascinated with the various birds of prey for years. He became a one-person traveling fount of information, visiting area ranchers whenever and wherever to explain why it was important to everyone's ecosystem that the birds be protected.

He also left his calling card for ranchers if they spotted an injured bird of prey, like "Otis," the golden eagle made famous when held high in the photo with the governor of Idaho. Maybe it was the other way around – Otis made Andrus famous?

Nelson also perfected a strategy adopted by power and transmission line companies so that birds of prey were not electrocuted when landing on power transmission lines. Nelson convinced these firms to put greater spacing between their lines for it was when an eagle or other birds with a large wing-span would touch a second line that they would be electrocuted.

Because of his extensive knowledge, Nelson was also a technical consultant to films and features on the "Birds of Prey" made in the 60s and 70s.

Morley Nelson. Photo courtesy Nelson family.

Once his friend became governor, Nelson made it a point to get acquainted with the press secretary, John Hough. Like Andrus, Hough too became fascinated with Nelson's efforts to restore to health these majestic birds, especially the golden eagles.

In the fall of 1972 Nelson dropped by the office to discuss with Andrus the fact he was starting to have problems finding homes for the birds he was restoring to health. Nelson wondered if there was some way the governor could assist. "I don't know what I am going to do," he said. "These birds deserve a good place to live out their days, but I just cannot find enough suitable places for them."

Andrus said he would like to help and would entertain any suggestion Nelson or Hough might come up with.

Hough put on his thinking cap and before long approached Andrus with the idea of writing his fellow governors across the nation. The opening line of the Andrus letter to his gubernatorial peers was a classic hook: What do you do with a wounded eagle? Andrus then requested their assistance in finding homes for Nelson's restored-to-health eagles in their state.

The reaction was mixed. Wyoming Governor Stan Hathaway, through an aide, gave a tart reply saying there were plenty of eagles in Wyoming and he did not need any from Idaho. Governor Reuben Askew of Florida and Governor Marvin Mandel of Maryland, on the other hand, were helpful and able to find homes for several eagles, much to the delight of Hough, Nelson, and Andrus.

Hough also put the Andrus letter in the press boxes for the AP and UPI wire services as well as the *Idaho Statesman*. One of the wire services did a small item which just happened to catch the eye of CBS television reporter Richard Threlkeld. He called Hough, said he had seen the item on Nelson, was intrigued and was planning to come to Boise to visit Nelson and asked if John would assist. Within the week Threlkeld was there and he and Hough went to Nelson's place in the Boise foothills.

Threlkeld was immediately hooked, called for a film crew to fly in, and the next day filmed and narrated what would become a 4 and ½ minute CBS Evening News story with Walter Cronkite on December 18th, 1972. As he left Boise, Threlkeld told Hough the story would run that week. He also told Hough to call him if any other network called to follow up on the Nelson wire story.

Of course, the story did not run and did not run. Hough began to worry it would never run. He contends he finally received an inquiry from NBC News asking questions and indicating they were going to fly a crew from Salt Lake City to Boise to do their story. Hough called Threlkeld who said thanks for the heads up and that night the story ran as the last item on the news with a great introduction by Cronkite.

Some, who know Hough well, do not put it out of the realm of possibility that the inquiry from a competing network might just have been manufactured. If so, Hough will never tell.

Andrus and Nelson were interviewed for the CBS news show and came across through the TV medium as the decent people they are; concerned about birds of prey. It was Andrus' first major appearance in a nation-wide medium but far from his last.

Hough was able to alert Nelson as well as the governor that the piece was going to be shown that night. He was also able to watch the program with Andrus. When the news show was done, Andrus turned to Hough and deadpanned "now that you've gotten me on national television don't rest for a moment, and get going on getting me on the cover of Time Magazine."

While Andrus was jesting with Hough, when I came aboard as Hough's successor I took the challenge seriously and did finally get the Boss on the *Time* cover, albeit as a composite of the 200 rising young leaders in America!

To draw further attention to this unique wildlife resource, Nelson and Hough convinced Andrus to hold Otis on an outstretched arm. In today's terms, the photo went "viral" instantly, with the Associated Press and United Press newswires moving the picture from the front-page of the *Idaho Statesman* to all their outlets, domestic and overseas.

It was the first of three pictures in which Andrus held a raptor during the next two decades that garnered national attention. In the first and second photos he was holding Otis – one could call both "Two Birds of Prey take each other's measure."

The third photo appeared on the front page of the *Washington Post* and came almost nine years later in the second year of Andrus' four-year stint as Jimmy Carter's Secretary of the Interior. This photo was part of an extensive campaign by Andrus using the his pulpit as Interior secretary to draw attention to Idaho's unique status in hosting the huge concentration of birds of prey, and the consequent need to protect their habitat and forage area.

Andrus tasked the Bureau of Land Management with securing a sufficient prey base for an expanded Birds of Prey Sanctuary in Idaho. BLM asked for assistance from the Secretary's Office of Public Affairs in drumming up publicity to build more public support for legislation expanding the Birds of Prey.

Public affairs (OPA) came up with good ideas including reintroduction of peregrine falcons (the first bird species ever given the "endangered species" designation under the ESA) into greater Washington, D.C. It made sense because peregrines love to feast on pigeons, of which there is an abundant supply around "the Beltway." We scheduled a public "release" of mature peregrines from the roof of the Interior Department Building at 14th and C Streets as well as set up nests. Then we invited the press to come by.

Old Harold Ickes, the longest serving Interior secretary (14 years), must have rolled over in his grave.

A *Post* photographer, and Barry Kough, the Lewiston *Tribune* photographer then on a visit to D.C., caught the same picture of Secretary Andrus, dressed in a fine suit, holding a young peregrine chick in his hands with the mother peregrine perched on his shoulder, carefully watching. It easily made the front page of the *Washington Post* and was the only time during the four years in D.C. the Interior secretary was pictured on the front page.

Film of a peregrine dropping out of the sky at a 100 mph, and hitting a pigeon, is dramatic and stunning. The hit often results in a literal explosion of the pigeon.

While most people detest pigeons – they are pesky, persistent, often disease-ridden birds – we found there are pigeon-lovers in this world. We heard from them all. We received numerous letters protesting the reintroduction program.

Southwestern Idaho's original "Birds of Prey" area was a 33-mile stretch of the Snake River and it was a continuing issue in Andrus' career as governor and as interior secretary. It also weaves through my checkered past as a journalist and his press secretary from 1973 to 1981.

My first column mention of the proposed Birds of Prey came in mid-July of 1971. The Bureau of Land Management within the Interior Department had proposed, and, they expected Congress would approve, setting aside 26,000 acres in southwestern Idaho to be dedicated to birds of prey.

No longer, for example, could one apply for land withdrawals under the Desert Land Entry Act or the Carey Act for conversion to cultivation as farm land. The 33-mile stretch, known locally as the Swan Falls Reach, was by no means totally sufficient to meet the birds' food needs, but it was a start.

On July 14, 1971, I reported then Interior Secretary Rogers C.B. Morton was expected to preside at a mid-August Idaho dedication ceremony to be attended by state and local dignitaries. Morton's staff and BLM officials saw this as an opportunity for the Interior secretary to do something positive for the environment. They also thought it would be non-controversial. The dedication was contingent on the House and Senate Interior oversight committees approving.

Their imprimaturs were expected, however, because support at a hearing in Boise on February 26, 1971, had been near unanimous with the recently elected governor, Cecil D. Andrus, leading off with his strong endorsement.

Andrus has always possessed an uncanny ability to come up with an easily retainable, memorable descriptive phrase. It is a gift, not a talent one can learn.

Thus, at the Boise hearing Andrus coined one of his classics by referring to the initial designation as providing protection for the "bedroom" area of the "house" for the birds, but that an expanded area would be needed to protect their food source, their prey base – "the pantry," which was truly needed for the long-term enhancement of the birds of prey population.

Also contributing to the success of the Boise hearing was the popularity of two recently released feature length movies, *Walt Disney's "Ida, the Off-Beat Eagle,"* and *Wild Kingdom's "The Valley of the Eagles."*

Interior Secretary Morton had announced earlier in the 1971 summer he intended to make Denver the department's "headquarters" from August 6 to September 6. This coincided with the Congressional recess. From Denver he planned to take short jaunts to various western states looking into and publicizing the myriad of issues Interior is involved with and its cooperative work with appropriate state agencies.

Interior spokesmen made it clear Morton would avoid "controversial" proposals, specifically mentioning the proposed inclusion of the White Clouds in the Sawtooth NRA, if it was not going to be designated a National Park. Additionally, they cited putting the

Middle Snake under a seven-year moratorium from any plans for dam-building.

Though Morton hoped to keep the media focused on "positives," the mere fact his spokesmen outlined issues and divided them, virtually assured what he wanted to avoid would happen. Nevertheless, the Interior Secretary did go ahead with the ceremony planned for mid-August in Idaho.

Another reason Morton withdrew the 26,000 acres was the hope the media would see it as a positive antidote to the growing controversy elsewhere over inadvertent poisoning of eagles by ranchers trying to protect their cattle and/or sheep herds from coyote predation. Using powerful poisons provided by the Interior Department's Predator Control Program, ranchers were devastating eagles, golden as well as bald, feeding off the coyote carrion.

A lingering question was, where did First District Congressman James A. McClure stand? The proposed withdrawal was in his district, after all. Despite the overwhelming favorable sentiment at the Boise hearing the astute McClure had held back from endorsing a Birds of Prey sanctuary.

Cautious by nature and yet still a conservation conservative, McClure's instincts were to hold back until all the players had been heard from – in particular, the Idaho Power Company. One suspects McClure knew in advance the company was going to propose two low-head hydro projects between Swan Falls and Guffey that would potentially generate 119 megawatts.

How would this impact the upcoming Republican Senate primary fight between McClure, former Second District Congressman George Hansen, former three-term Governor Robert E. Smylie, and a doctor/lawyer from Kendrick named Glen Wegner – all of whom would be duking it out for the Senate seat held by incumbent Senator Len B. Jordan?

During the August recess Jordan, who was expected to run again by Idaho's political insiders, had instead stunned the state by announcing plans to return home at the end of his term and ten years of senate service.

McClure announced immediately he intended to seek the Senate seat. As a matter of practical politics, he wanted to minimize any issue that could mushroom into controversy. There is no evidence McClure, or any of his office or campaign staff, contacted Morton to urge him not to participate in a "dedication" event. It's a good guess, though, that Morton gave due deliberation before deciding to move forward.

As a political issue, then, the Birds of Prey faded into the background for a few years. Andrus' 1974 opponent, Lt. Governor Jack ("Blackjack") Murphy, did allege Andrus was an "environmentalist" (a pejorative term). Murphy charged Andrus did not aggressively support expanding Idaho's agricultural land base through further utilization of the Desert Land Entry and Carey Acts. The charge never developed legs with the media or resonated with the public. Andrus went on to win re-election by the largest margin in Idaho history.

Good with a pencil and a calculator, Andrus knew that as a matter of economics further Desert Land Entry and Carey Act withdrawals needed ever-increasingly, costly electricity to lift water from the Snake onto the few bench areas left with potential for development. He was not surprised when Idaho Power announced plans for the Swan Falls/Guffey low-head hydro projects on virtually the same stretch of the Snake containing both the "bedroom" and the "pantry" for the Birds of Prey.

While a "sanctuary" for Birds of Prey may have disappeared from the front pages, it was not forgotten either by its proponents or by the ever-growing members of Idaho's nascent environmental community. Ways were found to focus more public attention on the Birds of Prey such as a "coffee table" book of stunning photography by Robert Beatty. Published by Caldwell's Caxton Printers under the sponsorship of one of Idaho's leading banks, Tom Frye's First National Bank of Idaho, the book portrayed well the area and the majesty of the raptors. Andrus gave away many copies of the beautiful book as Christmas gifts during the winter of 1974.

Four years later, the Birds of Prey area was again on the front pages. Pictures of now Interior Secretary Cecil D. Andrus, along with movie star Robert Redford and Andrus' successor as governor, John V. Evans, all on a float trip together through the "Birds of Prey" stretch of the Snake, flashed across the state and the nation.

Redford (second from right), Andrus (left) and others on the Snake River. Photo courtesy Bureau of Land Management.

The unusual attention was instigated by Spencer Beebe, a bundle of energy who headed up the Washington, D.C. office of the Nature Conservancy, one of Andrus' favorite organizations. At the time, a relatively new 501(c)(3), the Conservancy specialized in utilizing funds from its many wealthy contributors to buy and hold key parcels of land critical to future creation of environmental set-asides until government funds could be obtained to purchase the property.

Aware of the proposal for a Birds of Prey Conservation Area and its still strong public support, Beebe was also aware of Idaho Power's plans for dams and their potential threat to an expanded Birds of Prey area. Conservancy staff had made Beebe aware of five land parcels along the Snake that could be purchased. Once that was accomplished, the Conservancy purchase would stand square in the path of Idaho Power's plans for the Swan Falls/Guffey dam projects.

Beebe, a natural promoter, came up with the idea of drawing national attention to the Birds of Prey by doing a two-day, one night float trip utilizing the Interior secretary, Idaho's current governor, and a movie star – Robert Redford – as the draws. Beebe was the nexus; the one who knew all three.

At a meeting in Andrus' office in early 1978 the resources of the Bureau of Land Management's national office and the Idaho BLM state office were mobilized to support and promote the "resource inspection" trip.

Interior's office of public affairs also undertook the development of a booklet complete with raptor photography and maps which would be made available to news media covering the float trip. The booklet provided vital background information about the Birds of Prey, its genesis, current status, imminent threats, and future plans.

Critics often charged that OPA, in producing such documents, was "lobbying" with public funds, especially if a matter called for future legislation, as did the Birds of Prey. Such booklets were seen as advocacy pieces. The response is they are balanced, **educational** pieces consistent with the mission of a cabinet secretary's public affairs office.

A small task force within the OPA was created, led by Harmon Kallman and Ed Essertier, to work out all details with the Conservancy, Governor Evans' office, the Idaho BLM office (capably led by State Director Dean Bibles), and Robert Redford's staff. A two-day period, April 30th-May 1st, 1978, was bore-sighted as the target date and locked into place.

Several things stand out for what turned out to be a PR success for all involved, but especially a winner for the Birds of Prey area.

Redford flew into Boise in a private Cessna Citation jet to be met and picked up by the Interior secretary. Andrus was immediately impressed with what a genuinely unpretentious, decent, intelligent, person Redford is. He had no entourage with him. Beebe had briefed him well on the issues and he quickly displayed a familiarity with their nuances that pleased Andrus.

Idaho State BLM Director Dean Bibles had arranged a helicopter to take them to the put-in point on the Snake River from Interior's fleet of planes and helicopters, many located and maintained at the Interagency Fire Center at the Boise Airport. Governor Evans, Spencer Beebe, and the others accompanying Andrus and Redford, as well as the news media, awaited them at the site.

A decision had been made to hold the first press availability there even though it was a long jaunt from Boise. I worried we would not attract press but the fear was baseless. Never underestimate the ability of a movie star like Redford to draw news media from miles around.

The three principals all played their parts, but when it was over and folks were getting into their rafts, Bibles got off one of the best quotes, telling reporters "I don't really see how we can risk a population of birds found nowhere else in the world for a mere 119 or so megawatts of power."

Another indelible memory from that trip is "the hat." Andrus had forgotten to bring any kind of hat and as we were getting into the rafts it was a "bluebird" clear day with a bright sun beating down. I spotted the solution.

Perched on the head of Governor Evans' press secretary, Steve Leroy, was a 10-gallon felt Stetson. Having hired Leroy in 1973 to be the communications director for the Department of Law Enforcement, I felt no compunction reaching over and plucking his "donation" to the Interior secretary's well-being. So I appropriated it, handed it to Andrus, who, having no idea that I had commandeered it from someone else, immediately donned it.

Two other images are indelibly burned into the memory bank.

The first came at our stop for the evening at a pre-designated camp site set up by BLM. We had time to chat before dinner and, as the daylight was fading in the west, I captured a picture of Andrus, wearing the 10-gallon Stetson, holding a beer in his hand and talking with Redford about the Birds of Prey. It is a classic.

The other image is several of us, Andrus and Redford included, sitting around the campfire with a canopy of beautiful, bright stars overhead unobstructed by the lights of any city. The conversation ranged from casual to serious, but it was something to listen to two natural entertainers keep the rest thoroughly entranced.

Early the next morning, Redford departed by helicopter which disappointed the news media waiting at the pull-out point some 30 miles downstream. Redford, however, had accomplished Beebe's goal to draw national attention to the Birds of Prey and so hastened on his way to other endeavors.

Andrus and Evans returned by helicopter to Boise and then flew to north Idaho for a campaign fund-raiser for Evans that evening in Coeur d'Alene.

Evans, who had been Lt. Governor when Andrus was selected by Jimmy Carter to become the 44th secretary of the Interior, had become Idaho's 27th governor on January 24, 1977, following Andrus' resignation and his swearing-in as the Interior secretary.

Now standing for election in November, he was in full campaign mode and delighted to be able to snag the still popular former Idaho governor to speak at and raise funds for his ultimately successful campaign over Republican House Speaker Allen Larsen.

At a press conference in Coeur d'Alene before the fund-raiser, however, Andrus surprised the news media by revealing he would be coming back to Idaho after Carter's first term, that four years in D.C. was enough for him.

Making himself a "lame duck" with two years left did not strike some as something that had to be said then. It could easily be misread by Carter's Georgia Mafia as a sign Andrus wanted out. Andrus, though, comfortable in his relationship with Carter, was not worried. Later, after Carter's infamous "Malaise" speech when the President compounded his off-messaging by asking ALL his cabinet members to submit their resignations, Andrus called all his personal staff to tell them not to worry. In his case the "resignation" was *pro forma*, the President was not about to let him leave.

While Spencer Beebe's efforts to spike Idaho Power's dam plans succeeded, Congress dithered and dallied for another two years doing nothing to protect either the pantry or the bedroom of the Birds of Prey area. Andrus' patience began to wear thin, so much so that a frustrated Interior secretary utilized powers granted him within the BLM's recently enacted BLM Organic Act for the first time. In 1980, by executive order, Andrus withdrew approximately 483,000 acres of the Birds of Prey from entry by the Carey Act, the Desert Land Entry Act, and other laws that could alter the landscape.

The action imposed a 20-year moratorium and preserved the area's assets until Congress would hopefully take definitive action. It wasn't until 1993, in the next to last year of Andrus' record 14 years in the governorship, that Congress created the Birds of Prey National Conservation Area, and set aside 485,000 acres along the Snake as the pantry, cupboard, kitchen, and bedroom, almost the full house for Idaho's Birds of Prey.

Playing a key role in securing the legislation, besides the former Interior secretary, was Idaho's First District congressman, former Frank Church aide Larry LaRocco.

Thus, an action initiated by Interior Secretary Rogers C.B. Morton in August, 1971, by Public Land Order 5133, which withdrew from other uses 26,714 acres, finally culminated 22 years later with formal passage by Congress of a law that established permanent protection. President William Jefferson Clinton quickly signed the legislation into law.

Supporters of the Birds of Prey area recognize the lion's share of credit goes to Morton and Andrus; Morton because of his initial action as well as his 1975 order adding an additional 280,000 acres for placement in the "suspension" category with no change in status while BLM conducted a series of raptor research studies.

In 1977, the new Interior secretary, staying in touch with his friend, Morley Nelson, issued another Public Land Order increasing the study area to 515,000 acres. Finally, as part of prodding Congress to act, Andrus issued PLO 5773 designating 483,000 acres to be the Birds of Prey National Conservation Area in 1980.

Congress also finally recognized the pivotal role played by Morley Nelson, the driving force who early on had seen something in an obscure state senator from Clearwater County that he made a point of cultivating a friendship. In Public Law 111-11, in section 2301, BLM is ordered to rename the Birds of Prey posthumously after Morley Nelson – a truly fitting tribute for he was definitely the *sine qua non*.

There is a postscript that should be mentioned. When people think of Robert Redford they often also think of his fellow superstar side kick, Paul Newman. They starred together in movies such as *Butch Cassidy and the Sundance Kid* and *The Sting*.

Somewhere during Nelson's campaign to create the Birds of Prey area and save the world's largest concentration of these raptors, he captured the attention of Redford's side kick, Paul Newman. Nelson reportedly employed or had BLM employ for one summer of work in the Birds of Prey area one of Newman's daughters.

The story is that Dad Newman decided to visit the daughter. Suddenly, Owyhee County was reporting Newman sightings. The two most credible came from Marty Peterson and spouse, Barb, who have long owned a rustic cabin in the historic old mining town of Silver City deep in the Owyhee Mountains.

Peterson tells the story that he and Barb were sitting on the front porch of their cabin one warm summer afternoon when here came a station wagon up the road driven by Morley Nelson. His passenger was none other than Paul Newman.

The other credible sighting happened at the now closed Wagon Wheel Restaurant in the unincorporated town of Murphy, the county seat of Owyhee County. Most Idahoans are familiar with the picture of the county's only parking meter in front of the county courthouse and jail. It was also the abode for legendary, long-time County Sheriff Tim Nettleton, who often would jump in his Cessna 180 parked just beyond the courthouse on the dirt airstrip to patrol his vast county.

The proprietress (also named Marty) of the Wagon Wheel was a huge fan of Newman's. She had a large picture of the actor taped above the stove in the kitchen. She was working in the kitchen that same summer day when no one else was in the café and failed to hear a customer enter. The customer waited patiently and then walked into the kitchen.

Imagine Marty's shock and surprise when she turned around and there was Newman himself in the flesh.

The point of this chapter is that worthy as some goals are they still take dogged determination, patience and persistence to see the goal realized. As Andrus likes to say, success has a thousand fathers and it is amazing how much can be accomplished if one is willing to share the credit. He adds, "failure is always a bastard."

In this drama there were obvious stars, like Nelson, Andrus, Beebe, John Evans, and Robert Redford. There were also many quality supporting actors and actresses who can take private satisfaction in playing their part well – folks like John Hough, Dean Bibles, Congressman Larry LaRocco, Marty Peterson, Paul Newman, Harmon Kallman, and Ed Essertier.

Thus, a full 22 years after Andrus had testified at the Boise hearing, a goal he and Morley Nelson had started working toward while he was a state senator, and continued into his terms as governor and interior secretary was at last achieved. Some things just take a long time to gestate no matter how obvious the case for protection appears to be.

Like a resolute bird of prey, Andrus would say he "just kept his eye on the rabbit," or, more likely he would say he kept his eye on the "Townsend ground squirrel," the primary food source for Otis and many other Birds of Prey.

4 ▪ Idaho's 800 Pound Gorilla

Richard Nixon (left) and George and Connie Hansen campaigning in 1968 in Idaho. Photo by Barry Kough.

A few years ago a colleague came back from a business trip to Soda Springs, the county seat of Caribou County in the far southeastern corner of Idaho. It was an area first settled by Mormon pioneers heading north from Salt Lake City on "pioneering instructions" from Brigham Young, the second President, Prophet, Seer and Revelator of the Church of Jesus Christ of Latter-Day Saints.

I asked the colleague if he had noted the Mormon influence in the community.

His answer: "Not until dinner time when I went into a pizza place and ordered a couple of slices of pizza and a beer. I found out you can get pizza, and you can get beer, but not in the same place."

He had stumbled onto one of the many subtle and not-so-subtle ways Saints influence nearly everything in Idaho, from politics to economics, to life styles.

His story recalled another aspect of Mormon influence I stumbled on while working as a correspondent in Washington, D.C. (And wrote about in my biography on Andrus.)

As I walked out of then Congressman Jim McClure's office on a spring day in 1972, I offhandedly said to his administrative assistant, Dick Thompson, "I have to tell you, your boss just said he was opposed to 'release time."

"What's that?" asked Dick, who had never set foot in Idaho.

"In about three days Jim Goller will call and explain it to you," I responded.

McClure, in an unusual difference from other members of Congress had his chief of staff, stay home and operate out of the congressman's district office in the Old Boise Post Office Building.

Thompson, though an efficient manager of a D.C, staff well known for its constituent service, was in fact second in command.

If he had ever been to Idaho he would have known that "release time" was the practice in many Idaho school districts with a heavy concentration of Mormons, whereby students are released from classes for an hour to attend a religious education class at a nearby LDS seminary or institute.

I had gone to see McClure because I noticed he and his Second District colleague, Rep. Orval Hansen, had voted oppositely on the "Prayer Amendment." I wanted to know why.

JAMES A. McCLURE
1ST DISTRICT, IDAHO

1034 LONGWORTH BUILDING
(CODE 202) 225-6611

DISTRICT OFFICE:
805 IDAHO STREET, ROOM 319
BOISE, IDAHO 83702
(CODE 208) 343-1421

JAMES A. GOLLER
DISTRICT ASSISTANT

Congress of the United States
House of Representatives
Washington, D.C. 20515

November 19, 1971

COMMITTEES—SUBCOMMITTEES
INTERIOR AND INSULAR AFFAIRS
IRRIGATION AND RECLAMATION
PARKS AND RECREATION
MINES AND MINING

POST OFFICE AND CIVIL SERVICE
POSITION CLASSIFICATION
POSTAL OPERATIONS

RICHARD K. THOMPSON
ADMINISTRATIVE ASSISTANT

Mr. Chris Carlson
% A. Robert Smith
328 Pennsylvania Avenue S. E.
Washington, D. C.

Dear Chris:

I have never had any occasion to be disturbed by your report of any interview. I do want to take this occasion, though, to correct an impression which I apparently gave you in our recent conversation on the prayer amendment. You reported in your column that I was opposed to "release-time" and I am afraid somehow that my comments created an impression which I had not intended.

When I mentioned the example of release-time as a form of support of religion or recognition of religion by the government, I intended it to be in the context of other examples such as federal aid to colleges, some of which are church related institutions, and the federal aid to secondary schools which sometimes goes to parochial schools.

While I don't believe I mentioned it, another such example would be the tax exemption which is granted for property used for religious purposes. It was not my intention in giving those examples to indicate my opposition to any of them but to indicate that the prayer amendment for voluntary prayer in public buildings is much less a "recognition of religion" than these other practices which are supported by the government.

I am very much concerned that the report does not accurately reflect my views, and I am very sorry that apparently I did not make myself clear when using those examples. Because I believe it is important that people know how I feel on these issues, I am issuing a statement to each newspaper which carries your column. I want you to know, and I want them to know, that I am in no way critical of you for the statement in your column. It was my fault, not yours, that I didn't state it more clearly.

Sincerely,

James A. McClure, M. C.

McClure letter on release time.

The column was challenged by McClure and Goller, who realized how George Hansen, the former Second District Congressman who gave up his seat in 1968 to mount an unsuccessful Senate campaign against Frank Church, would use the column within the LDS community to raise questions in the upcoming Senate primary.

Though ostensibly one is not supposed to campaign in wards and stake houses because the LDS church wishes to maintain not only a non- partisan status, but also its tax-exempt status, Mormons in good standing can call on a bishop in his home to discuss politics and politicians. And some political meetings do in fact happen at stake houses.

Hansen had made hundreds of copies of my column, circled the appropriate graphs and than left a "bunch" with each bishop, fully expecting the bishops to pass them along. George was actively working his brethren because McClure was not LDS.

Goller knew it was a problem made more challenging by the fact that I had not misquoted his boss. When he called a few days after the column appeared, he neither asked for a retraction nor criticized my reporting.

Instead, all the newspapers that carried my column received a letter (I was copied) in which McClure "explained" he had misunderstood the question and now wanted to set the record straight: He was not opposed to "release time." Goller then hand-carried or mailed copies to every LDS bishop in Idaho.

The story is illustrative of the 1001 ways the LDS church exerts perceived and actual influence over the daily lives of Idahoans. "Saints" and "Jacks" (the euphemisms for practicing and non-practicing Latter Day Saints) constitute approximately 25 per cent of Idaho's electorate but they exert a disproportionate influence in the affairs of state.

This influence can be positive or negative. One need only look at Idaho's heavily Republican, extremely conservative legislature. A plurality of the members is LDS.

What is disconcerting, though, is that little is written or discussed openly about this high degree of "influence." The Church's "views" on various issues matters to its members, but they also impact non-members. The LDS Church is the classic 800 pound gorilla in the room. Everybody sees it but no one wants to discuss it.

This is partly because in polite company one still is not supposed to discuss religion or politics. Additionally, there is an implied attitude that if one is not of the faith they cannot possibly understand the faith. One may, as I have, read *The Book of Mormon, The Pearl of Great Price, The Doctrine and Covenants* and a dozen other books or studies of Mormonism, but that does not remove the stigma of being a gentile.

BYU-Idaho in Rexburg is now the fastest growing four-year college in Idaho. Its undergraduate enrollment of over 14,000 students has quickly passed Idaho State University and the University of Idaho in total enrollment. Only Boise State, with over 20,000 students, is larger.

Education is a good example of mixed Mormon attitudes, and of a vital subject not often discussed openly for fear one may be accused of bigotry.

Practicing Mormons profess strong support for education in principle. It is a major part of their belief system, a faith that sees each person evolving into their own god-like status based in part on one's acquisition of knowledge. They give new meaning to the term "life-long" learning.

Their well known emphasis on family, however, can and does impact their attitudes about educational value. It is no coincidence that surveys show Idaho and Utah to be two of the highest states with home schooling and two of the top states with the lowest state support for education on a per pupil basis.

Yet schools in Utah and Idaho are heavily influenced by LDS pressures. In Utah, non-Mormons joke about their state having the largest tax-supported parochial school system in the nation – and they don't mean Catholic.

Mormons value education and life-long learning but that does not always translate into strong support for adequately funding public education. This is paradoxical and this "mixed message" should be discussed but seldom is.

LDS legislators, when challenged on this paradox, point to the "Institutes" often built next to public schools, where LDS students can attend a religious education class during the extra period at the end of the normal five-day school week, or mid-day at those districts that are on the four-day-a-week schedule. These Institutes are built entirely with private funds and staffed largely by volunteers as well as part-time employees.

In Idaho, school boards, in theory, are "supreme" given that "local control" is a venerated value. In practice, however, the state of Idaho's Office of the Superintendent of Public Instruction issues many mandatory guidelines. Nevertheless, local boards do exert power and influence.

State and federal courts have upheld the legality of "release time" because the school district and the LDS Church go to great lengths to ensure there is no crossover expenditure of public funds. Nor are classes in religious education credited by the SPI towards the number of credits required to graduate.

This is due to Institutes not being certified by the state. Neither are their course offerings accredited. This stands in contrast to the Catholic schools in Idaho, where teachers have to be certified by the state and the curriculum state-approved.

Here are a couple of key points: Because local control at school boards appears to be paramount, it is possible, under exceptional circumstances for a local school board in a heavily LDS school district to grant credits for classes in religious education or history.

Even more to the point, if a student desires to attend BYU or any of its branch campuses (BYU-Hawaii, BYU-Idaho), a prerequisite for admission is having a specified number of religious education credits from an LDS seminary or institute.

Private colleges and universities set their own standards for admission and graduation, just as they can decide whether to accept other colleges' credits towards a diploma.

"Release time" is not as simple as it first appears. It is a critical element in the church's support of education, but it warrants constant monitoring. For example, Idaho, like some other states, intends to require at least two online courses as part of the course work required for a high school diploma.

Don't be surprised if classes "on-line" in LDS religious institutes make the approved list. Take a guess at which college or university offers the most "on-line" classes?

You are right – Brigham Young University.

Did the "release time" issue cause Jim McClure any real problems in his statewide race for the retiring Len Jordan's senate seat? Not exactly. He won the 1972 GOP Senate primary by 9 points, 36 percent to 27.8 percent, over George Hansen, then went on to defeat the popular president of ISU, Dr. William E. "Bud" Davis, by 20,000 votes with a significant margin coming right out of southeastern Idaho where previous polling had shown Davis in a much better position.

In the Republican primary, however, McClure did not do nearly as well as he did in the general. In the primary he received neither a majority nor a plurality of the votes cast in the heavily LDS Second Congressional District. The "release time" issue may have been one reason why he fared rather poorly with LDS voters.

The thumping was especially bad in the LDS counties of Madison, Jefferson, Bonneville, and Bannock. One could easily conclude that having to spend time on the issue the column raised was a distraction from McClure's basic pitch.

In 1972, Ada County had not yet been split between the First Congressional District and the Second Congressional District. McClure's performance in his key counties (Ada, Bonner, Kootenai, Nez Perce and Payette) more than compensated for his poor performance in the second district where the only county he captured in the primary was Twin Falls.

George Hansen's numbers and margins were startling nonetheless. In Madison, Hansen captured 1,400 votes to McClure's 400. In Bonneville he beat McClure by 4,000 votes to 1,800. In Bannock, McClure lost to Hansen, 2,654 to McClure's 690. And in Jefferson county it was 1,737 to 392.

Margins like these can be interpreted in only one way: The Sunday before Election Day in wards and stake houses across southern Idaho bishops and elders gave a brief testimonial to what a good "brother" George Hansen was without making a formal endorsement..

Thus, the LDS Church neatly sidesteps the charge that it dictates to its membership how to vote. It does not "dictate" the vote, but the "testimonials" carry the power of suggestion. It may not be as strong a monolithic vote as some critics like to portray it, but the numbers certainly suggest if it is not monolithic it certainly is a strong "bloc" vote.

LDS practices and beliefs impact Idaho in a variety of other, not immediately apparent, ways. The LDS Church encourages its members to patronize the businesses of members over non-members, for example. This may make sense to brother and sister Saints, but in practice there's no real competition in a majority LDS community between a Les Schwab tire franchise run by a Mormon and an OK Tire outlet run by a non- member. But all good Republican "saints" will tell you how good competition is.

A non-Mormon will sometimes hear a Mormon describe another as a Mormon "in good standing" or one that has a "temple recommend" from his bishop. It means the person is one with high morals and a solid reputation for honesty. It also invariably means they fulfill the pledge to tithe 10% of their "before tax income" to the Church. Many bishops sit down with their members under their guidance every two years and review how things have gone in their lives from a personal standpoint as well as reviewing their income tax form to monitor adherence to tithing.

With a bishop's "temple recommend," a Mormon is allowed to visit or get married in more than 100 LDS Temples around the world.

The architecture of the newer temples, especially where expensive white slabs of marble are utilized, capped off with the Angel Moroni at the tip of the highest spire, are simply stunning. Three in particular are noteworthy: the Washington, D.C. Temple, the Boston Temple and the San Diego Temple.

The Salt Lake City Temple holds a special place in the hearts of Mormons akin to St. Peter's in Rome for Catholics. It reflects the architecture of an earlier period but is stately, classic, and graceful in appearance.

The LDS Church is almost alone today on the American religious landscape as one that maintains a strong streak of Calvinism: that is that "temporal success is indicative of spiritual success." In other words, being a successful businessman is *prima facie* evidence one's spiritual house is in order and he has been marked for favor by God. Some of the fundamentalist Mega-churches also adhere to this Calvinistic view.

The LDS Church reinforces its Christian social ethic in many ways. Members are encouraged to belong to Rotary and Kiwanis clubs and to give back to the community, with their treasure, time and talent. Civic involvement for Mormons also includes voter participation, and in political parlance more than the average, Mormons are largely "four for four" voters. This means they participated in the last four straight opportunities to vote down to and including school board elections.

Saints take pride in taking care of their own. Thus, they maintain storehouses of supplies that members and families in good standing can draw on if they've hit a temporary bump in the road. Every adult Saint is expected to actively volunteer in Church activities; whether it is working at a cannery for a few hours each week producing supplies for the poor, serving as a Cub Scout den mother and everything in between, there are numerous opportunities for volunteerism.

In 2012 *The Bloomberg News* ran a detailed analysis that reflected poorly on the amount of dollars collected by the LDS Church and then reinvested in society through charitable donations and activities.

The Methodist Church, for example, puts back 26 percent of what it collects annually as compared to the 2 percent for the LDS church. LDS spokespersons, though, correctly point out that the study did not reflect nor quantify the enormous number of volunteer hours put back into the community by Saints in good standing. Time, after all, can be more valuable than money.

The LDS Church has long been commended for its emphasis on "family life" and the setting aside of one evening a week as "family home evening" in which the entire family participates in a group activity.

It is no coincidence; either, that in many communities across the country men and women in the LDS church are encouraged to be active in the Boy and Girl Scout organizations. Predominantly in the West, when one sees an announcement that a young man has obtained the rank of Eagle Scout, often he is a member of an LDS family.

Likewise, look at an application form for an ROTC scholarship to attend college or an application to go into an officer training program. Invariably, there is a question asking the applicant if they were ever in the scouting movement. The thought is, being a scout reflects well on having been taught the importance of discipline, the acceptance of accountability, the value of responsibility for others, and, the core value of group loyalty.

In the past, many officers in the U.S. Marine Corps came out of southern states with strong backgrounds in conservative religions; but today, more and more Marine officers are LDS. There are no coincidences.

All of this originates from a deep sense of patriotism. Despite the history of the early years of conflict with both state and federal governments, today's Saint manifests an extraordinary degree of old-fashioned patriotism. For most Mormons, the United States in general and Utah in particular are the biblically forecast new "Zion." They believe this nation is and has been singled out by God for special favor and that the Constitution is divinely-inspired.

For the LDS Church, it all starts with the family unit. Utah and Idaho stand out in the face of a national decline in the traditional family unit of dad and mom, and their biological children. That traditional unit in some cities is as low as 15 percent of the population. Utah and Idaho though still have significantly higher numbers of the traditional unit.

Additionally, Mormon families have a higher than the national average rate for adoptions because babies put up for adoption are viewed as freed souls in need of a nurturing environment. This is consistent with a major tenet of the LDS faith that emphasizes the importance of providing an earthly form for spirits waiting in heaven to become individual souls beginning their own journey towards a god-like status.

LDS families take seriously the Biblical injunction to be fruitful and multiply. That exhortation plus the emphasis on providing more earthly forms for waiting souls is what led Mormon forefathers to embrace polygamy. Setting aside for a moment one's belief whether polygamy is moral, in the early days of a persecuted church there was a practical as well as humane side to the practice.

Again, citing Biblical accounts of brothers taking on the widow of a deceased brother, polygamy was viewed as a humane practice that provided for the widow and her surviving children before the advent of welfare and government programs like Aid for Dependent Children.

Critics of course charge that it was nothing more than an elaborate scheme by lusty old men to exploit their position of power in the age-old way of gathering more women to demonstrate their position as well as more recipients for their seed in the survival of the fittest competition.

Regardless of one's views on the practice, it became the focus point for general societal condemnation across the nation and subsequent justification for persecution during the early formative years of the LDS faith. It ultimately became the single political issue standing in the way of Utah's admission into the union of states.

The issue was unsatisfactorily resolved in 1890 by the then LDS president, Wilford Woodruff, issuing "The Manifesto," which bound Mormons to obey the law of the land regarding marriages. The Mormon-dominated Utah Legislature adopted laws banning the polygamy practice and providing penalties for those that would not conform. On January 4, 1896, Congress admitted Utah as the 45th state. For years thereafter, though, authorities in various LDS dominated counties, particularly the more rural ones, looked the other way while some still engaged in the practice.

It should come as no surprise then that having been persecuted for their beliefs about marriage in the past, LDS Church authorities are strongly opposed to efforts by the gay and lesbian community to change the definition of marriage from its historical meaning of the union of one man and one woman with part of the purpose being propagation of the species.

For the LDS Church, this is a serious undermining of the institution of marriage. In Idaho and Utah, despite strong libertarian streaks in collective political philosophies, laws expanding the rights of minorities based on gender and sexual preference are carefully scrutinized and generally not well received. Recently, however, the Church has not opposed fringe benefits for gay couples and Utah now allows civil unions.

A new test of just how tolerant the LDS Church may have to be in an atmosphere where a majority in America are more accepting of the gay and lesbian life-style, is the recent decision by the national board of the Boy Scouts of America to drop its opposition to homosexuality as a reason to deny membership to young gay scouts. The Scout Board did, however, maintain a prohibition on Scout adult leaders being gay. Whether this compromise sticks remains to be seen. In the West, especially, Mormons are a major presence in many local and regional Boy Scout Councils.

Whether intentional or not, the LDS Church has in place a system that encourages early marriage and the getting on with the religious imperative of a couple to bring more "spirits" into this world.

Some critics say it is insidious how well it works – most of the time. At age 13 every young man is encouraged to enter the "priesthood" as part of his growth. Both young men and some women start planning also for their proselytizing mission of two years, usually around their 19th birthday (The age is being lowered by one year which could have a profound impact on freshman college enrollment rates at BYU campuses and the campuses of public universities in Idaho and Utah).

Most male Saints – and many females – fulfill this obligation. While one is on a mission, he or she is isolated from the opposite sex. No dating is permitted, contact with the opposite sex is restricted, and this all happens during a time when psychologists tell us in particular a young man's sex drive is at its peak.

Take a look at the engagement and wedding announcements in the papers that serve Rexburg, Idaho or Provo, Utah. The number of announcements is simply staggering. The explanation is simple: When these young men have completed their mission, many are set to resume or start their pursuit of higher education. Waiting for these "return missionaries" are the daughters, or sons, of members in good standing who throughout their formative years have been encouraged to look for suitable spouses from the ranks of return missionaries. To put it mildly, neither gender, with hormones raging, stands a chance.

Marriages grounded in pure lust, though, seldom last. Despite its emphasis on the primacy of the family unit, according to the 2010 Idaho and Utah census data, Mormons as a whole have a slightly higher divorce rate than the general population. When children are involved this leads to slightly higher child support costs for the federal government's AFDC (Aid to Families with Dependent Children) program. State support is somewhat stingy. There is social stigma in both states for those on welfare.

Social workers also tell us that the incidences of spousal and child abuse are higher in Utah and Idaho than in the general population.

On balance, though, Saints in good standing walk the talk and are benefits to any community. This is due, in part, to the expectation that a good Saint adheres to Section 89 of *the Doctrine and Covenants*, which prohibits the consumption of alcohol, coffee, and tea. At a minimum this means a Mormon in good standing is much less likely to receive a citation for "driving under the influence."

There are notable exceptions, though, as Idahoans discovered in late December of 2012 when Senator Mike Crapo, a former bishop, was cited with a DUI in Virginia.

Adherence to Section 89 does not mean a good Mormon will never drink, for many do in the privacy of their homes. There also have been more than a few LDS legislators who, when they get to Boise and away from the eyes of their home communities, have been known to have a bottle in their desk drawers.

Senator Crapo pled guilty, was fined, given a suspended sentence and forbidden to drive a car for a year. As one who professed publicly not to be an alcohol consumer, he sorely disappointed many of his supporters because in public he said and did one thing but in private he acted differently. It is that kind of hypocrisy that can get a Mormon elected official in deep trouble with his base constituency.

In Utah, there is a term for some public officials, such as Crapo. They are said to be "500-mile Mormons." Once 500 miles or more away from home, they imbibe.

The state of Idaho itself has somewhat of a checkered past with regards to its attitudes towards the "Saint" community. Idaho's original Constitution, largely because of the polygamy issue, forbade Mormon's the vote. The anti-Mormon clauses were largely ignored and ultimately repealed in 1972 at the insistence of Governor Andrus.

Whether there exists a subtle bias against a Mormon ever serving as governor is difficult to prove, but the fact is Idaho's first practicing LDS governor was Arnold Williams who inherited the governorship in 1945 when Charles Gossett resigned and had Williams appoint him to a vacant U.S. Senate seat. The voters tossed both out in 1946.

John V. Evans, who took office in 1977 upon Andrus' resignation to become Jimmy Carter's Secretary of the Interior, was raised LDS and when he was elected in his own right in 1978 he became the first Mormon elected to the governorship..

Even then, some say Evans was known as a" Jack" Mormon and the absence of a "Saint" being elected governor is still there – although several have tried. Other statewide office and U.S. senate seats have all been held by "Saints." So perhaps the absence of a practicing Mormon in the governor's chair is a quirk of history.

The bottom line for any aspirant to high political office in Idaho though, is that they best have a good understanding of the LDS community, and respect and appreciation for its achievements.

And they should be aware of such practices as "release time."

Likewise, any gubernatorial aspirant should have a good understanding of Idaho water law. Mormons have a long history in the development of irrigation systems to bring water to crops and have long dominated both state water departments in Idaho and Utah as well as the Federal Bureau of Reclamation within the Interior Department.

It was no accident that Andrus selected his own state water director, Keith Higginson, to be his Reclamation Director. Besides being a talented administrator, Higginson was also an outstanding representative of his Mormon faith.

Andrus, as the "grey eminence" of what remains of the Idaho Democratic Party, is often visited by aspirants to higher office. Occasionally, he will look at the person and ask if they have visited any member of the "Committee of Nine?"

Most just get a blank look and say, "What is that?" This is a sure-fire indicator to Andrus that they are not yet ready to present their prospective candidacy to Mormon Idaho let alone the rest of the state.

The Committee of Nine refers to the nine water masters who run the federal irrigation projects in the Upper Snake River basin. All are LDS and most have been bishops. Within the southeastern Idaho farm community, and the LDS Church, they are influential and can make or break a candidacy.

There is irony in the fact that in the early days of the LDS Church, most Mormons were Democrats because much of the Church's conflict with the federal government came in the post-Civil War years to the end of the century. Virtually, all the presidential administrations during those years were Republican, with the exception of Grover Cleveland's two non-consecutive terms.

As early pioneers of dams for irrigation purposes, Mormons were strong supporters of the 1902 Reclamation Act which, along with the Homestead Act, further incentivized people to get their 960 acres and develop it.

Having the government after 1902 subsidize their ability to bring water to their fields from dams constructed by the Bureau of Reclamation further solidified the predilection of many Mormons to support the Democratic Party. Though the 1902 Reclamation Act was signed by the trust-busting T.R. Roosevelt, it was pushed by the Democrats in the Congress.

Times have changed though, today the majority of Mormons, whether in Idaho, Utah, or Wyoming are conservative Republicans.

Besides being aware of this history, there are other "little things" an aspiring politician can do when in a heavily LDS county that will indicate to Mormons the candidate has some modicum of understanding about who they are and why there are differences.

When at BYU-Idaho, for example, officeholders are always served as their liquid refreshment the ubiquitous red punch. One should never ask for coffee, tea, or Coca-cola out of respect for Section 89 of *The Doctrine & Covenants*.

On balance the Mormon influence in Idaho is a net positive.

Anyone running for office ought to be as familiar as possible with the people who call themselves, "Saints." Whether it is "release time," water laws, or returned missionaries, the more an aspiring politician can learn about the LDS community the better.

And in November of 2012 the nation gave serious consideration to the notion of electing a Mormon president. Mitt Romney, former governor of Massachusetts, Bain investment billionaire, savior of the Salt Lake Winter Olympics, son of a beloved Michigan governor, a solid member of the Church of Jesus Christ of Latter-Day Saints, a former bishop in the Boston stake, received 47 percent of the popular vote.

Had he stuck to his economic message and emphasized earlier his presumed skill to address the nation's fiscal challenges, and not gotten himself diverted into the social issues on which he incontestably flip-flopped, he might have pulled off an upset. As it is, he becomes another chapter in the fine book *They Also Ran*, first penned by Irving Stone, providing mini-biographies of presidential losers in American history.

Romney will not be considered one of the more interesting losers. His historical footnote will be his religion and his loss definitively displaying that the nation has truly become multi-cultural and diverse.

Romney carried the "white vote" nationally, 59% to 39%, and still was trounced because he lost the minority vote, 72% to 28%.

LDS Church President Thomas Munson, his councilors and the Quorum of 12 Apostles that run this entity that combines the spiritual and the temporal in what can only be called an original American religion must have salivated at the thought of a Mormon president.

Post-election analysis of the results, however, would indicate that in many respects Romney's Mormonism did indeed hurt his candidacy, especially with southern Evangelicals, many of whom appear to have stayed home. The LDS Church's long-time ban on African-Americans being eligible for the priesthood hurt Romney's candidacy with that element of the nation's minority vote as well.

Even in the LDS dominated state of Utah, where Romney of course won easily, astute observers picked up that the total Republican vote for Romney was significantly less than what John McCain received in 2008. Some of Mitt's LDS brothers do appear to have had reservations.

There's a story yet to be written that will detail the numerous ways the LDS Church and its many adherents supported – legally in most respects – their favorite son.

This tacit support has to be bittersweet irony for former Idaho Attorney General Larry EchoHawk (1990-1994), who, in early 2012, resigned his position as the assistant secretary of the Interior for Indian Affairs and answered the "call" to become a member of the LDS Church's chief legislative body, the Quorum of 70.

EchoHawk appeared to be the first Native American with a serious shot at becoming governor of a state. A quality candidate, of sober demeanor, thoughtful, intelligent, and articulate, a former U.S. Marine and an outstanding defensive back at Brigham Young University, he had built a solid record as Idaho's attorney general.

Polls gave him a substantial lead over the presumptive Republican nominee, former Lieutenant Governor Phil Batt, who also ran against John Evans in 1982. Batt, too, was a quality candidate, a moderate Republican who, like his good friend Cecil Andrus, likes to solve problems.

Before taking another run at the governorship, Batt had personally taken on the task of rebuilding Idaho's Republican Party. Traveling the state at his own expense, he visited every county, meeting with the party chairs and precinct committee people, interviewing and identifying those committed enough to help rebuild the base of the Republican Party.

Republican hegemony in Idaho ever since 1994 is directly attributable to his efforts. Still, while he steadily cut into EchoHawk's lead, he lagged behind as the election drew near. Amazingly, in the first poll over a year before, EchoHawk led Batt 48 percent to 32 percent, and with two weeks to go, Batt still was behind, 48 percent to 44 percent.

It was then EchoHawk's campaign made a fatal mistake which at first glance did not appear problematic. EchoHawk had a campaign fund-raiser in Salt Lake City in an LDS Church office building near the Temple. Clearly the fund-raiser was designed to tap into presumed support for a fellow Mormon. When the fund-raiser was reported by *The Salt Lake Tribune*, many Idaho Mormons took offense at EchoHawk blatantly appearing to use Church connections.

Some folks debate just how much support this really cost EchoHawk because southeastern Idaho Mormons tend to the Republican anyway. There's a tendency to vote for a non-Mormon Republican over a good Democrat Mormon, as Richard Stallings found out in his race for the U.S. Senate in 1992 when he was defeated by Boise Mayor Dirk Kempthorne. In 2010, Democratic gubernatorial candidate Keith Allred, an LDS Church member, was pole-axed in southeastern Idaho by Republican C.L. "Butch" Otter, a Catholic.

While some may say the EchoHawk fund-raiser did not really cost him that much support, the one person in the best position to know, the beneficiary of the *Tribune*'s reporting and follow up editorializing, Phil Batt, left little doubt about how essential he felt the story was to his successful election.

Batt, shortly after his election, called Jay Shelledy, the *Tribune*'s editor and a person Batt had known previously from the former's years working in Idaho for the Associated Press and the Tribune (Lewiston and Moscow) Publishing Corporation. Batt thanked *The Tribune* for his election. Batt told Shelledy the story had turned the tide for him. Shelledy told Batt the story was meant for Utah consumption and, in fact, caused a stir in that state as well.

Batt was reflecting the fact that tracking polls showed a sudden shift his way and the only event that he could attribute it to, given the dates, was the coverage in Idaho of *The Tribune's* fund-raiser story.

Two decades later the presidential campaign of Mitt Romney was working, subtlety where possible, its LDS connections and network. The truth of the matter is that whether professing a party preference or not, the LDS Church has been embroiled in politics wherever it has been, from its beginnings. Its founder, Joseph Smith, himself ran for President.

Its second president, Brigham Young, was a gifted leader and had he decided he wanted to be president of the gentiles in the United States may well have been able to accomplish it.

Not since Brigham Young led the remnants of the LDS Church from Illinois and Missouri to Utah in 1846-47, and held them together by the sheer force of his personality after the death of founding prophet, Joseph Smith, has there been a Mormon as prominent as Mitt Romney.

Young was an up-by-the-bootstraps and school-of-hard-knocks graduate who learned how to inspire and lead. Had he channeled those abilities in a driven, single-minded manner towards obtaining the presidency, he might well have achieved the goal – but not as a Mormon. Polygamy was simply too big of an obstacle to overcome and Mormonism was viewed as a peculiar religion at best and at worst, a cult.

Mitt Romney picked up the presidential standard that had fallen from his father, Michigan Governor George Romney's, grasp in 1968, and continued the quest for a Mormon to achieve the country's highest elective office. He came close, but that only counts in horseshoes.

Few doubt his effort was nothing less than the result of a years-in-the-making single-minded quest that long lurked in his heart. During the campaign, President Obama accused Romney of having campaigned for six years for the office. The truth is it is more like 18 years and dates back to his unsuccessful challenge of Ted Kennedy for the Senate in 1994.

His public and private moves since that time had been taken with the quest for the presidency as the refractory and backdrop. It is obvious he became schooled and disciplined. Spouse, Ann, shared his ambition and likewise was schooled and disciplined to the demands of the long campaign. She, along with their five sons, became an active, articulate and popular surrogate for Governor Romney on the campaign trail.

A major reason Romney lost some political pundits firmly believe was his high standing within the LDS Church and his failure to overcome the bias of many Evangelical and fundamentalist Protestants against Mormonism, which they view as a non-Christian quasi-cult.

Romney is respected and revered by almost all Mormons as being just about the best example one can find of all that is good and great about being Mormon. A returned missionary, a faithful husband and a fine father, a decent, kind and compassionate person, a dutiful tither of 10 percent of his before-taxes income, a good bishop, a man who lives a Christian life and walks the talk.

To have detailed the various ways the LDS Church – well within its Constitutional rights to use its funds as a form of free speech – could and did support Romney usually brings letters of denial and righteous indignation. Nonetheless, the Church in subtle ways signaled its support.

A quick review is illustrative of just how the LDS Church can and does influence political outcomes in Idaho and, in doing so, testifies to the reality that separation of church and state is a nice ideal in the Constitution. In reality, the LDS Church knows everything is political to one degree or another. The only challenge is to practice the art of politics without jeopardizing its tax-exempt status.

For example, a national television campaign portraying the many fine points about the Mormon social ethic and urging people to get to know more about Mormonism ran nationwide for weeks, a year before the presidential primary season began. No coincidence.

The weekend following the 2012 Republican National Convention in Tampa in wards and stakes across the country people stood up to give testimonials about how well their religion was represented and portrayed. The implications were obvious: Mitt, Ann, and their children had done a fine job of reflecting the importance of Mormonism in their lives.

The conclusion had to be obvious to all Mormons: Vote for one of us.

They did in droves and by huge margins in states like Idaho, where despite being just 25 percent of the electorate Mormons are nonetheless extremely influential. One can reasonably guess that 80 percent plus of tithe-paying Mormons in good standing voted for Brother Mitt and Sister Ann.

It was a foregone conclusion because of their heavy LDS population Wyoming (12%), Idaho (25%) and Utah (66%) were locks for Romney. Members of LDS wards were indispensable workers for the Republican Party across the country, but especially in western states like Nevada, Colorado, Montana, and Arizona.

As far back as 2006, the LDS Church's leadership had signaled its approval of Romney's run and made decisions to support, mostly behind the scenes, his candidacy.

Former Utah Governor Jon Huntsman Jr., and his billionaire father, Jon Huntsman Sr., themselves Mormons, found out the deep degree of the Church's preference for Romney after Huntsman Junior resigned as the nation's ambassador to China to seek the Republican nomination.

Much bitterness was generated behind the scenes over this blessing of one Saint's candidacy over another's. Polls in Utah reflected the Church's ability to influence voter attitudes. Governor Huntsman, though popular (and having won an overwhelming re-election), was chagrined upon learning Utah surveys showed a 2:1 preference for Romney.

Huntsman Jr. had earlier competed against Romney for the coveted spot of taking over and saving the 2002 Salt Lake Winter Olympics, a contest which Romney won. The resulting dislike between the families is now legendary and it is a safe bet neither is on the other's Christmas card list.

In October of 2006, the *Boston Globe* broke the news of Romney's political operatives holding secret discussions with LDS Church leadership. In their fine and balanced book, *The Real Romney*, reporters from *The Boston Globe*, Michael Kranish and Scott Helman, wrote that "e-mails showed that Romney's political operatives, family members, and church officials had discussed building a grassroots political organization using alumni chapters of Brigham Young University's business school around the country."

They go on to say that Jeffrey Holland, a former BYU president and one of the 12 Apostles who govern the Church with the First Presidency (the president plus his two councilors) was tasked with handling the initiative and was the one who suggested using the BYU Management Society to help build a supporter base for Romney. The group at the time had 5,500 members in 40 chapters across the country.

Embarrassed by the publicity and knowing Romney could never win as the overt LDS candidate, the Church played down the matter, but nowhere is there any evidence that it changed any of the various ways it intended to help one of its own win the Big Enchilada.

It is no doubt true that LDS properties were not used for blatant political partisan purposes, but Mormons, noted for their organizing abilities, easily could congregate at someone's home or a public meeting place, get their assignments for deploying teams to do "door drops," for example. Others manned phones, scanned Facebook and Twitter for likes, linked up like minded folks and reminded them of volunteer opportunities galore to help use the increasingly multiple modern communication tools and marketing information at their disposal.

The Romney team wisely handled the issue of his personal beliefs by refusing to go down that path. Questions about Mormon theology and beliefs were simply referred to Salt Lake City for LDS Church authorities to respond. Late in the campaign, the Romney's strategically allowed the media to follow them one Sunday when they attended a nearby ward meeting.

It gave the media enough wherewithals to see that an LDS Church service is fairly standard Protestant fare. As Election Day grew closer the subject of standard "crock of baloney" LDS beliefs was never brought up or out. Romney basically received a free pass on this one.

Idaho could have benefited mightily from its special relationship with Romney had he won. The Romney National Campaign Finance Committee was co-chaired by wealthy Idaho Falls businessman Frank VanderSloot, founder of the Melaleuca Company, a manufacturer of vitamin supplements and other health aids.

VanderSloot personally donated several million dollars to the Romney campaign, one of many LDS business leaders across the nation who opened their checkbooks and sent liberal sums to the Romney effort. In addition, VanderSloot "loaned" and paid the salaries of some of the key campaign aides for the "Romney-Idaho" effort including the savvy state chair, Dom Watkins, son of former Idaho Falls State Senator Dane Watkins.

All of Idaho's Republican leadership and major officeholders lined up behind the Romney effort, some no doubt thinking they were sure to be rewarded with appointments to key administration posts. Leading candidates for significant positions were thought to be State Superintendent of Public Instruction Tom Luna, who saw his "Luna Reform Laws" soundly repealed by Idaho voters.

U.S. Senator Mike Crapo, a key member of the Senate "Gang of Eight" who was deeply involved in negotiations to keep America away from the rapidly approaching "fiscal cliff" of disaster was another many thought might be in line for a major appointment if Romney had won and before his fall from grace. Governor Otter himself was said to be interested in becoming Interior Secretary following the path of former Idaho Governors Cecil Andrus and Dirk Kempthorne. Luna and Crapo are coincidentally members of the LDS Church.

Then there is the special case of Jack Gerard. The Idaho boy from Mud Lake is considered by many to be almost singularly Mitt Romney's go-to guy in Washington, D.C., and has been for a number of years. A former natural resources aide to Senator Jim McClure, a former president of the National Mining Association and in late 2012 the $6 million-a-year president of the American Petroleum Institute, Gerard could have had almost any position he wanted had there been a Romney Administration.

Even Gerard's critics concede he is an incredibly competent, savvy "inside-the beltway" operator who would command everyone's respect. And hailing from what most Idahoans see as little more than a bump in the road in Jefferson County (Mud Lake) between Salmon and Idaho Falls. Gerard was raised in an LDS household. He is a member of the Quorum of Seventy, the second most influential governing body of the Church.

If Idaho's long experience of co-existing with a strong Mormon influence carries one conclusion for the many Americans never exposed to the LDS Church, it is that the pluses far outweigh the minuses. The LDS Church practices a Christian social doctrine, taking care of their neighbors, affirming the paramount importance of family, promoting keeping sex in the confines of marriage, volunteering and displaying deep devotion to patriotic endeavors – all positives.

It is unfortunate so many non-Mormons hold such distorted views regarding Mormonism, calling it a cult and refusing to recognize its basic Christian ethic. One can dispute tenets of a religion without condemning it outright.

They should not, however, diminish the accomplishments of what is the fastest growing church in America. It can and does lay claim to being an authentic home-grown American religion.

The influence of the LDS will continue to grow. Nor have we seen the last serious Mormon challenger for the presidency.

In fact, there is another rich, handsome, intelligent, articulate, successful Mormon out there in the land of characters who may see a president when they look in the mirror – former Utah Governor Jon Huntsman, Jr.

At least that was the "conventional wisdom" until Huntsman, late in 2012, announced he was joining a group called "No Labels" that works to achieve bi-partisan consensus in resolving today's many challenging issues. This move probably precludes his ever trying for the Republican presidential nomination again, especially in the Republican Party's raw meat primaries.

If so, keep an eye on Utah U.S. Senator Mike Lee, a favorite of the Tea Party wing of the Republican Party. Shakespeare once wrote: "Keep an eye on yon Cassius. Methinks he hath a mean and hungry look."

5 ■ Who Is The Lioness of Idaho?

From top left, clockwise: Verda Barnes (courtesy Martin Peterson); Helen Chenoweth (congressional); Louise Shadduck (courtesy of Shadduck family); Gracie Pfost (courtesy College of Idaho); Bethine Church (courtesy College of Idaho).

The politics of Idaho, both state and federal, have been quietly but effectively impacted by strong women, despite the election of only two to Congress and none to the senate or governor' chair.

A glass ceiling appears to be in place for those two positions, but the "lesser" state offices like treasurer, superintendent of public instruction, and auditor have been administered well by females.

In 1972, I wrote a column about three influential women most Idahoans did not know a thing about. All were the chiefs of staff: Verda Barnes (Senator Frank Church); Gwenne Lewis (Senator Len Jordan); and, Louise Shadduck (Congressman Orval Hansen)..

At the time the 1972 column was written, the Idaho congressional delegation had the highest percentage (75 percent) of women in Congressional chief of staff (Or administrative assistant) positions in the nation.

Each was a Phi Beta Kappa, articulate, intelligent, competent, and a capable administrator.

Today, I find myself asking a key question: If William E. Borah was Idaho's most famous officeholder in the first half of the 20th century and was known as the "Lion of Idaho," who would we designate as the "Lioness of Idaho?"

(Author's note: Retired Coeur d'Alene Pastor Mike Bullard has written a solid biography on Louise Shadduck. I was one of many that sat for an interview with him. I mentioned working on this chapter of the book and that I was going to call it "The Lioness of Idaho." Additionally I told him I was personally leaning towards saying that if we had to narrow it down to one recipient I was going to designate Ms. Shadduck. Pastor Bullard recently requested and I readily granted him permission to use the phrase for the title of his book and asked if he could copyright the phrase because of its tie to his book. I gladly granted him such permission and heartily commend his book to the reader.)

If elected office is the only criteria, than hands down it has to be one of the two women elected to Congress, Gracie Pfost (1952-1962) or Helen Chenoweth (1984-2000).

If being influential within political circles or transformational in some sense on the Idaho political scene is a prerequisite, there are numerous others that should be considered. A partial list includes:

Gwen Barnett – She played a leading role in the Republican Party as the national committeewoman. Single-handedly she turned the party to the hard right where it continues to dwell today. A female "Grover Norquist" before there was a real Grover Norquist, she took aim at the liberal Republican governor of Idaho, Robert Smylie, who most could see had aligned himself with New York Governor Nelson Rockefeller.

Her hero was conservative Arizona senator and presidential candidate Barry Goldwater. Reputedly, Barnett is the person who recruited a little known but true blue conservative senator from Sandpoint, Don Samuelson, to challenge Smylie in the August 1966 primary. To the amazement of the political class in Idaho, Samuelson stunned Smylie and won the nomination. Sometime during these years, Barnett took up with Roland Wilber, the Idaho Republican chairman. Each divorced their spouse and the couple moved to Oregon where she faded away.

Bethine Church – Should be ranked in the first tier of candidates for the "Lioness" designation. She is the daughter of a former Idaho governor, Chase Clark (1940-1942), with an uncle that had also been governor, Barzilla Clark (1936-1938), and another uncle, D. Worth Clark (1940-1946) held the Senate seat her future husband would hold for 24 years. She came from the most distinguished Democrat family in the state. It came as no surprise that she had politics in her DNA. Devoted to her spouse who she nursed through an incredibly painful bout with cancer in 1949, many say she willed the future senator to live and simply would not let him die.

Bethine Church not only brought this same tenacity to Idaho politics, she also was the Senator's closest political advisor and his best sounding board. Justifiably, she was viewed by Idaho's political cognoscenti as the third senator for the state. A better politician and a more natural campaigner than Frank Church, she could have won elective office herself. Watching the Senator enter a room anywhere in Idaho, one would notice Bethine was leading, inevitably first at greeting someone, she would say to the Senator, "Frank, you remember Pete Wilson," thus providing him with that key piece of information, a person's name. She celebrated her 90th birthday on February 17, 2013.

Though confined to a wheel chair she remains mentally sharp and still participates in Idaho Democratic affairs.

Sandy Patano – The longtime Idaho chief of staff to former Senator Larry Craig, she is the textbook model for the best and right kind of staff person a member of Congress ought to have representing him or her back home. Smart, witty, a million-dollar smile, an incredible memory for names and a master of the smallest of details, she almost single-handedly kept Craig in office. She could have had the First District congressional seat for the asking when Butch Otter left it to run for governor. No one in the Republican Party would have challenged her had she decided to run. She chose not to out of motherly concern for her teenage daughter, Jordan; she knew well how consuming the life of a member of Congress can be. Candidly, she said she was at a time in her life when she did not want to spend hours on planes flying between the district and the nation's capitol. She and her significant other, former Lt. Gov. Jack Riggs, are considered one of the top power couples in the state.

Ruthie Johnson – She oversaw Jim McClure's northern Idaho office and understood the importance of constituent service. Active in Republican Party affairs, she was a staunch conservative. Her claim to fame, though, was that years earlier she had met the late David Broder, the *Washington Post's* lead political reporter. Her disarming folksy manner hid a keen mind for politics. She became one of Broder's many sources and a year rarely went by without Broder calling Ruthie to pick her brain for insights.

Wendy Jaquet – One of Idaho's best state legislators, she represented the district comprising Blaine County. Raised in Seattle, she cut her teeth on politics in the cutthroat world of San Francisco where some of the nation's toughest and smartest politicians have been raised – from Phil Burton, to Nancy Pelosi, and Willy Brown. She and husband Jim came to Idaho when he accepted the position of city manager for Ketchum. A voice for reason and common sense, she decided life was too short to keep tilting at the ridiculous but entrenched Republican windmills and retired after a distinguished 14-year tenure.

MaryLou Reed – Another talented legislator, she served in the Idaho Senate for 10 years, representing Kootenai County. A graduate of Mills College, she and her attorney husband, Scott, have been active in Democratic politics for years. Both were supporters of Frank Church and Cecil Andrus. Among their remarkable children is Bruce, chief of staff for Vice President Joe Biden, former executive director of the Democratic Study Group, an aide to President Clinton and the ghostwriter for Bill Clinton's acclaimed speech on behalf of President Obama at the 2012 Democratic National Convention.

Though more a "wine and cheese" liberal than a lunch-bucket Democrat, Lou Reed is always thoughtful, a good listener, and a true progressive. She remains active in the civic affairs of Coeur d'Alene and writes a monthly column for *The Northwest Inlander Weekly*. Lou is also one of four co-founders of Idaho's premier environmental advocacy group, the *Idaho Conservation League*, founded in 1973.

Michelle Stennett – In 2012 she was elected to the Minority Leader position by her State Senate Democratic colleagues. She represents the district comprised primarily of Blaine County, having been selected to replace and finish the term of her late husband, Clint, who died in office. Trained in marketing and advertising at the University of Oregon, she has a business background including a position as marketing director for a regional airline that flew in and out of Hailey. She also assisted her late husband in running their ranch. Personable, intelligent, articulate, she may be the most viable person Democrats could run as their candidate for governor in 2014.

Shawn Keough – The long-time veteran Republican State Senator who represents Idaho's northern-most district, Keough is also the executive director of the state's Associated Contract Loggers. Though Keough is a conservative, she is considered to be somewhat of a rarity---a true pro-education Republican.

She sits on and has co-chaired the legislature's Joint Finance-Appropriations committee which has given her the opportunity to become an expert on the state's budget. Thoughtful, she is also a good listener and has built a loyal following in and around her home town of Sandpoint. During the 2012 election cycle she withstood an abortive Tea Party challenge financed by a major utility and a more right wing legislative colleague.

Should the Republican primary for governor in 2014 attract a wide field, many are urging her to seek the nomination feeling that as a pro-education Republican she could attract support from independents and Democrats if she could emerge from the Republican Party's conservative-dominated primary process.

The unfortunate and nasty primary challenge has reportedly considerably soured her on politics.

Marguerite McLaughlin – Another former Democratic state senate leader, she was the long-time state senator from Cecil Andrus' hometown of Orofino in Clearwater County. Andrus has said on more than one occasion she would have made an outstanding governor. A few years back he tried to talk her into running, but her husband, Bruce, was combating an ultimately fatal illness. The senator not only would not run for governor, she left the legislature to care for him.

Besides being a "lunch-bucket" Democrat, like Andrus, she was a strong supporter of state support for public education. She also was a true master of the state budget. She dug into the nitty-gritty and knew every line of the document that guides state spending. Because of this she commanded the respect of her colleagues on both sides of the aisle.

In the fall of 2012, Idaho political historians Randy Stapilus and Marty Peterson released a book they had written entitled *The Idaho 100*. It was their list of the 100 most influential Idahoans in the history of the state and included several figures from before Idaho's 1890 admission to the Union.

They also listed the criteria by which they determined who went on their list, one such major measurement being the person's transformational role in history. Neither of Idaho's two female members of Congress, Gracie Pfost and Helen Chenoweth, made the list. Nor did Bethine Church or Louise Shadduck make the grade. However, Gwenn Barnett and Verda Barnes did, with Barnett being the second highest female listed. Barnett would be a candidate for the "Lioness" designation, although the cases for Louise Shadduck, Verda Barnes, Bethine Church and Gracie Pfost are all more compelling.

The case for Shadduck is the strongest. She was the first female executive assistant to any governor of Idaho, but in her case, because it was Idaho's first post-war progressive governor, Dr. C.A. Robins (of St. Maries), Shadduck, by Robins' own admission had a profound influence on the many progressive initiatives he undertook.

She then worked for Governor Robins' two immediate successors, Len B. Jordan and Robert E. Smylie. Smylie made her director of the Department of Commerce, which she transformed into the aggressive state marketing agency it is today. She held sway there for 10 years.

Louise also served as chief of staff to Senator Henry Dworshak, and later held down a similar position with Second District Congressman Orval Hansen.

Though she never held a public office, she wielded considerable influence from other posts such as president of the National Federation of Newspaper Women. (She was a trained journalist who worked for the *Coeur 'd Alene Press* and the *Spokesman Review*) and as the first director of what became the Idaho Forestry Association.

The key to her influence was not just smarts, but an incredible memory for names, and unfailing courtesy and discretion. She knew everyone. She jammed into one life half a dozen careers and could have retired at several points but chose to stay active in Republican affairs until the day she died at age 93.

She wrote a number of interesting books on subjects ranging from a history of doctors in Idaho to a biography of Andy Little, a turn of the century Idaho sheep and cattle baron, and the grandfather of the current Lt. Governor, Brad Little.

What few people know, save University of Idaho Dean Catherine Aiken, is that Louise did seek public office in 1956, taking on First District congresswoman Gracie Pfost. It was the first time in the history of the Republic two women were the GOP and Democratic nominees in a congressional race.

In a 1972 interview, Shadduck said she had no regrets about the race. "I learned more in that brief time than any other comparable period of my life. It was a good clean campaign. Most of all, we proved that two women could run a credible campaign against one another."

Marty Peterson, a former key staffer to Senator Frank Church, Governors Andrus and Evans, and the longtime director of the University of Idaho's government affairs program, believes Verda Barnes should wear the crown. In a 2012 article that appeared in the Lewiston *Tribune*, he made the case for Verda Barnes (reprinted with permission):

Few readers will have ever heard of Verda Barnes. That would have pleased her. If she were alive, she would have insisted I not write this. Over a span of four decades, Verda Barnes' impact was felt by Idahoans throughout the state, even though few were aware she existed.

Born in Willard, Utah, in 1907, she moved with her family to a farm near St. Anthony the next year. After graduating from high school, she attended Albion National School and than Brigham Young University. Married briefly in the early 1930's, she had a daughter, and as a single parent, spent much of the 1930s living in Boise. With the repeal of prohibition, Governor C. Ben Ross appointed her the first director of the newly formed Idaho Liquor Commission.

In the days before form letters, she received a letter from James A. Farley, the Postmaster General and Chairman of the Democratic National Convention. Farley had managed Franklin Roosevelt's first two presidential campaigns. Widely viewed as being responsible for FDR's political ascendancy, he reportedly was exploring his own prospects in 1940.

Farley, however, sent out a national mailing challenging people to become part of Roosevelt's "New Deal." Barnes, assuming it was a personal letter, took up the challenge and, with her young daughter, moved to Washington D.C. She quickly became involved with organized labor, working as a political organizer with such groups as the Amalgamated Clothing Workers and the CIO.

Then she went to work as an assistant to Interior Secretary Harold Ickes, followed by a stint at the newly formed Securities and Exchange Commission working for William O. Douglas, who later became a Supreme Court Judge. Around this time she began compiling a legendary list of influential personal contacts throughout the federal government and Idaho.

Barnes was active in the Young Democrats, eventually becoming national vice chairman, which led her to become acquainted with Franklin and Eleanor Roosevelt. In her later years, one of the few pictures in her office was of Eleanor Roosevelt. FDR gave her the advice that became her operational hallmark. "A good staff person" Roosevelt said, "should have a passion for anonymity."

In 1945, she went to work for the newly elected Idaho Senator Glen Taylor. Following Taylor's defeat in 1950, she became an assistant to Congressman Harrison "Pete" Williams of New Jersey.

Her roots were in Idaho however, and with the election of Frank Church in 1956, she joined his staff, serving first as his governmental liaison, and then became his chief of staff in 1964. In that position she became Church's chief political strategist and the de facto chief political strategist for the entire Idaho Democratic Party.

Rumor had it that Barnes never slept. She was tireless. During political campaigns, it was common for key campaign workers to get a call at 6 a.m. wondering why they weren't at the office. Barnes would spend much of the day working on the telephone, talking to contacts throughout Idaho and Washington D.C.

Even when she was in Washington, she generally knew more about what was going on in Idaho than anyone else. Republicans were in awe of her, knowing that in a particularly tight race, her arrival in Idaho meant generating an additional 10,000 votes that would otherwise not be.

Without Barnes' political efforts, Frank Church would have been a one term Senator. He only lost after she retired and then passed away in June of 1980. That November, Church lost to Steve Symms by a mere 4,000 votes.

Her most lasting legacy though was the rise of Cecil Andrus, whom she helped secure the Democratic gubernatorial nomination from the State Central Committee after primary winner Charles Herndon was killed in a plane crash.

Although Andrus lost the 1966 election, four years later Barnes was back using the statewide voter identification program she had put together for Church in 1968 along with much of Church's campaign volunteer base, plus the recruitment of several Church staff members working in a "boiler room" effort, she played a pivotal role in Andrus' election in 1970. That opened the door for the most successful political career in Idaho history.

Barnes suffered a stroke and died on June 9, 1980. She is buried in the Parker, Idaho cemetery near St. Anthony.

Bill Hall, the then editorial page editor for the Lewiston Morning Tribune noted in an editorial, "They say Verda Barnes died in her sleep the other night. But that's preposterous, Verda Barnes never slept."

Since the "Lion of Idaho," William E. Borah, was an elected Idaho Senator (1907-1940), a case can be made that any aspirant to the title "Lioness of Idaho" also has to have been elected to public office.

If so, the clear winner is one of only two women to serve Idaho in the Congress, five-term Congresswoman Gracie Pfost (pronounced "post") who represented the First District from 1953-1963. The mere fact that she could win and then hold the office through four re-elections in and of itself during the 1950s, when few women were being elected to anything, speaks volumes for her talent and tenacity.

The late Helen Chenoweth was tenacious also. Swept into office in 1994 along with dozens of other Republican freshmen who signed on with Georgia Congressman Newt Gingrich's "Contract with America," Chenoweth made a name for herself, but was more the object of ridicule than the subject of sober reflection. Quick with a quip, she was a Tea Party Republican before there was a Tea Party. Chenoweth supported the "sage brush rebellion," a view which called for the privatization of public lands and a downsizing of the federal presence in people's lives.

Her talk of black helicopters prowling western skies and her pooh-poohing endangered species designation for salmon, saying she could walk into any Albertson's and buy plenty of canned salmon, marginalized her and rendered her ineffective.

To her credit, though, unlike her colleague to the immediate west in the Fifth Congressional District of Washington, George Nethercutt, she honored the clause in the Contract in which signatories had promised to serve only three terms and retire.

Congresswoman Pfost, on the other hand, was a respected member of Congress and held onto her seat in the face of tough opposition. Because of her relentless support for a publicly owned and operated single high dam in Hells Canyon, the media referred to her as "Hells Belle." She believed strongly in public power, which put her at immediate odds with two powerful special interests, the Idaho Power Company and Spokane's Washington Water Power.

Both firms supported three smaller dams in Hells Canyon to be owned by Idaho Power. The ensuing acrimonious debate lasted a decade. She ended up being out-maneuvered and lost a key vote in the Interior and Insular affairs subcommittee in the late 1950s. Thus today one sees Brownlee, Oxbow, and Hells Canyon dams on the Snake, but fortunately no High Mountain Sheep Dam.

In 1962, hoping the Senate would be a better venue, Pfost gave up her safe House seat to run for the Senate seat vacated by the death of Henry Dworshak. She lost a close race (51% to 49%) to former

Governor Len B. Jordan, a supporter of private power and its three smaller dams approach, as well as a supporter of High Mountain Sheep **IF** built by private power.

Legendary Beltway Democratic operator Robert Strauss once famously said every politician likes voters to think they were born in a log cabin and pulled themselves up by the bootstraps. In the case of Gracie though, it was the truth.

Biographical sketches note that she was born in a log cabin in the Ozark Mountains of Arkansas in 1906. The family moved to Idaho in 1911 where she attended school until age 16, quitting and taking a job at Carnation Milk in Nampa. There she met and married her supervisor, Jack Pfost, who became her life long political partner.

In 1929, she graduated from Link's School of Business in Boise which led to temporary work in the Canyon County Clerk's Office, quickly turning it into a permanent job. From there she jumped into local county politics and for the next decade served as Canyon County auditor, clerk, and recorder. In 1941 she was elected Canyon County treasurer and served another decade.

During the 1940s and 1950s she owned a successful real estate business as she steadily got more involved in state and national politics. In the 1950s the First District congressional seat opened up with Democrat Comp White Sr., from Clark Fork, deciding to retire. White had held the seat since 1932 but lost it in 1946, then gained it back in 1948. In 1950, Pfost won the Democratic nomination but lost the general election by 783 votes to 72-year-old Republican Dr. John Wood of Moscow.

With the help of Eleanor Roosevelt, who criticized Wood in her popular national column for his efforts to derail the United Nations, Pfost won a rematch in 1952 by 591 votes (out of 109,000 cast) despite the landslide election of Dwight D. Eisenhower. She and Jack never looked back.

At various times she was described as tough, tenacious, calculating, a spitfire, but she was a worker who did her homework. From 1955 to 1961, she chaired the important public lands subcommittee of interior and insular affairs.

A relentless campaigner, she challenged her 1954 Republican opponent to a log rolling contest at a county festival in Orofino. She lost the log roll but won the election by 9,000 votes. Her constituent service was legendary – every high school graduate received a personal congratulatory note and every new parent received a book on child care.

In the historic 1956 battle of the first time two women squared off for a congressional seat as major party nominees, she defeated Republican Louise Shadduck, herself a legend, by 10 percentage points.

Other legislative interests included support for Alaskan statehood and for U.S. Postal Service employees, a federal school construction bill, and legislation to prop up a sagging agricultural commodities market.

Despite Jack's sudden death in 1961, she went ahead with the Senate race. After losing, President Kennedy appointed her to the Federal Housing Commission. Unbeknown to many, she suffered from Hodgkin's disease and died prematurely on August 11, 1965, at Baltimore's Johns Hopkins. She is buried in Meridian.

Which one, then, of these two "finalists" should be given the "Lioness" title? The answer depends on which criterion is most important. If one believes major political office is an indispensable requirement, then the nod goes to Gracie Pfost. If one believes a life-long impact on the Idaho political scene, but more behind the scenes, then the nod goes to Louise Shadduck.

History will ultimately decide, but both have legitimate claims and both can have the title justifiably.

6 ■ Thirty Pieces of Silver?

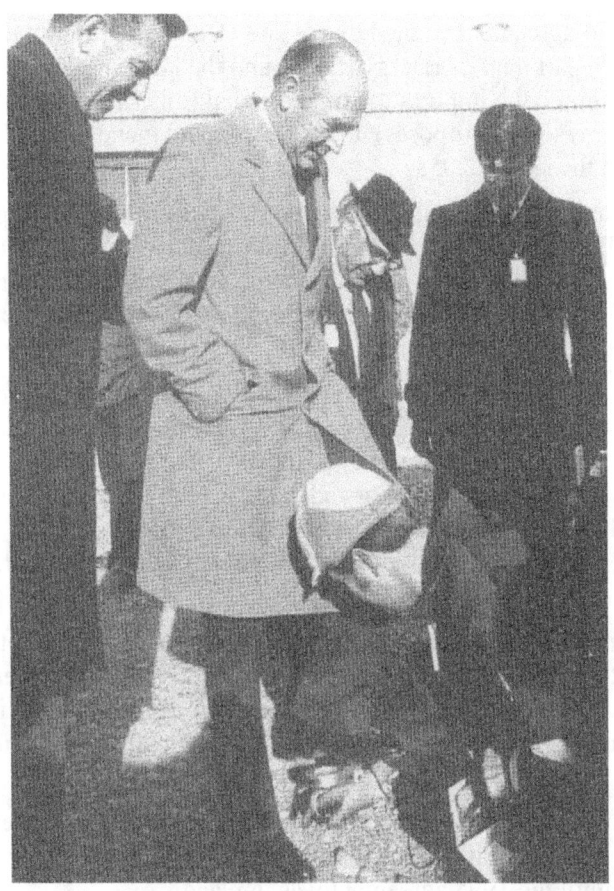

Governor Cecil Andrus at the Idaho Nuclear Engineering Laboratory gets a check for radioactivity of his shoes, while press secretary Chris Carlson (right) looks on, and site maneger Glenn Bradlee (left).Photo courtesy Chris Carlson.

In December of 2012, former governors Phil Batt and Cecil Andrus saw through the smoke screen of wishful thinking by blind Idaho National Laboratory partisans who, with dollar signs dancing in their eyes, thought they could hornswoggle them into accepting amendments to Governor Batt's 1995 nuclear waste disposal agreement.

The Batt agreement, signed by the site manager, representatives from the Department of Energy (DOE) and the United States Navy, severely limited the importation of additional (other than a small amount for research purposes) nuclear waste and mandates it all be gone from the site by 2035.

Idahoans ought to thank the members of Governor C.L. "Butch" Otter's LINE commission for being, choose your word, dumb or naïve enough to think dangling a carrot of vague, unspecified additional economic development might possibly entice Idaho's current leadership to amend the 1995 agreement.

There would be hell to pay. Governor C.L. "Butch" Otter would buck two governors who he served as Lt. Governor and cross their emphatic "hell no" response to even the hint of amending the agreement. While Butch appears adamant, declining federal investment in the state is an admittedly powerful incentive to consider amendments, at least to those that economically benefit in southeastern Idaho.

Batt and Andrus understand Idaho has the *only* agreement of any state not to be turned into an interim waste or possibly permanent waste repository. The 1995 agreement gives Idaho the only leverage it has. It is reinforced by having been held up as binding in a Federal court of law.

To deal away a "hole card" would be the height of folly when dealing with a Federal government which did not begin to keep its promises until the 1995 agreement was in place.

Andrus was emphatic in his letter of December 7, 2012, to the LINE Commission chair, Commerce director Jeff Sayer. He told Sayer he had read all 50 pages including the recommendations and "nothing in the (LINE Commission) report warrants any amendment for any reason to the Batt Agreement of 1995. ..."

Batt followed suit immediately with his strongly worded letter to the *Idaho Statesman* which ensured folks would see the two governors from different political parties tied together at the hip on this matter.

It was meant to signal a non-starter to anyone who might try to make this a partisan issue. The former governors had been talking and coordinated their responses. One could hear the gnashing of teeth in far away north Idaho emanating from the INL boosters in Idaho Falls.

What was the LINE Commission thinking by issuing a progress report with such a non-starter in it thereby giving Batt and Andrus the opportunity to kick it off the table? The result was predictable.

Was this a deliberate strategy by Governor Otter and Director Sayer to use this as a "teaching moment" to curb the INL boosters who think in an era of shrinking federal budgets they can buck the trend and generate many more federal dollars for the INL? Doubtful.

Sayer ought to make it abundantly clear to any others who comment not to waste their time trying to make a case for any *quid pro quo* that would involve first having to amend the Batt agreement. He hasn't and he won't, however. He thinks the politics dictate keeping his options "open."

There are other problems with the LINE Commission's progress report and wish list, though. Candidly, it looks like the proverbial Christmas Tree with new baubles being added all the time. Congress used to concoct these when, at the end of a session, they would pass a catch-all appropriation bill to keep government running and add pork chop after pork chop.

The first question that needs answered is where is the money going to come from, whether federal or state, to pay for all these items? At a minimum a budget estimate ought to be attached to each and potential sources of funding identified. Then, the list prioritized with the Commission's view as to what is feasible.

Secondly, where do INL boosters get the notion the INL site can avoid the budget cuts coming for every federal department and program? It appears some may be trying to set up the Batt agreement as the cause for these inevitable cuts.

Third, INL site boosters in southeastern Idaho make much ado that a couple of counties in New Mexico have responded positively to becoming the final repository for nuclear waste. The implication is they could steal the Lab's work because they will be cooperative with the Feds.

The fact is, though, no other *state* has given a tentative yes. A decision to be a permanent repository will not be a local decision only.

Likewise, much has also been made of six southeast Idaho mayors sending a letter to the LINE Commission saying Idaho ought to take a look at selling the state's future for 30 pieces of silver just to see what all it might get. Their constituents might be more impressed if these six could even agree on just one site for a southeastern Idaho regional airport.

That would do more for economic development than amending the Batt agreement in a Faustian bargain with a devil that has proven time and again it cannot be trusted.

Ever since Andrus, early in his first term, saw the reinjection wells in use at the INL site, he has understood the threat to the vast Snake Plain Aquifer that underlies the place. He saw immediately the need to assure Idahoans their environmental and economic future was secure from radioactive pollution whose half-life is measured in thousands if not millions of years.

There is no question that because of Andrus and Batt's resolute insistence that the aquifer be protected by removal of all waste above it by 2035, progress has been made at the site. Both governors, as well as their successors, have kept the pressure on to the point that the Waste Isolation Pilot Project (WIPP) site in New Mexico is operating and taking in Idaho's poorly stored and packaged transuranic waste.

Other benchmarks have been met. The only recent setback was failure to meet the deadline for removal and calcification of all the remaining liquid waste at the site. Regardless of good intentions, the state should impose the penalties for this failure also.

Furthermore, the LINE Commission should have paid more attention to one of the briefings it received in October, 2012, from a hydrology expert, DEQ's Gerry Winters, who presented a fact-ladened power point update on the state of groundwater conditions at the INL.

While somewhat technical, the bottom line was validation of the tough stance Andrus and Batt have taken with the DOE while still enabling beneficial and economically sound projects to go forward.

Two of the slides contained graphs on radioactive particle concentrations: one was of Strontium -90 in groundwater by the INTEC site; the other was tritium in US Geologica Survey (USGS) monitoring wells 104 and 106 on the southern perimeter of the site.

Both graphs showed concentrations well below safe drinking water standards and a steady decline over the years.

Those graphs are all that warranted the one-line sentence in the LINE Commission progress report on page 13, which read "the risk to contamination of the aquifer continues to decline." Amen.

I first became aware of the Idaho National Laboratory in the mid-'50s when we lived in Idaho Falls. For a brief period my father worked at the site and, like hundreds of others, rode the bus to his post and back. All the activities were "top secret." Dad rarely talked about what he did "out there."

During the summers of 1966 and 1967, I went to summer school in the morning at Idaho State University so as to graduate from Columbia in three years. In the afternoons, I drove laundry routes for my uncle, Fergus Briggs, Jr. He owned and operated Pocatello's National Laundry & Dry Cleaning Company, which did business throughout southeast Idaho.

Once a week I drove a laundry truck out to the sites of experimental breeder reactors, EBR-I and EBR-II, to collect employee laundry for cleaning and return. Nuclear power always holds one in awe because of its mystery, and the breeder reactors were especially mysterious because they were supposed to be the next generation reactors that would consume the waste they generated as ever-lasting fuel in an endless cycle. The dream remains unrealized.

In 1971, while working as a reporter in Washington, D.C., I came across a censored government report on the first (and so far) only three fatalities associated with running any aspect of a nuclear plant. It occurred at the INL and received little media coverage at the time.

It appeared to post-accident investigators that at a small reactor site run by the U.S. Army, one of the individuals there deliberately pulled the control rods from a reactor core too quickly resulting in an explosion, the deaths of the three technicians, a discharge into the air of radioactive material and a sizable amount of nuclear contaminated material that had to be buried immediately.

It remains the nation's only fatal nuclear accident. After writing a column I thought nothing more about it.

My next encounter with the subject and the site occurred shortly after I became Andrus' press secretary in January of 1973. In October of 1973, the newly named INL Site manager, Glenn Bradlee, walked into my office to talk about setting up a tour for Andrus of the INL Site. Bradlee wanted Andrus to get better acquainted with INL activities and the critical role played in southeastern Idaho.

Andrus put it on the schedule and we soon flew over to Idaho Falls for the tour.

It was both fascinating and historic. While Bradlee did his best to keep Andrus focused on the economic potential of the research at the site, Andrus was noticing the poorly packaged and ruptured barrels of transuranic waste. What really caught his attention, though, were the reinjection wells. He saw right away a potential public relations nightmare in sending trace amounts of radioactive particles straight down into the Snake Plain Aquifer.

He realized that activity had to stop and told Bradlee just that. On the way back to Idaho Falls he also added coordination with the site and monitoring of site activities to my list of responsibilities. Andrus knew the press would play a major role in the coming years.

Shortly thereafter this new duty required assembling a Blue Ribbon Commission to review a proposal from the Atomic Energy Commission looking at 15 sites across the nation, including Idaho's INL, to serve as the nation's repository for spent nuclear fuel rods and other waste from the country's atomic energy plants.

Besides reviewing the proposal (named WASH-1535), the Commission was to hold hearings around the state and take public comment. This would be followed by a presentation of findings to a Federal review panel at AEC headquarters in Germantown, Maryland.

Andrus accepted the suggested approach, then phoned and asked a list of folks to serve. The key selection was the chairman – Idaho State University President William E. "Bud" Davis. The previous November Davis had been the Democratic nominee for the Senate seat being vacated by Len B. Jordan, and had lost a hard-fought battle to Congressman Jim McClure. It was an interesting choice, but it worked out well.

In Germantown, Davis testified that the people of Idaho unanimously did not want to be the nation's nuclear waste repository. In addition, Idaho's commission concluded it made no sense to transport spent fuel rods back and forth between an interim storage site and then a permanent site once found and developed.

The recommendation was to expand interim storage capacity on sites of nuclear facilities and with more diligence get on with finding the permanent repository. That is the course that has been followed.

Fast forward some 40 years. The "Lion in Winter," Andrus, still has a roar and a bite, especially when it comes to the issue of getting all nuclear waste off from above the Snake Plain Aquifer. His successor, Phil Batt, completed the job Andrus had begun of negotiating a deal with the INL, DOE, and the Navy, permitting the receipt of a limited amount of nuclear waste from the Navy, and a limited amount of spent fuel rods for research purposes.

The *quo* of this *pro quo* is an absolute commitment not to miss deadlines established by the agreement and the removal of *all* waste from above the aquifer by 2035. Of course when the Batt Agreement was signed in 1995 the Federal government fully expected the chosen location, Nevada's Yucca Mountain, to be open for business and operating by then.

Critics of the Batt agreement are still saying in the absence of any designated repository, Idaho's waste won't be going anywhere so the state may as well accept its fate and negotiate a better deal with the Federal government. This still means amending the Batt Agreement to which both Andrus and Batt have said, as pointed out earlier, "hell, no!"

As to the possibility of no action, Andrus says the monetary penalty (a fine of $60,000 a day) as well as public pressure will force DOE to start removing all the waste.

"Where it goes, is not my problem. That's the Fed's problem. In 2035, though, I trust there'll be a worthy successor to the legacy Phil Batt and I have left, and there'll be a governor who knows the importance of getting all waste off the site from above the Aquifer," Andrus adds.

Though Andrus has never said anything publicly, I cannot help thinking that he has been disappointed at the tepid activities of the Snake River Alliance, the environmental group in Idaho with the lead mission of protecting the aquifer. He senses the inertia in contesting a relentless Federal government which slowly wears opposition down. The public no longer seems as alarmed as it was when he first entered this fray in the mid-70s.

This is more than a legacy issue for the former governor. Anyone who knows him knows he plays to win, whether it is a game of hearts or the right outcome to a policy debate. In poker parlance he always has an "ace in the hole."

Those who think they can subdue his and Batt's opposition to amending the Batt Agreement of 1995 underestimate their tenacity and determination. One ace Andrus believes he can and will play if necessary is his ability to find a party with legal standing that could haul the Department of Energy into federal court if Governor Otter and the state reverse field and try to amend the agreement.

The other ace one suspects Andrus has is the lead witness he will bring before the court to testify for the inviolability of the Batt Agreement, the signatory for the INL, its manager in 1995 and DOE's lead negotiator, John Wilcynski. Put your money on Andrus and Batt.

7 ■ Betwist and Between

John Evans. Photo by Barry Kough.

There is an unpayable debt I will forever owe to Cecil Andrus. Everything I have accomplished, everything I am today I owe to his seeing something worth educating and molding some 40 years ago. Next to marrying my wife, the smartest decision I ever made was to tie my career to his coattail and go along on an incredible ride.

There is another distinguished former Idaho governor I also owe a deep debt of gratitude – John V. Evans.

As my tenure with the Department of the Interior was winding down, knowing that regardless of the election outcome Andrus was returning to Idaho and all his personal staff had been instructed to plan accordingly, I put out a hundred "fishing" lines. I thought some company somewhere engaged in natural resource conversion would see the value in snagging one with my expertise.

I figured wrong. Some, like Bill Rucklehaus at Weyerhaeuser and Wendell Satre at Washington Water Power, were kind enough to interview me. Since I was facing a hefty mortgage payment and the need to put food on the table without any income and little in savings, I appreciated their nominal interest.

In January, 1981, I kicked into gear my "fall back" plan, flew to Boise and met with the now-elected in his own right Governor John Evans. I asked him to name me as Idaho's first appointee to the newly created Northwest Power Planning Council. This entity had been established by the recently enacted Northwest Power Planning and Conservation Act.

The four northwest states roughly comprising the Columbia River Basin would each have two representatives on the council which was charged with developing a five year plan for meeting the region's power needs with an emphasis on conservation measures. Additionally, it was charged with developing a plan for restoring, protecting, and enhancing salmon and steelhead runs being depleted largely by the operation of four dams on the Lower Snake River. (See the next chapter).

John Evans did not owe me a thing and I knew not to presume that he did merely because of my association with his predecessor. I made a straight-forward pitch to him why I should be appointed and how that appointment would serve the people of Idaho as well as his Administration.

To his credit, he thought about it for a day, consulted with several others, called me back to his office and tendered the offer which I quickly accepted. Though I only served nine months (the first appointed from any of the four states and also the first to leave), I played a role in shaping the council for the future, ensuring Idaho's upstream rights were protected, and positioned myself for transition to the private sector within the year.

The nine month stint though kept the wolf from the door and one does not forget that in an hour of need someone other than Cecil Andrus had faith in my abilities to continue to serve Idaho.

While John Evans would never be mistaken for the charismatic Andrus, and suffers somewhat when comparisons are made, he nonetheless was a solid, capable governor who carved a worthy legacy and was elected to the office twice by the people after having initially inherited the post.

Evans is one of those people gifted by the Creator with "forever young" looks. I used to say Evans photographed ten years younger than his age while Andrus photographed ten years older. The elder of the two, though, is Evans who was born six years earlier than Andrus.

It was while working as the political editor for the *Idaho State Journal* in the fall of 1969 that I first met State Senator John Evans. He hailed from Malad and had first been elected to the senate in 1952. Ironically, two of his senate colleagues, State Senator Cecil Andrus and State Senator Bill Roden from Ada County, used to argue about whom the youngest was ever elected an Idaho State Senator.

Andrus ostensibly was the winner having been elected at the age of 29 in 1960 from Clearwater County. John Evans, being a quieter, self-effacing type, never bothered to correct either of them by pointing out when elected in 1952 he was 27.

In 1958, however, Evans left the state senate even though he had been elected majority leader during his last term. He and his spouse, Lola, were the parents of five children and he felt the need to be closer to help with their upbringing. With hardware and supply businesses in town as well as a farm outside of town, and a pioneering bank (D.L. Evans) to manage he had varied interests to take care of. In 1960, though, he did run for and was elected mayor of Malad. It is a matter of record that from 1952 until 1986, when he was defeated in his bid for the United States Senate, Evans never lost any race he entered.

Evans comes across to many people as an easy-going, decent, straight-shooting, straight-talking kind of guy, and he is indeed all of those things and more. What he masks almost deliberately is a keen, incisive intelligence and a first-rate Stanford education, having matriculated there in 1951.

Born in Malad on January 18, 1925, the progeny of pioneer LDS stock, he was raised there and indoctrinated in the family LDS faith along with the family interest in the successful regional bank founded in 1904. Somehow the bank managed to keep its doors open during the Great Depression – no mean feat in those times. With the advent of World War II and following his graduation from Malad High with the class of 1943, he enlisted and served in the infantry during WWII.

Returning from the war, like millions of other veterans, he used the G.I. bill to finance his way through Stanford University. As the eldest son in a pioneer LDS family one might presume he would have attended Brigham Young University. His father, however, had attended Stanford and so the future governor followed his dad's footsteps. Another brother also attended the challenging and highly regarded "Harvard of the West."

John Evans, though, is the only family member to have graduated from Stanford. That he by-passed BYU and chose the more challenging Stanford says much about his independence and his penchant for challenges.

The political bug also bit him early for he first stood for election to the state senate a little over a year after graduation and returning home to assist with the family's varied enterprises.

In 1968, after an absence of ten years, he returned to the state senate.

In October, 1969, Evans was in Pocatello for an appearance before the Bannock County Democratic Central Committee along with Twin Falls attorney Lloyd Walker and State Representative Vern Ravenscroft, from Tuttle, a small community in the Magic Valley just off of I-84 northwest of Twin where he ran his Penta-Post company. All three were "exploring" candidacies for the 1970 gubernatorial nomination to challenge an already weak Republican incumbent, Don Samuelson.

That evening, all made solid presentations and appeared capable of defeating Samuelson if they won the August 1970 Democratic primary. The unspoken elephant in the room, though, was State Senator Cecil Andrus, the 1966 standard bearer who had moved down the Clearwater from Orofino and returned to the state senate from Lewiston.

Andrus was then traveling the state conducting his own assessment of whether there was a fresh face, such as Idaho State University President William E. "Bud" Davis, Democrats could unite behind in 1970 or whether he should again seek the nomination. Of the three that spoke to the Bannock County Central Committee that fall evening, Evans was the only one shrewd enough to back off once Andrus made his intentions clear. As it was, Evans held the senate Democratic minority leader post, having been elected at the beginning of the 1969 legislative session.

I interviewed Evans several times by phone when doing articles on issues the 1970 legislature would be facing since he was the senate minority leader. He was what reporters characterize as a good interview – accessible, open, always providing concise and thoughtful answers to one's questions. He was not overtly partisan and never came across as an ideologue.

In 1974, the lieutenant governor's job opened up when the Republican incumbent, Jack Murphy, a rancher from Shoshone, announced he was going to challenge Andrus for the governorship. Within a matter of weeks there were three candidates from each major party who cast hats in the ring.

Of Idaho's thirty-two governors (through the end of 2012), nine had served previously as lieutenant governor and the post has always been viewed as a stepping stone to the governorship. Under Idaho's constitution, the lieutenant governor assumes all the powers of the governor when the governor leaves the state. Thus, by law the governor has to notify the lieutenant governor when he leaves the state and when he returns.

More than one governor, when facing appointing someone of the opposite party to a legislative vacancy or a board or commission, has procrastinated on making a choice, then left the state on official business (usually) having achieved an understanding with the lieutenant governor who in turn makes the selection.

Despite the governor and the lieutenant governor more often than not being from opposite parties, this constitutional requirement for a degree of "shared responsibility" has led to solid working relationships between the two office holders. During the years current Governor C. L. "Butch" Otter was serving as lieutenant governor while Andrus was governor (the second time around), Otter would always elicit a chuckle from audiences when he inevitably would tell folks his initials, C. L., stood for "Cecil's Lackey!"

It was Otter's way of saying it was not the easiest job being number two to a dynamic master of the political art such as Andrus. Otter also served as lieutenant governor to Phil Batt who was elected as Andrus' successor in 1994. Following Batt's one term, Otter also served as Dirk Kempthorne's lieutenant governor for two years before his 2000 election to Congress from Idaho's First Congressional District.

If Governor Otter decides not to seek a third term, and many speculate he will not, it is a foregone conclusion Lt. Governor Brad Little will be a prohibitive favorite to succeed him. Some pundits, however, speculate Little may be too moderate for the hard right wing of the party which might recruit First District Congressman Raul Labrador to challenge him in the Republicans-only primary.

Whether any of the six candidates for lieutenant governor in 1974 had any inkling Andrus might leave office before completing his term to serve in a cabinet position following the 1976 presidential election is open to conjecture. It seems unlikely since there had never been any elected official from Idaho tapped by a president to serve in the cabinet. (Two native Idahoans did serve, one in Cal Coolidge's cabinet and Ezra Taft Benson served in Dwight Eisenhower's cabinet.)

Odds are all six were guessing Andrus would only want to serve two terms and so each hoped by winning the second post to then be viewed as the most likely successor.

The three Democrats were state Senator and Minority Leader John Evans, from Malad; former state Senator Ray Rigby (1965-1972), a distinguished water lawyer and former LDS Bishop, from Rexburg; and, former state Senator Nels Solberg (1967 to 1972) who ran an insurance business in Grangeville.

The three Republicans were former state Rep. Pat Harwood (1965-1968) from Caldwell; Hope Kading, a prominent socialite and moderate Republican from Boise active in educational affairs; and the recently converted state Representative Vern Ravenscroft, from Tuttle, who had served in the state House of Representatives as a conservative Democrat since 1963.

Of the three Democrats, Evans easily had the most legislative experience and as a current member of the legislature and in leadership had more name-recognition as well as more familiarity with current issues. His strategy was a state-wide one centered on the more populous counties and an ability to tap into local organizations of current legislative members who knew and respected him.

As a rancher, Evans could speak knowledgeably on agriculture issues. As a banker, he could talk and walk fiscal conservatism. As a former mayor, he could discuss with ease issues facing cities both large and small across Idaho. Though raised LDS, some considered him to be a "Jack Mormon."

If a practicing member of the LDS religion, he certainly did not wear it on his sleeve, nor did he come across as Ray Rigby did in adhering to Section 89 of the *Doctrine & Covenants* which prohibits the consumption of alcohol or other strong drink. Evans was perfectly capable of having a beer with the boys if he was campaigning in a bar in Kellogg or Orofino.

He was intuitively aware that Idahoans, especially in the north, were mistrustful of the LDS Church and Mormons. As of 1974, Idahoans had never elected a practicing Mormon to the governorship. Only one had served as governor – Arnold Williams, who as Lt. Governor in 1945 had become governor upon Charles Gossett resigning the governorship to fill a vacancy in the U.S. Senate created by the death of John Thomas – courtesy of appointment by the former lieutenant governor now turned governor by inheritance.

The voters did not take kindly to such a self-aggrandizing deal and tossed both from office the first chance they had in 1946, decisively electing Dr. C.A. Robins from St. Maries as the first-ever governor from north Idaho, and Henry Dworshak from Burley to the U.S. Senate. Another factor angering voters was the late Senator Thomas had been a Republican, but the shenanigans of Gossett and Williams, both Democrats, switched the Senate seat to the other party.

The lesson taught by the voters has never been lost on future Idaho governors and lieutenant governors. No such "deals" have ever been tried since. That Evans actually ended up inheriting the job legitimately was as much a surprise to him as to others in the political arena.

The point, though, is John Evans earned the position by virtue of hard work as a legislator who strove for consensus and compromise with others. Being a genuinely kind and decent person who enjoyed meeting people and helping to solve their challenges stood him in good stead with the voters as well.

Rigby was counting on his reputation for probity and extensive knowledge of water law, as well as his unspoken good standing within the LDS Church, to garner him a significant lead in the LDS counties of southeast Idaho. He hoped to hold his own in southwest Idaho and the Treasure Valley (Ada and Canyon counties) where fully a third of the Idaho electorate resided and an area where Mormon influence was steadily growing.

One mistake Rigby made was conceding north Idaho to former state Senator Nels Solberg. It was thought north Idahoans would vote for the regional favorite son, but Solberg never really caught fire. The beneficiary was Evans who aggressively went after Democratic voters in Nez Perce, Kootenai, Shoshone, and Benewah counties.

None of the candidates appeared to spend much money, and each largely self-financed his skeletal campaign effort. The Sunshine Law was not adopted by the voters until the following November, so it is difficult to pin down expenditures especially some forty years later. A good guess is Evans had more resources and as a sitting legislator could call on businesses to contribute more easily than either Rigby or Solberg.

It should be noted that Andrus stayed out of the primary. He considered all three to be friends and was not going to play favorites. Indeed, he also considered two of the three Republicans, Pat Harwood and Hope Kading, to be friends as well.

When the smoke cleared from the August 6 primary, Evans won by almost 5,500 votes over Rigby and 13,000 more votes than Solberg. His strategy of running statewide and concentrating on the larger, more populous counties worked well as he decisively won all except Bonneville County which Rigby captured by a thousand-vote margin.

Final totals were Evans, 25,309 votes; Rigby, 19,823 votes; and, Solberg, 12,097 votes. The Malad senator decisively won Ada, Bannock, Canyon, Kootenai, and Nez Perce counties. Rigby's strategy of building up a huge margin in southeastern Idaho's predominantly

LDS counties simply did not materialize beyond his base of Jefferson, Madison, and Bonneville counties.

Evans either narrowly won or ran even with Rigby in all the other LDS counties such as Bear Lake, Caribou, Franklin, and Cassia. He also won his home county of Oneida with 518 votes to 39 for Rigby and 5 for Solberg. It has to be gratifying when those that live closest to you and have known you the longest validate that they still think highly of you. Thus, both Rigby and Evans were "validated" by their home counties.

Just in case there is any observer out there that still doubts the impact of LDS testimonials just before an election that produce a substantial bloc vote, results from Rigby's base should give you cause for pause. In Rigby's home county of Madison, the former bishop trampled Evans, garnering 1,793 votes to Evans 80 and Solberg's 29. That translates into Rigby getting an astronomical 95 percent of that county's Democratic vote.

In Fremont county, Rigby won with 954 votes to Evans 78. In Jefferson, he won with 677 to Evans 93, and in Bonneville he won with 1,719 to Evans 758. Evans, however, negated almost all those margins by winning Bannock County by three thousand more votes than Rigby, 5,453 to 2,589.

To the surprise of some, the Republican primary was not close at all – the recently converted Ravenscroft ran away with the GOP nomination and was also the largest vote-getter in either party, garnering 38,218 votes to 17,339 for Hope Kading and 12,712 for Pat Harwood. The "Tuttle turncoat" won all 44 counties.

A deceptive side note that gave Jack Murphy a brief moment of hope that he might have a shot was the fact that "Blackjack" polled only about 4,000 fewer votes in the statewide primary than did Andrus, with the final primary tally being 58,778 for Andrus and 54,950 for Murphy. This simply reflects a higher number of Republicans in Idaho and a higher number participating more so than normal in the primary.

The national context of this particular primary should be kept in mind also, especially on the Republican side. Two days before the primary the Supreme Court ruled that President Richard Nixon had to turn over to the special prosecutor the White House tapes whose secret recording had sensationally been revealed a short time earlier by Alexander Butterfield.

Less than three days after the election Nixon announced his resignation. Times were not good for Republicans even in Idaho.

The final contestants were now known, however, and the candidates hit the August county fair circuit immediately as well as the major regional fairs. It is not an absolute requirement candidates for governor and lieutenant governor in Idaho be able to ride a horse and look good doing so, but it sure helps.

All four (Andrus and Evans, Murphy and Ravenscroft) knew what they were doing around horses, which was good because at some fairs they would be asked to bring the colors in with the color guard at the start of the fair's rodeo.

Now that Evans was the nominee, Andrus could and did embrace him closely. He cut a joint television commercial for Evans, read several radio scripts supporting his election and endorsed the production of Andrus/Evans bumper stickers and Andrus/Evans pins.

To the degree possible, campaign appearances were coordinated and Evans chief campaign aide, Cary Jones, was the liaison between Larry Meierotto and me as we carried out our co-campaign management duties. Evans' daughter, Martha, and his long-time secretary, Tina Prophet, comprised the rest of his campaign team.

For Andrus, the prospect of Ravenscroft serving as his lieutenant governor was simply unacceptable. Such was the relationship between the two that Andrus knew he could not trust Vernon nor would he ever be able to leave the state even for a day in Vern's hands let alone turn the office over to him should he be tapped for a cabinet post.

Ravenscroft was running a solid campaign though and the mid campaign fall poll conducted in early October, while showing Andrus with a commanding lead, also showed Ravenscroft with a narrow lead over Evans.

It was then Andrus made the game-changing decision. He ordered his campaign team to turn over virtually all of the already paid for television slots for the last two weeks to the Evans campaign (except for his traditional ask-the-voters-for-their-vote commercial running the weekend before Election Day).

Thus, thousands of dollars of campaign television was donated to the Evans effort enabling Evans to run at almost a market saturation level his three TV commercials. The gambit worked because when the smoke cleared late in the evening of November 5th, Evans had won the race for the second spot by almost 17,000 votes over Ravenscroft, defeating him by a count of 133,307 to 115,184.

No one could deny Evans had been the beneficiary of some incredible largess as well as Andrus' stunning standing with the voters. Andrus crushed Murphy by the still-largest winning margin in a gubernatorial race in modern Idaho history, a 72 – 25 percent margin. Andrus' vote total was 184,142 to Blackjack's 68,731 votes.

Evans carried almost all the major population counties and in the others he ran fairly close (the three "urban" counties Ravenscroft carried were Twin Falls, Canyon, and Bonneville). Even in the southeastern Idaho LDS-dominated counties that Rigby had taken so overwhelmingly Evans made substantial gains, winning Franklin by 200 votes while losing Fremont by only 300 votes.

It was a very happy John and Lola Evans who joined Cece and Carol Andrus at the election night gathering in the ballroom of the old Hotel Boise.

I have several fond memories of John Evans primarily from a trade mission to Japan in the fall of 1975 sponsored by the northwest region's Title V Commission. The name is derived from a section of a Federal economic assistance bill designed to assist states in selling products overseas.

West Virginia's wily master of pork, Senator Robert Byrd, was the godfather of the legislation that provided funds with very few strings attached to states or regional groupings of states. Idaho was joined with Washington and Oregon in its Title V commission.

At a quarterly Title V Commission meeting in Salem in the spring of 1975 it was decided that each governor would lead a delegation from their state comprised of some legislators and a handful of business leaders on a ten-day business development trip to Japan.

Washington Governor Daniel J. Evans, nearing the end of his record three consecutive terms as that state's chief executive, was the titular head of the delegation. He was also near the end of his term as chair of the National Governors' Association. Oregon Governor Bob Straub led that state's delegation.

Andrus, who had served during the Korean War, at the Iwakuni Air Base in Japan, and had also traveled there previously, decided to stay home and named Evans to lead Idaho's delegation. He called me into the office one afternoon and said he was also sending me along with instructions to provide Evans with the same degree of service I always provided him.

Having always wanted to visit Japan (ever since my Oriental Civilization class at Columbia), I was delighted to go. Other members of Idaho's delegation included veteran Democratic State Senator Cy Chase from St. Maries, Democratic State Rep. Marion "Swede" Davidson, from Bonners Ferry; Republican State Rep. Herb Fitz, from New Meadows; Lt. Governor Evans' wife, Lola, and Administration Director Wayne Mittleider.

The trip began inauspiciously. Shortly after our Northwest Orient 747 lifted off the Sea-Tac runway the plane's pilot/captain came on the speaker to announce there was a glitch somewhere in the system, we were going to have to circle once we rose to 10,000 feet where we would commence dumping the plane's fuel to lighten our landing weight before putting down back at Sea-Tac. From 10,000 feet the fuel supposedly all evaporates before it can hit the ground.

Once on the ground they would either find and fix the glitch or substitute a back-up 747. It was a nice fall day around Puget Sound, and we all took turns sitting in the window seat watching the earth unfold below as the fire hose tips of each wing were gushing a fan-like spray that occasionally cast a rainbow.

While some members of our contingent displayed anxiety until we all were safely back in the airport lounge, most took their cue from the plane's pilot who sounded calm and relaxed. While one realizes this is part of their training, it is nonetheless reassuring. I call it the "Chuck Yeager" voice – a slight drawl, a studied nuance, the cool, calm, collected reassuring sound of someone saying relax, he is in control and you all are safe.

After a ten-hour delay we were again airborne on a replacement 747 but as we flew the schedule was being redone to fit in all the tours and meetings our hosts had planned.

Several vignettes from this trip will forever be branded into my memory – some funny, some sad.

One of several surrogate children Governor Andrus has adopted over the years is a strapping young fellow from Meridian, Wayne Mittleider.

He had worked in Andrus' 1970 campaign and then Andrus put him to work first in the Communications shop of the Division of Administration and then moved him up the chain of command.

Mittleider is one of those can-do, jack-of-all-trades people every governor needs because of their ability to take on and complete most any task, large or small, simple or difficult that a governor hands to them. Andrus sent him along to help handle the logistics of the trip.

One quirk of the Japanese language is an inability to pronounce the letter "L".

Thus, Mittleider's name was always pronounced Mitt-rider by our hosts. In part because he and I were the only two young folks on the trip we spent time together getting better acquainted.

As we got better acquainted I realized Andrus had sent Mittleider along to distract him from a deep grief he was carrying over the death of a beloved younger brother, Ray Mittleider, who had died the previous January on Super Bowl Sunday. Both brothers had been exceptional football players at Meridian, and Ray, who was a star high school quarterback, had been recruited by Boise State.

He was expected to start by his junior year, but leukemia cut short his life. Sometimes one realizes their role is to be a good listener and I recall Mittleider and I sitting in the bar car of the Bullet train, sipping Kirin beer looking out at the scenery as the train sped along at 200 mph. In particular the route seemed to pass a number of Japanese Shinto/Buddhist graveyards which prompted ruminations and discussions between us about life and death, the afterlife, and other attendant subjects. It turned out, I felt, to be good therapy for Wayne, but to this day I know there still exists a deep wound in his heart at the loss of Ray. It is a grief that while unspoken will always go on.

To their credit both John and Lola Evans also sensed this sadness within Mittleider and each in their own kind way "mothered and fathered" him as we went along our way. In subsequent years, Mittleider became one of John Evans trusted behind-the-scenes advisors.

Two other memorable events occurred which also say much about Evans willingness to try something new, and that he possesses that vital sense of humor most politicians need to survive.

Towards the end of the trade mission I concluded in many respects we had been hermetically sealed away in large western hotels and then escorted everywhere by our hosts during various business as well as cultural tours. I felt we were missing out on any authentic non-westernized experience.

So I booked the governor and Lola, Cy Chase, Swede Davidson, Mitt-rider, Fitz, and myself into a genuine Japanese *ryokan*, or inn, for one night outside of Osaka. The rest of the delegation looked at us askance as we walked out of another western-style hotel tower, piled into several cabs and off we went.

We had fun. No one spoke a word of English at the *ryokan* and indeed the proprietors were a bit startled when we rolled up to their door. The rooms, however, had been paid for and our hosts set about introducing us to the normal routine for any Japanese overnight guest.

First, they indicated we were to get out of our clothes and to cleanse ourselves thoroughly. I'll never forget sliding open one of the numerous *shoji* sliding doors used to divide the various *tatami* floor rooms and there was Cy Chase sitting in what can only be described as a fairly large bucket of steaming hot water, his legs draped over the edge as one of the Japanese hostesses scraped and cleaned away the day's perspiration from his back.

He was enjoying himself, as did the rest of us when it was our turn. Once washed and dried, we each were given a nice robe to put on, along with slippers, and then ushered into a separate room for dinner. We all knelt beside a table and those that had not yet mastered chop sticks had no choice but to do so because there was no silverware.

Courses were brought in on one large platter and either placed on a "lazy susan" in the center of the table or carried around to each of us to take our portion. Traditional *saki* was provided as well as Japanese beer and of course the ever present green tea. It was a wonderful meal.

At the ryokan in Japan. Photo by Chris Carlson.

The entire group kicked back, relaxed and some of us may have even gotten slightly inebriated. We told stories, laughed at how ridiculous some of us looked, and finally in the wee hours of the morning were escorted to our separate rooms where we slept on slightly higher *tatami* mats piled on the floor.

Every one that went to the *ryokan* thanked me for the experience and for being adventuresome enough to figure out how to obtain an authentic Japanese experience. It proved to be the highlight of the trip for all.

The other memory I have was somewhat of a rotten joke I decided to play on Governor Evans, being confident I could get away with it and that in the end he would have a good laugh also.

Like many well-to-do Idahoans, John Evans is pretty darn tight with a buck. This is a quality we like in our governors, especially when it comes to spending our tax money. However, in personal situations where one person is going to pick up the tab for a meal or a round of drinks, he is one of those folks who seem to take a little time fumbling for and finally pulling out his billfold.

So I decided to have some fun with this.

Along with Governor Dan Evans and Governor Bob Straub, Lt. Governor John Evans was invited to a rare audience with the Japanese Emperor, Hirohito. This had not been on the original schedule and was rightly viewed as a high honor for our entire delegation. John was genuinely excited about the visit and asked me to prepare a news release upon his return, when he would give me a few quotes, and to then get the release to Boise and on the AP and UPI wires for statewide distribution.

Keep in mind there was no Internet in 1975 and so one either sent something via Western Union or placed an international phone call. "How quickly do you want it there, governor?" I innocently asked. "Oh, right away, Chris, as soon as you can get it to Boise, get it to Boise," he said. "Okay, will do, Governor," I replied.

So I sent a 400 word press release about his meeting with the Emperor via Western Union, top priority, and I had the $380 charged to his room. Early the next morning I grabbed Mittleider and said, "Come with me, Wayne. I think you'll enjoy sitting in the lobby with me watching the governor check out."

So we were in the lobby of the Tokyo Hilton a few minutes before the governor and Lola got there to check out. Sure enough, like the lovable tightwad he is, he was carefully going over every charge on the bill. Suddenly, like Mt. Fuji erupting one could see him start gesticulating, pointing at an item on the bill, demanding that the clerk explain it, his voice rising, eyes bulging, slowly getting incensed at how he thought he was being gouged.

Mittleider and I were rolling on the floor laughing.

Finally, you could see the clerk's explanation starting to register with him. He looked around and spotted Wayne and me sitting across the lobby trying to look innocent, came charging across the lobby and as he got closer trying not to yell but in a somewhat commanding voice demanding, "Chris, Chris, what's this $380 charge you put on my bill?"

"Why governor, you ordered me to get the press release on your meeting with the Emperor to Boise as quickly as possible, so I did. It cost $380 to get it done!"

Suddenly, it clicked with him, and he started smiling, and then started laughing at his folly. He knew too that I'd pulled a good one on him.

Within 18 months John Evans was rewarded for his loyalty to Andrus as well as his shrewdness in having sought and won the post of lieutenant governor. He became Idaho's 27th governor on January 24, 1977, upon Andrus' resignation to become Jimmy Carter's Secretary of the Interior.

I remember the genuine joy and happiness on his and Lola's faces as they greeted Andrus and me at the Boise Airport upon our return from Plains, Georgia. They led a large and enthusiastic crowd greeting Andrus' return that also included as many Republicans as Democrats, all Idahoans proud of Andrus' selection. Among the Republicans at the airport that evening was Senator Jordan and his wife, Grace, as well as state senators Lyle Cobbs and Dean Summers, and state Rep. Jack Kennevick.

Evans would be governor for the next ten years. Many Idahoans have forgotten those were not the easiest years in which to preside over a state that started suffering along with the rest of the nation during the recession that began towards the end of the Carter Administration. Inflation and high energy costs took their toll.

Evans was a steady hand on the tiller throughout. There was also an element of luck in which person the Republicans chose to challenge him when he stood for election on his own in 1978. The challenger was the speaker of the Idaho house, Allen Larsen, who hailed from Bingham County..

Larsen was a wear-it-on-your-sleeve moralizing Mormon who campaigned on imposing his moral strictures along with other traditional Republican planks regarding no taxes and running state government like a business. Needless to say this did not go over well with most of a libertarian leaning electorate that subscribes to the separation of church and state.

Evans crushed Larsen, garnering 169,540 votes to Larsen's 114,149. That is a 59 – 40 percent margin. Evans justifiably took pride in a significant endorsement of his first two years on the job. During his tenure he basically followed the Andrus formula of strong support for public education, reasonable conservation programs, aggressive recruitment of out-of-state businesses but no subsidies, and strict adherence to the state constitutional requirement of balancing budgets annually and no accumulation of debt.

Like Andrus, Evans subscribed to the statement that first one had to make a living, but then they wanted a living worthwhile. One of his notable successes as governor was negotiating a major water rights agreement with Idaho Power. As noted in a previous chapter, he also stood with Andrus in protecting and expanding the Birds of Prey, fully supported the establishment of the Hells Canyon and Sawtooth recreation areas, and backed the establishment of the central Idaho wilderness.

One issue that plagued his tenure was right-to-work. Evans vetoed several right-to-work laws passed by the Idaho legislature, maintaining his loyalty to the various unions from teachers to the electrical workers at the Idaho National Laboratory who faithfully backed him in his races. His 1982 race for a second full term revolved around the "right-to-work" issue and the ability of farm workers to unionize.

His opponent was Lt. Governor Phil Batt, a solid, moderate former Republican state senator from Wilder who had in 1978 easily defeated Bill Murphy, the man Evans had chosen to fill his old office upon his becoming governor. Murphy was a former veteran state representative from Wallace in north Idaho and a former Andrus chief of staff for a brief period.

Batt hammered away on the right-to-work issue as well as his opposition to a farm worker's union and came close to ousting Evans, losing to the incumbent governor by slightly over 4,000 votes. Evans' total vote was 165,365 to Batt's 161,157 total, or a margin of 51 percent to 49 percent.

Evans actually polled 4,000 votes less than he had taken in 1978.

A man not to be kept down for long, Batt returned to the legislature, and in 1990 set about to reorganize the state's Republican party turning it into the juggernaut that it has been ever since. And in 1994 he achieved one of his life ambitions, succeeding his good friend, Governor Andrus. For reasons known only to him, Batt chose to serve only one term.

In the meantime, Republicans were smart enough to put right-to-work on the ballot as a referendum thereby guaranteeing it would be a major issue in Andrus' comeback campaign where he was being challenged by Republican Lt. Governor David Leroy and in Evans' challenge of Steve Symms for the U.S. Senate seat Symms had won from Frank Church in 1980.

For once labor did not deliver for Evans. The right-to-work measure won easily, 54 percent to 46 percent. Andrus was still popular enough to withstand the tide, narrowly winning by 3,357 votes over Leroy. Evans, on the other hand, suffered his first ever defeat.

He lost to Symms, 52 percent to 48 percent. The vote totals were 196,958 for Symms, and 185,066 for Evans. In defeating Leroy, Andrus had taken 193,429 votes to Leroy's 189,794 votes. In other words, approximately 8,000 Republicans who voted for Symms then switched and voted for Andrus for governor.

In January of 1987 John Evans turned the governor's office back to Cecil Andrus, who would go on to win a fourth term in1990. By the time Andrus turned the keys over to Phil Batt in January of 1995 the Democrats under the stewardship of just two men, Andrus and Evans, had held the office for 24 consecutive years.

Idaho underwent terrific transformation during those years moving from a part rural, part urban state to a decidedly more urbanized one. Its population almost doubled and the economy began the painful shift from a resource-based economy to one with high tech manufacturing moving to the forefront with businesses like Hewlett-Packard and Micron springing up in the greater Boise area.

During his ten years with his hand on the tiller most would say John Evans hand was every bit as steady as Cecil Andrus'. The people were well served by both. John and Lola Evans can look back with justifiable pride at the service they rendered Idaho for the ten years John held the governorship.

Following Andrus' inaugural the Evans's moved to Burley where the former governor took over the presidency of the expanding family bank, the D.L. Evans Bank.

The story goes that when Governor Evans returned to the family-owned bank and attended his first board meeting, he was asked what title he would like to have. With a twinkle in his eyes he responded, "Well, I've had the title of governor, of senator, of chairman, but never president. I think I'd like "Mr. President" as my next title."

As of this writing the former governor is still mentally sharp but is confined to a wheel chair at the age of 88. His devoted wife of so many years, Lola, remains in good health and loyally at his side.

His epitaph when his time comes should be either "Well done, thou good and faithful servant…" or "To whom much is given, much is expected. He delivered."

8 ▪ The Toothless Tiger

The first formal photo of the Northwest Power Planning Council, spring of 1981. Carlson is second from right, standing; Bob Saxvik is second from right at the table. Photo by Robert Lenaghen.

My first editor at the *Idaho State Journal*, Lyle Olson, would occasionally walk up to me with copy of a story I had submitted, and say, "Chris, you buried the lead in this story. Don't do that." He was always correct, sometimes painfully so, to my chagrin.

No burying the lead:

The Northwest Power Planning Council has lost whatever usefulness it once had, is no longer coming close to the purpose its proponents originally envisioned, and it should be abolished.

Now let me explain why.

As the first person appointed to the NWPPC by any of the governors of the four states within the Columbia River Basin, and as the catalyst for ensuring Idaho and Montana's upstream water rights were acknowledged and protected from day one, I believe I have more than incidental credibility to pronounce the Council to be a colossal failure.

The Northwest Power Planning Act in fact outlines a simple mechanism for abolishing the Council. Three of the four northwest states' governors merely have to request in writing to the Secretary of the Interior that it be abolished and it's done. The governors should act, now before the Council wastes any more ratepayer money.

Candidly, it has been a gargantuan waste and its shortcomings in not producing a viable plan to restore wild salmon and steelhead fishery runs decimated by the four lower Snake River dams is prime reason to put the Council out of its misery. They shoot horses with broken legs, don't they?

The council has broken legs, as well as arms, feet, hands, and head. It too should, in an act of compassion, be eliminated. The governors should act, and act now.

It should have been judged a failure many years ago. That it hasn't attests to why it is so difficult for governmental entities to sunset themselves. First, some history on the early days of the Council, the initial politics, and the seeds of failure, is warranted.

The Act itself is largely the product of two of the sharpest legal and political minds to have ever darkened Capitol Hill: Rick Redman and Brett Wilcox. Redman is a former partner in the law firm of Preston, Gates & Ellis, and, more importantly was the legislative director for one of Congress's most powerful senators, the state of Washington's Warren G. Magnuson. Maggie, as he was affectionately called by staff and friends, and the state's junior senator, Henry M. " Scoop" Jackson, were called by colleagues "the Gold Dust Twins," because they were so effective at channeling federal largess to the state of Washington over a number of years.

Redman, when still a young staffer, wrote an excellent book called *The Dance of Legislation,* an account of how the health care issue was turned into legislation in the 60s. It has become a textbook used in many college political science courses across the nation.

Wilcox, every bit the intellectual equal of Redman, was the executive director of the Direct Service Industries Association, the 13 largely aluminum and nickel producing companies in the northwest which bought their power directly from the Bonneville Power Administration rather than through a public or private utility. They comprised the industrial customers of BPA, the federal marketing agency of mostly hydroelectric power produced by the system of dams in the northwest on the Columbia and Snake River systems.

BPA's other major customer groups are the commercial and residential classes. Each class consumed roughly 1/3 of the power marketed by BPA. Redman, Wilcox and their clients, represented by each company's power manager, were concerned about long-term access to this relatively inexpensive power, which, in the case of the aluminum industry is literally one of the raw ingredients in a pound of aluminum.

It did not take a rocket scientist to recognize population growth alone across the region would inevitably put pressure on industry's share of this public resource. To critics, the Northwest Power Planning and Conservation Act of 1980, largely drafted by Redman and Wilcox, but massaged by dozens of lawyers and power managers, was a not too thinly disguised effort to ensure industry's share was protected well into the future.

One of the keys was an elaborate power switch which for the first time permitted the residential customers of private utilities to also benefit from the low power costs of the hydro-based federal system.

Two other compromises welded onto the package were: A commitment that a new entity, the Power Planning Council, comprised of two representatives from each state, would draw up a five-year power plan that estimated the region's power demand; and a five-year resource plan, including a large element of conservation and later, other renewable resources, that would be on line to meet the demand.

The final compromise was the Council was charged with developing a plan to restore decimated salmon and steelhead fishery runs. The needs of the fish were to be put on an even basis with the needs of power supplies. Here is where the Council clearly has failed miserably.

During the late 1970s, of the four northwest states only Oregon and Washington had up and running, well staffed energy offices. Folks within each office were aware of the Power Planning Act. In particular, a state like Oregon had a person like Roy Hemingway assigned to monitor the progress of the bill and work with the state's congressional delegation to ensure its interests were protected.

Members of Idaho's private and public utilities were less aware, but aware nonetheless of the proposed legislation as it was gestating. Other than a staffer or two within the state of Idaho's public utility commission, there was little awareness anywhere else in state government up to and including the office of the governor.

During the waning days of the Carter Administration I had added, with Andrus' consent, to my duties as director of the Office of Interior Public Affairs the role of Western Field Director. This necessitated a move back west and I and my family bought a home on Bainbridge Island across from Seattle. The Interior department's western field office was housed on the 29th floor of the Jackson Federal Office Building in downtown Seattle. I commuted to work on the ferry, and then walked the few short blocks to the office.

Candidly, I was not aware in the slightest that there even was legislation creating a Northwest Power Planning Council until I noticed a news item that President Jimmy Carter had on December 5th, 1980, signed into law a bill entitled the Northwest Power Planning and Fisheries Enhancement Act. Intrigued, I did some research and became engrossed.

Drilling down on the bill's creating a "northwest power planning council," I targeted one of Idaho's (Each state had two appointments) two appoitments as my "back up" plan for employment. When nothing materialized from my job search by the first of January, I booked a flight to Boise after obtaining an appointment with Governor John V. Evans.

I also placed a call to my old friend and Japan traveling companion, Wayne "Mitt-rider", who had become since that 1975 trip a key behind-the-scenes advisor to the governor. I explained to Wayne the purpose of my visit and was gratified by his encouragement. Serendipitously, he was sharing an apartment with the governor's chief of staff, former Burley radio station owner and state senator, Bob Saxvik.

I was confident that Governor Evans had not been made aware of his new appointing power, nor would he know much yet regarding the new power planning act. This was a function of insufficient staffing on energy matters across the board in Idaho's public sector. It put me in the enviable position of being able to be the first to explain the purpose of the legislation as well as the purpose of the council it created.

I pitched Governor Evans on why I thought I should be one of the two appointees and how my appointment would help his administration and him. Briefly I outlined a plan I had formulated in which I was sure in the setting of the budget I could get the consent of Oregon and Washington's council members to allocate a proportionally larger share of the operating budget to Idaho and Montana to assist us in staffing up so as to be more informed contributors.

The reason I was so confident was I knew if Montana's appointees stayed with me on a gambit I had in mind we had two big chits we could play – the location of the council headquarters office and the chairmanship.

Saxvik sat through my presentation, listening quietly. Governor Evans asked for a couple of days to mull it over and to make a few calls to friends and allies in Idaho's energy sector to see what they knew about the bill and its authority. After I left the governor's office, Saxvik put in a pitch for being appointed to the other position.

Leaving nothing to chance, I asked Mittleider to pay a visit to Governor Evans and Lola (Evans almost always obtained Lola's counsel before making any major decision) at their home to do some low-key lobbying. He did so with satisfying results. The next morning Evans called and invited me to drop back by the office.

Once ushered into the governor's office (with, as usual, the door left wide open so any visitor or the media could see who he was meeting with), Evans got right to the point, saying he had given it a good mulling over and decided what I had to say made a great deal of sense. Thus, he was offering the two positions to Bob Saxvik and to me. We each accepted on the spot.

I suggested to the governor he allow me to draft for his legal counsel a first cut at an executive order creating the Idaho power council positions and that I provide a draft of a press release for his communications office to post for the news media. He readily agreed.

There was one last question. I asked Evans at what level did he want to set the salary for Saxvik and me? Evans said he had not given that much thought and asked if I had a recommendation. I explained to the governor that the legislation itself had some "guidance," that there was a section in which if a governor failed to name council members from his state the BPA administrator would designate two and the salary would be set at the equivalent of the federal system's GS-18.

Evans said that sounded good to him. "So let it be said, so let it be done," I said, quoting a favorite line of mine uttered by the Egyptian Pharaoh played by Yul Bryner in *The Ten Commandments*. I smiled and thanked the governor and was also thankful that Saxvik had not asked just what a GS-18 meant in dollars. Evans was a classic "tight with a buck" kind of guy and I suspect he had little idea just how much a GS-18 earned.

A GS-18 in 1981 at step one was close to $100,000. Overnight, Saxvik and I became two of the highest paid public employees in the state of Idaho.

Upon departing, I immediately commandeered one of the governor's secretary's typewriters and wrote out the executive order, then drafted the press release to be issued the following day. Then I called my wife at home on Bainbridge and told her to put the house up for sale, that we were moving back to Boise and her husband would have a pay check coming the day after my service in the Carter Administration ended on January 20th.

To say the least, she was relieved to get the news. Like millions of Americans with three young children we lived from paycheck to paycheck and with two moves across the country in four years, had nothing left in savings. Governor Evans appointing me to the newly created council was a life-saver.

I also knew though that inevitably the Legislature would insist on confirming whomever the governor nominated because the post was too high-profile for them not to insist. Evans, being a long-time member of the state Senate, would in all probability acquiesce to the Senate confirming any governor's appointees.

While I knew Evans would support and fight for my nomination, the best course for all was to try and finesse a delay in the confirmation until the following year. That would give me a year to prove my spurs to utility folks in Idaho, both public and private. It also would give me time to travel the state to visit all the members of the Senate in their home districts in a more relaxing less visible forum – at their kitchen tables.

An unlikely ally in this effort was the state attorney general, David Leroy. He and I started jogging together over the noon hour and sometimes after work. He enjoyed picking my brain on a variety of subjects and without my asking, when asked by the Republican Senate caucus regarding the ability of Saxvik and I to serve a year without being confirmed (or being rejected) until the following session, Leroy issued an informal, verbal opinion that we could serve the year without any onus falling back on the state.

Thus, I bought some time. Fortuitously, I was able to arrange to live in Boise in an apartment shared with Mittleider and Saxvik at a rather nominal charge. My wife and I decided she and the kids would stay on Bainbridge until the house sold and then move to Boise. I resolved to get "home" every weekend, and as the Council was inundated with invitations to tour projects all around the northwest the expense of whether I flew to Boise was virtually the same as flying back to Seattle on the weekends.

Make no mistake, though, as the long-time walking, talking spokesman for Idaho's most successful politician ever, I was an inviting target for conservative Republican state senators like future Pro Tem Senator Reed Budge, from Soda Springs. (Andrus had once quipped "Reed Budge – can't read and won't budge." The senator of course had never forgotten). They were sharpening their long knives, but it was easier to wait a year than force a fight right away with Governor Evans. They could wait.

Neither was the largest private utility in Idaho, the Idaho Power Company, enamored with me. I was viewed as strictly a political appointment with no energy knowledge. On this they were mistaken. I had quickly started educating myself plunging not only into Northwest Power Planning Act and its history, but well known texts on energy issues both national and regional.

This did not stop Logan Lanham, Idaho Power's influential government affairs director, from sidling up to me on a flight from Portland to Boise to give me an energy quiz ("Chris – what's the difference between an AC transmission line and a DC transmission line?"). I knew better than to take the bait. Once I started down such a path he would have a question I would not yet know the answer, so I politely declined to play his game.

I could understand the concern because the Council inevitably would review the "exchange" portion of the act which allowed private utilities for the first time ever to have limited access to lower-cost public power for their residential customers. This feature was literally worth millions of dollars.

Shortly after Evans announced the formation of the Idaho Power Council and that Saxvik and I were Idaho's initial appointees we set about building a budget and a modest staff to assist us. We interviewed several folks for the staff director's post, a staff secretarial position, a staff attorney and a staff economist.

We also drew up a basic budget for the Idaho Power Council office and were pleased to come up with a reasonable amount of $500,000 a year to operate.

I was quite pleased at how quickly "Saxee," as I nicknamed him, and I were able to work together, dividing up areas of responsibility, collaboratively working and communicating well. I was most pleased at our agreeing on who should be staff director – Bob Lenaghen.

Lenaghen, a former state legislator and long-time union leader from Pocatello, was the person who in November 1969, first introduced me to a young, aspiring state senator from Orofino, Cecil D. Andrus. In the years since he had loyally served both Andrus and Evans in a number of posts.

We knew it was important that we embark on a proactive program of introducing ourselves to the key energy constituents around the state. So, we scheduled sessions not just with energy constituents, but with conservation advocates, environmental groups, such as the Idaho

Conservation League (which was spearheading the "save the salmon" effort), and Idaho's Native American tribes.

Everywhere we went we made presentations on the Act and its mandates for a five-year energy needs/resources plan. Additionally, we discussed plans for conservation and fishery enhancements. Many of the interest groups held winter meetings in Boise to coincide with the legislative session and we would be invited to "sniff sessions."

Not too long after Evans' announcement, Montana Governor Ted Schwinden announced his appointments to the Council: Keith Colbo and Gerald Mueller. Colbo, like Saxvik, had been serving as Schwinden's chief of staff and prior to that headed up several state agencies. Mueller was the energy wonk who had followed the development of the Act from his previous position on the staff of Montana's Public Service Commission.

Within hours we were on the phone discussing the four of us meeting at the Idaho Falls airport to develop a unified, coordinated strategy for the upriver states to be united on as we went into the first organizational meeting of the new Council. Idaho and Montana had common interests not the least of which was to assure legislators, always a bit paranoid, that we were not about to allow the two more populated downriver states to divert the increasingly precious water produced within our borders.

We agreed on a time and place and within days were in Idaho Falls hammering out our unified positions. We knew the downriver states of Washington and Oregon would want the Council's headquarters to be either in Portland or Seattle. It was also a safe guess that Washington would want the chairmanship for the most distinguished appointment of the initial eight appointees – former three-term Governor Daniel J. Evans.

The downriver four needed at least one of the upstream four's vote to obtain those two items. Idaho and Montana needed proportionally a higher share of the Council's budget in order to set up offices and hire some staff to enable us to be as well briefed and prepared as our downstream counterparts who were supported by large state energy offices.

The four of us resolved to stay together. I was designated to lead the strategy as it would play out at our first meeting in Portland. We made no effort to keep our upriver group meeting a secret so word spread quickly to the downriver four.

Oregon Governor Vic Atiyeh's initial appointees to the Northwest Power Planning Council were Roy Hemingway, like Mueller an energy wonk who had been active in the development of the Power Act, and a distinguished retired jurist, Judge Herb Schwab. Washington Governor John Spellman's other appointee besides Dan Evans was a talented businessman and retired Army colonel, Chuck Collins.

Hemingway was reportedly furious when he heard about the meeting, feeling that it was injecting politics from the get-go into what he felt should be a totally apolitical, objective, fact-driven exercise. He quickly fingered me as the ringleader, the one who had injected dirty politics.

When we first met in Portland he was cold and distant with me. In my view, he was incredibly naïve and a bit idealistic if he thought politics was not going to be woven into the fabric of virtually everything the Council did. The selection of the BPA administrator, for example, is a patronage position which traditionally goes to the northwest's senior U.S. senator of the party holding the White House at the time a vacancy is created. Historically, whenever the presidency changed the BPA administrator would resign so a new one could be appointed.

The out-going administrator was Sterling Munro, the long-time chief of staff to Washington Senator Henry M. "Scoop" Jackson. With Ronald Reagan having defeated Jimmy Carter the previous November, the incoming BPA administrator, Peter Johnson, the former chairman of Boise-based Trus Joist Corporation, had been selected by Idaho's senior Republican senator, James A. McClure, who also would be taking over the Senate's Energy and Natural Resources committee.

We "upriver states" felt the Council had to establish quickly its independence from BPA even though our budget would be provided by ratepayer money under the Administrator's office funds. It should be pointed out also the governors of the two upriver states were Democrats and the governors of the two downriver states were Republicans.

The upriver four also envisioned the Council functioning as the board of directors to BPA including the clear setting of policy to be followed by the administrator. For his part, Earl Gjelde the "Acting" Administrator, and then Peter Johnson, Sterling Munroe's appointed replacement, saw the Council as merely an advisory body.

Unfortunately, led by Dan Evans, the Republican four eventually opted to the advisory side of this issue.

Hemingway, also an attorney, held a third view which he later articulated in a 1983 article published in the spring issue of Lewis & Clark College's distinguished Environmental Law Review edited by Michael Blumm. Blumm was then and still is a leading analyst of the Act and its impacts on the region. In the article, Hemingway called the Council a unique experiment in President Reagan's policy of the New Federalism in which the federal government would "share" power with the four northwest states.

News flash for Hemingway – the unique experiment has failed miserably, another testament to the "Golden Rule," which states he who has the gold rules. BPA is the source of the money (ratepayer generated revenue) and unfortunately for the states and the region the Council from the beginning started down the path of irrelevance and failure.

Thus, the scene was set for the Council's first meeting on April 28th, 1981. Following opening comments by or from the governors, Judge Schwab (as temporary chair) quickly moved to the selection of a permanent chairman. Chuck Collins nominated his colleague, Dan Evans and it was seconded by Hemingway. I nominated Saxvik and it was seconded by Colbo. The vote was taken and to the surprise of those watching, it was a 4/4 tie.

Collins then made a motion for a 15-minute recess. He and Evans approached me and wanted to know why we were not deferring to the obvious and backing Dan Evans. I said there was going to have to be some old-fashioned horse-trading take place, that if Washington wanted Evans to be the chair they had to commit to supporting a much larger budget than the Power Act's language capping spending for the Council to be no more than .02% of BPA's projected annual firm power sales. A much larger budget was needed, at least initially so the upriver states could be properly staffed and the Council central office properly staffed.

Dan Evans rather imperiously looked at me and sanctimoniously said he had never in all his years in politics cut deals, that he always analyzed each matter purely in terms of what was in the public interest. He turned and walked away. Not sure I believe that. It is hard to imagine a governor serving 12 years and never cutting a few deals. It sure explains also why he did not re-up for the Senate seat he occupied after the death of Scoop Jackson.

I said to Collins something like, "well, if Oregon will vote with us for a better budget I guess they will get both the headquarters in Portland, which they clearly wanted and the chairmanship."

Collins said to give him a minute, walked over to Hemingway and Schwab to explain the situation. Hemingway, even more disgusted with my "politicizing things," walked away but Schwab told Chuck it was a deal.

Collins came back to me and said the deal was done. We would get the budget we desired if Evans was named chairman and the central office was set up in Portland. We shook on it and with the recess ending we reconvened. I withdrew my nomination for my colleague, Mr. Saxvik and made the motion for a unanimous vote to name Dan Evans the chair.

So let it be said, so let it be done.

Interestingly, none of this is in the official record which merely states that Dan Evans was unanimously elected chair and Bob Saxvik, vice-chair. Neither is there a tape recording of the historic first meeting. It seems that the taping of Council meetings did not begin until its third meeting. Isn't that interesting?

In late 2011 I saw a write-up on the beginnings of the Council in the newsletter put out by the Council's communications office. It was an interview with Governor Evans in which he conveniently ignored the jockeying and merely recalled his unanimous selection. I sent him an e-mail politely reminding him of the history. He pointedly chose to ignore me thereby insuring that this account of what really happened would be written.

The Council developed its initial work plan rapidly which included staffing up. Ed Sheets, a former staffer to Senator Warren Magnuson, was hired as the Council's first executive director. While bright, energetic, and plenty smart he retained the post for almost 20 years, which surprised me. Just as almost all the Council members were replaced by new governors or having served two three-year terms, were not reappointed, change was deemed healthy. It would have been true for staff.

Sheets, to his credit, if not necessarily to the BPA ratepayers', was an absolute genius at drafting up and then selling a real "Cadillac" staff set-up to the Council members (not a hard sell) and to BPA (a bit harder sell). The initial plan presented had a budget total of $6,063,000.00 It included staffing of 33 central office full-time employees.

This amount of money was .059 mills per kilowatt hour of anticipated annual firm power sales, approximately three times the amount the law stipulated. The law, however, also allowed for the BPA Administrator to waive the cap, which is what Peter Johnson and each succeeding administrator has done every year since.

In fairness I cannot heap upon Sheets all the blame for the Cadillac instead of the Chevy model, especially when it came to the public affairs/press relations office. We all tend to play to our strengths and mine of course, in my view, was the public information/outreach/public affairs component.

For Fiscal Year 1982 I made sure the budget included slots for a central office press shop of at least seven people with generous compensation and extra hefty budget allocations for lots of get acquainted travel around the region and sufficient funds for the initial outlays for brochures, fact sheets, and other basic tools a good information shop would need.

I also made sure that since we figured Idaho's office would need a budget of at least $500,000 that meant that each of the other states would also receive a like amount whether they needed it or not. Thus, I accept my share of the blame for foisting off on the northwest a Cadillac that I never dreamed would be fed by champagne every year since. I guess I thought sooner rather than later it would be put on a beer budget. I was wrong.

In Fiscal Year 2002, the budget document itself for the Council had more than doubled in pages from 34 to 77 which tells one much right there. The budget, 20 years later was $7.8 million or .078 mills per kilowatt hour of projected annual firm energy sales.

For that 20 years the Council's budgets had averaged $6.7 million annually with the percentage of firm sales fluctuating from between .061 mills per kwh to .083 mills per kwh. In the eyes of many the Council also experienced classic mission creep.

Rather than adhere strictly to the scope of work in the Act, many feel the Council strayed into an oversight role of various BPA contracts especially those dealing with fish and wildlife studies. Five-year power need plans and projections of how those needs will be filled are not all that difficult to draw up.

What to do in the interim to keep everybody busy was to appropriate for itself a questionable oversight role of numerous BPA contracts, especially those dealing with trying to restore wild salmon and steelhead runs as mandated by the Act. This has been a bonanza and the gift that keeps on giving every year.

One would think that there are only so many trips the Council can make around the region and only so many projects it can look at, but we all know that is not the nature of any bureaucratic entity. The first law is to preserve itself and to keep finding work to justify its existence.

So, for Fiscal Year 2014 its budget is $10,359,000 or .086 mills per kilowatt hour of projected annual firm energy sales. The public affairs budget is $1.389 million or 13%. The fish and wildlife program is 24% or $2.451 million and the Power Planning is 33% of the budget at $3.405 million. The state offices are 30% and each office now spends around $769,000 annually.

The executive director today is another veteran of the Hill in D.C., Steve Crow, who worked for Senator Mark Hatfield. The central office is up to 40 positions and each state office has around five folks counting the council members so total staff is around 60 folks.

If one projects the first 20 year average of $6.7 million per year through the next 13 years the Council in its 33 years of existence has expended, one has a total of approximately $221.1 million, which is on the conservative side. And what is there to really show for that number?

Have the wild runs of salmon and steelhead been improved? Not really. The Federal District Court keeps rejecting the Biological Operating Plans put forth by BPA after lengthy consultation periods with various other federal agencies ranging from the US Fish and Wildlife Service, to NOAA, to EPA to the BLM and the US Forest Service not to mention various state agencies and mandatory coordination with Native American tribes because of their treaty rights.

Want to take a guess at what BPA lists as having spent in total from 2002 to 2012 for a fish and wildlife program whose objective is following the federal mandates to restore the wild salmon and steelhead runs in the Columbia River basis? Try $7.3258 Billion dollars – that's correct, "b" as in billions. The average is $665.98 million per year.

And for what? Federal Judge Redden is retiring, but has found all three Biop plans to date to be insufficient. The dollars expended and wasted alone dictate the Council be abolished and a radically different approach be undertaken (See Chapter 11).

None of us involved in the Council's creation ever dreamed it would turn out this way but facts are facts.

The council's first communications director was John A. Wilson, from Seattle. An award winning investigative television journalist for KING-TV John also worked for David Brewster's *Seattle Weekly* and eventually for the *Seattle Times*. He was a superb communications director and later down the road I helped hire him as a consultant in the Gallatin Group's Seattle office.

As enthusiastic as any of us present at the creation, I suspect he would agree with me also.

The initial work plan had us traveling frequently around the region visiting energy projects, fish hatcheries, and aluminum mills and holding a monthly meeting with the public invited, on a rotating basis in each state of the region once every four months.

The first official photo of the council was taken when we held our first meeting in Boise in the chambers of the Boise City Council. The new act required extensive public participation which meant we heard from many folks at each stop about what the Council should be doing.

In Boise, two of my Columbia classmates testified before the Council. Conley Ward, from Caldwell, an attorney as well as a commissioner on the Idaho Public Utilities Commission testified regarding ensuring input from the PUC to the Council; and, Pat Ford, from Idaho Falls, now headed up the Idaho Conservation League. He testified on the importance of quickly moving to develop a salmon and steelhead program that truly enhanced the runs and the numbers, as the Act required.

All three of us had entered with the Columbia College Class of 1969, though I accelerated my semester loads as well as attending Idaho State in the summers to obtain additional credits so that I could and did graduate with the Columbia College class of 1968.

Another classmate of ours was a brilliant attorney, Dale Goble, from Boise, who after graduating from Columbia obtained his law degree from the University of Oregon. At the time of the Council's formation he was an associate professor at the University of Idaho's College of Law. In 1986 he wrote a brilliant article for Blumm's publication making an almost irrefutable case for the constitutionality of the NW Power Planning Council.

Goble delved into the critic's approach on the legality of the council from the separation of powers stance as well as those, like Hemingway who were calling it a manifestation of the Reagan Administration's "new Federalism." His conclusion that the Council was indeed a legal body was upheld by the 9th Circuit Court of Appeals.

For me, the issue was never whether the Council had been formed legally. The issue was whether the Council was approving and overseeing programs that truly enhanced fishery runs as required by the law. An additional issue was whether the Council was operating in a truly independent manner and fulfilling its "board of director's role" overlooking the BPA budget and its conservation progress.

The verdict is in and has been for many years. The wild runs of non-hatchery salmon and steelhead have continued to steadily decline despite the Council approving and BPA spending over $7.3258 billion on various fish and wildlife efforts during the last 11 years alone (2002 through 2012). The results are just not there and despite good intentions and well-funded programs the Council simply has not met its mandate to enhance the wild fisheries.

Likewise, the Council has failed miserably to drive BPA policies and programs through exercising tough oversight on BPA's budget and how it allocates funds generated from the sales of power. In my view, BPA quickly detailed a number of folks to work with the Council and its staff and effectively co-opted the Council to the point of inability to act independently.

I should point out that my tenure on the Council is probably the shortest of any state's appointee. I served nine months and resigned upon receiving an offer from Seattle's Jay Rockey Public Relations to set up a government affairs consulting practice and also service several energy intensive clients and two pipeline clients.

It was rapidly becoming clear I would face tough sledding at obtaining confirmation by the Idaho Senate not because I had not proven to be qualified; rather, it could and would have been argued that I was not yet a real resident of Idaho. Our home on Bainbridge simply was not selling given a depressed housing market. While I had a legal residence at the apartment I was renting in Boise, it was apparent to many that almost every Friday I was flying to Seattle to be "home" with my family for the weekend.

The argument would have been made that the state of Washington had three members while Idaho had only one. It would have been all about perceptions.

My resigning also allowed Governor John Evans to avoid a clash with Idaho's legislature. The Senate in particular was running a bill which would mandate one member from each party and a significant reduction in a council member's compensation. Had I stayed I would have fought both provisions, and undoubtedly would have lost.

My initial replacement then was former Republican House Speaker Larry Mills, a retired Boise-Cascade executive. He was eventually replaced by Senator Jim McClure's long-time Idaho chief of staff, Jim Goller. My old colleague, Bob Saxvik, still holds the longevity record for service on the council – 15 years.

Saxvik undoubtedly does not share my sentiments regarding the irrelevancy of the Council and the need to abolish it. Goller, however, before he passed away a couple of years ago, confided to me that he too felt the Council had failed both in exercising real oversight over BPA and in fulfilling the absolute mandate to enhance the salmon and steelhead runs of non-hatchery fish.

All it takes is for three of the region's four governors to say end it and it is gone. If they take a little time to review the issue they will reach the correct conclusion and abolish what has become a boondoggle of epic proportions and an absolute waste of ratepayer funds.

Recently, for example, Idaho Power Council member Jim Yost was reportedly interjecting himself into the negotiations between Canada and the United States on drawing up a new Columbia River Basin treaty with our neighbors to the north. While Canadians have long felt the current treaty was far more beneficial to the United States than to Canada, and it is an important element in how the dams on the Columbia are managed, there is absolutely no basis within the Power Planning Act for the Council or a member to inject themselves.

This is the purview of the U.S. State Department and the nation's representatives on the International Joint Commission. Yost injecting himself is a classic sign of "mission creep" – that wonderful bureaucratic practice of seeking to justify existence by appropriating more and more duties whether part of a charge or not.

Yost, however, is one of the more qualified by background and experience to sit on the Council. Far too often of late the Council has become viewed as a place to put faithful political supporters or former powerful legislators needing to "pad out" and expand their retirement benefits. Critics viewed my appointment to the Council in this light.

Jokes are heard in governors' offices, and even reporters have been overheard saying that they would love an appointment to the Council. After all, the only requirement seems to be to love to travel and to stay awake while on manufactured tours or holding public in-put sessions on the latest five-year plan.

It is easy to see why many of the interest groups view the Council as irrelevant to what is really going on in the energy arena – an anachronism that may not even be salvageable by reconstituting it through the Office of the Secretary of the Interior.

What happens if the Council is abolished? Does BPA keep spending hundreds of millions each year on fish and wildlife?

The answer to the second question is a qualified yes, as long as there is an Endangered Species Act and a Northwest Power Planning Act, and as long as NOAA and EPA take a keen interest in anadromous fisheries, lots of money is still going to be spent – some wisely, some unwisely. The issue though is, do the agencies really need the Power Council looking over their shoulder? The answer is no.

The answer to the first question is complicated, but may provide reasonable grounds to re-open the Power Planning Act specifically with amendments intended to change the Council into a more useful, effective body. As the law stands now, if three of the four governors say abolish the council, then it goes. However, it is replaced by one that is appointed by the Secretary of the Interior.

It might be less filled with political patronage types, and less partisan types, but there would still be a Power Council. And it would still be misdirecting millions in spending.

Allow me to suggest some amendments to the law with regard to the Power Council (I leave it to energy and power wonks like Wilcox and Redman to decide whether the entire Act should be re-opened).

My suggestions are:

1. Recognize and ratify the governors' nullification to the present Council.
2. Put in its place a new Council comprised of 13 individuals, two from each of the northwest states to be appointed from a list submitted to the Secretary of the Interior by the governor and the congressional delegation of each state. A third person from each state shall be nominated and given to the Secretary from the Native American community of each state. The 13th member will be chosen by the Interior Secretary to represent northwest Native Americans living outside the northwest. This 13th member also will help to prevent tie votes from occurring. These positions will be part-time, non-partisan positions and each member will serve a fixed term of four years with a limit of three terms of service being the maximum.
3. Compensations will be set at 50% of the GS-18 Federal step.
4. The Council shall have its mission redefined to be that of serving as the Board of Directors of the BPA, and the priority purpose of the agency will be to commit to an accelerated schedule of repayment of its debt to the Treasury with the goal to be debt free as soon as possible. There will be no arbitrary cap placed on the board's budget other than a requirement to be "reasonable and prudent."
5. Once BPA's debt is repaid the agency shall then engage in an equitable revenue sharing plan to be developed by the BPA "Board of Directors" for each northwest state, recognizing that hydroelectric power is the region's natural resource advantage just as oil is for Texas and Louisiana, or coal for West Virginia and Pennsylvania.
6. Directors can be removed for cause. Appointment of the administrator will devolve from the Department of Energy to the Board of Directors. Each administrator can serve up to three five-year terms.

If this happens just maybe Roy Hemingway's vision of a "New Federalism" will indeed come to pass.

9 ▪ Give a Boy a Gun, Revisited

Carlson goes hunting in Hells Canyon. Photo by Jack Canavan.

The call came mid-morning in late March or early April of 1997. On the other end was a former Northwest Power Planning Council colleague, Chuck Collins, one of the first two state of Washington appointments to the Council.

A brilliant and charming person, Collins had the gift of taking complex issues and rendering them into digestible, understandable parts which the average voter could understand – and usually would agree with. Collins would have made a terrific candidate for the U.S. Senate or governor with this God-given gift.

He deliberately eschewed seeking high public office, but a number of governors, both Republican and Democrat, were impressed enough with this gift that he was constantly being called on to provide public service primarily through the giving of his time and talent. Besides serving six years on the NWPPC courtesy of an appointment by Governor John Spellman, he had also been named to the powerful statewide Board of Higher Education by Governor Booth Gardner.

I served on the power council nine months but still managed to know Collins well. We had respect for each other's perspective. Since establishing the Gallatin Group in 1989, with offices in Seattle and Spokane, as well as Boise, Portland, and Helena, we had spoken infrequently.

Collins wanted to talk about an initiative he was supporting and whether I would be interested in providing some political counsel. He underscored their effort had financing and that I could focus on the objective. There was big money behind this effort, he said.

He was correct about the money: Bill Gates, the founder of Microsoft was the campaign angel.

Collins was wrong about the issue, and the need for Initiative 676, a trigger lock and transport piece of proposed legislation.

Concerned about increasing gun violence, especially around schools, Collins and his friends felt the matter should be put to a vote.

As he explained it, everyone purchasing a hand gun would have to take an approved gun handling and safety course and also purchase a trigger lock to be placed in the handgun whenever one transported it away from home.

I asked the $64,000-dollar question: "Are you talking prospectively going forward or retroactively?" When Collins said "retroactively," I replied instantly, "No way, Chuck. You're dead if you try to make it retroactive."

Collins disagreed saying they had a poll done by one of the region's most reputable polling firms which showed that this version of additional gun control would be acceptable to the average voter.

I told Collins not only was I not interested in providing advice, I would also actively oppose the initiative if it contained retroactive features.

"You're stirring up a hornet's nest, Chuck, and you're going to get stung badly," I said, adding, "They'll come in out of the valleys and hollows scattered all over this state. You'll get your head handed to you."

Was I ever correct! Later in September, I attended a Spokane rally put on by the National Rifle Association, the number one defender of one's second amendment rights to keep arms in one's home and be ready to carry them. The NRA's top dog, Wayne LaPierre, was there. I went largely to see how it was handled and what they did.

The NRA rally brought together over 5,000 people, every one of whom left the rally with a bag of campaign "goodies" – materials explaining how they could make calls and work their neighbors. The key "talking points" were outlined along with suggested phone lists. The bag had bumper stickers, lapel pins, suggested songs and the words for chants. Every attendee took the packet and with a look of steely determination set out to do their part. It was stunning and only served to reinforce my sense that the initiative was headed for a colossal defeat. And it was. The voters kicked it in the creek by a 70 percent against and only 30 percent for margin.

What really helped to consign the proposed initiative to the trash heap, though, was the punitive punishment language for failure to comply with the act. If one owned a handgun, kept it in his home for personal protection and rarely if ever took it anyplace, they nonetheless had to purchase the trigger lock and take the gun safety class.

Otherwise one would be committing a felony and subjecting their weapon to probable confiscation. Thus, whether one was obtaining a concealed weapons permit in the state made not a whit of difference. One had to provide police with evidence of having purchased the trigger lock and taken the gun safety class even in order to maintain their ownership.

In the eyes of gun owners this was beyond universal background checks and the closing of the gun show loopholes. This was absolute registering of all one's firearms, much as autos have to be licensed and registered, and was providing police authorities with a list of gun owners who could be targeted and forced to yield their weapons if that's what society's majority decided.

It did not take a visionary to recognize an obvious next step could be a state requiring one to purchase liability insurance. The analogy to car ownership, registration, licensing, and providing proof of insurance would be complete.

Idahoans are fiercely protective of what they see in the second amendment to the Constitution as an absolute right for individuals (in theory citizens who could be called to form militias to defend the country) to keep and bear arms so as to be able to defend both home and country against external aggressors.

Unfortunately, the boogie-man aggressor most often cited is our own Federal government. The fear is that someday a Congress, dominated by urban congressmen and liberals in both parties, will pass legislation authorizing the confiscation of one's private weapons.

This leads to statements like that of former NRA chairman and famous movie actor Charlton Heston, who loudly proclaimed, "Let them come and try; they'll have to strip the rifle from my cold dead hands!" Of course the gun owner faithful went nuts at this call to arms.

This paranoia about our own government is admittedly baffling. Most law enforcement folks are veterans who while in the service took an oath to defend the Constitution and that includes the second amendment. It's hard to imagine any who laid their lives on the line for this nation would willingly participate in any society-wide scheme for confiscation of personal weapons.

When I hear this fear-mongering, I often think of a statement I heard one time at a political rally by Idaho's then Superintendent of Public Instruction, Roy Truby. He said, "I have a hard time understanding people who say they love their country but hate their government." So do I.

Make no mistake, though, there are many, sensible, rational, and reasonable members of the NRA as well as the general citizenry who are genuinely concerned that the future will bring not only gun registration, but include a ban on private ownership of weapons, especially handguns.

That the politics of gun control matters in Idaho is really quite simple. One better be for the supremacy of the second amendment and better not support too many restrictions. And so in Idaho successful office-holders, even a liberal like the late Senator Frank Church, are counter-intuitively for gun rights. The Churches would often say so publicly. In D.C. this undoubtedly led to them being dropped from a few social lists.

Regardless, though, this counter-intuitive support for gun rights and the NRA helped to keep card-carrying liberals like Senator Church and House Speaker Tom Foley in office for many years. For many voters gun rights was not just an issue, it was the only issue.

Periodically, horrible tragedies like the killing of 20 school children and six adults at Newtown Elementary in Connecticut galvanize advocates for more controls on weapons into demanding even more restrictions. The groups are aided by a media that loves conflict and tragedy, but also not so subtly has an agenda of its own.

Led by a well-meaning president and vice president intent on doing whatever they can to try and prevent future slaughters of innocent young school children, Congress is again engaged in a debate over adding additional restrictions that will do little to inhibit the nut case from securing weapons but only serve to exacerbate the efforts of the law abiding to pursue their interest in owning and using weapons either for hunting or sport shooting or simple personal protection.

Thus, some members of Congress pontificate about closing the gun show loophole and considerably expanding the background checks before one can sell an arm to another. They also denounce purchase of automatic rifles, "assault weapons" such as the AR-15, a combat semi-automatic rifle used by the military since early in the Viet Nam war and a weapon designed to kill. Except for a ten year period when the Brady Bill contained a ban on assault rifle sales (which Congress chose not to renew in 2005) people have legally been able to purchase them for personal use, either sport shooting or another weapon to keep in their locked gun closet for personal protection purposes.

At the end of the day most will be surprised if there are any new restrictive measures, and not because of the power and money the NRA can muster. More it will be a reflection of the political realities existing in many western states where there are many Democrats, both senators and congressmen, standing for re-election who do not want gun rights to become an issue in their effort to get re-elected.

Like many westerners, especially those who live in a rural area where it would take a sheriff's deputy a good hour to respond to an emergency call for assistance, I own a couple of rifles though I seldom hunt for deer or elk, a shotgun (I do bird hunt and shoot trap at the Coeur d'Alene Skeet and Trap Club where I am a member), and several handguns.

I keep all the weapons in a double locked gun closet, and when I transport the pistols or shotgun to a gun club for practice I carry them in a locked case with the magazine, or other ammunition carried separately. I believe I have an absolute right to defend my home and family from an intruder up to and including using lethal force.

During the many years I backpacked I also carried a .45 with me not so much to defend myself against a rogue bear, or a moose that might charge, or even a wolf or a cougar that might be coming too close, but more for the high-on-drugs two-footed creature that I have encountered several times deep in Idaho's back country.

As the epidemic of drug use increases, especially in rural America, I view this as a reasonable precaution that any prudent person should take. Urban dwellers, where a call to 9-1-1 can produce police within minutes may have a hard time understanding this, but one only has to run into a druggie once in the backcountry, or see a meth-crazed addict trying to steal anything of value to feed the insatiable habit to fully understand the necessity of carrying. I have had a concealed weapons permit for 20 years.

In short, I am a legal, law-abiding gun owner and make no apologies. The great Catholic theologian, St. Augustine, in 400 A.D. wrote the definitive tract on the right of a Christian to take a life in defense of his own life. While I would deeply regret having to take another life that was threatening mine or my family, I'm not about to be a sheep meekly submitting to being led to slaughter. Nor am I a wolf relishing to kill. I see myself more as a sheep dog with sharp teeth fully ready to protect my family and my life.

The .45 or shotgun are weapons I am fully prepared to employ if I have to do so. I don't feel I need an AR-15 automatic military use rifle but if someone else feels the need to have one, it is a weapon the law allows.

Unlike second amendment purists, I do recognize, and the courts have sanctioned, government's ability to restrict certain weapons and forbid them being made available to the public. We would not allow, for example, nor grant any individual the ability to own, a weapon of mass destruction such as a miniature atomic bomb. Rocket propelled grenades and shoulder carried surface-to-air missiles are other weapons that should not be generally available to the public though one can see where law enforcement officials should have a more complete and lethal arsenal.

Many card-carrying members of the NRA support these reasonable restrictions. While the NRA sometimes appears to go too far in its defense of the second amendment, I'm glad the organization exists as a watch-dog to stand guard against efforts by do-gooders to come up with additional restrictions on law abiding gun owners that do nothing to stop the insane or criminals who care not a whit for my life or for laws that supposedly inhibit their ability to procure and use weapons against innocent others.

Extremism in defense of liberty can be a vice if it turns into tyranny just as the do-gooders of the world can do much more harm than even the evil motivated can.

As is always the case, the challenge is to find the reasonable middle ground that reflects balance and respects constitutional rights. That presumes people on the extremes recognize the importance of compromise, respect each other, and genuinely are sincere in listening to the other side and then try to find the common ground.

Unfortunately, there appears to be little incentive to seek the middle ground. The unfortunate truth is the extremes are where funding is generated to perpetuate the cause and those leading the charge of the cause. There are few financial rewards to those that compromise, reach the middle and carry things forward in a positive manner.

Everything truly appears to be becoming more polarized, not less. Every interest group appears to be falling into what I call the fallacy of the either/or. Any student of history knows that is not the path forward in a democracy. Compromise has always been at the heart of the political process. Cut it out and you truly do have a war-like environment where no prisoners are taken and those with opposing views are branded as traitors.

Ironically, those liberals seeking more restrictions on guns are starting to adopt tactics first perfected by largely conservative groups opposed to abortion, i.e., they are attacking the issue incrementally by going to the margins of the issue to start to achieve the longer term goal.

By that I mean rather than engaging in an all-out frontal assault on gun rights they are presenting reasonable-sounding perfecting amendments. A good example is legislation being proposed in some states that will require a gun owner to obtain liability insurance. Again, the analogy is to auto ownership.

Both sides look to the 2008 U.S. Supreme Court decision, *DC vs. Heller*, which while it recognized the individual right to keep and bear arms also acknowledged that many 19th century prohibitions on carrying concealed weapons were also lawful under the second amendment. Court observers felt it was significant that the Supreme Court had declined to say whether, and to what degree certain restrictions on guns would still be allowed.

It wasn't all that long until a Federal District Court – in this case the 10th Circuit in Denver – ruled that carrying a concealed weapon is *not* protected by the second amendment. This ruling came in late February of 2013.

The issue on the margins that gun control proponents appear to be going after is that of whether a citizen can carry a weapon out of his home and off his property, period. In other words, they may concede one has a right to own a weapon for self-defense but argue that in society's best interests one can only have that weapon in his home and on his property. If he wishes to hunt, or target practice the requirement will be registration, mandatory trigger locks, liability insurance, gun safety courses, the whole ten yards all designed to discourage gun ownership without actually forbidding it.

While gun control proponents take heart in the 10th Circuit ruling, opponents take heart in the Chicago Circuit's ruling that flat said Americans do enjoy a constitutional right to carry loaded weapons outside their homes. Back to the U.S. Supreme Court we'll go.

The state of Idaho holds a somewhat infamous place in the minds of those who follow the gun debate due to a tragic encounter in January of 1981 along the south Fork of the Owyhee River in the Owyhee desert southwest of Boise.

Claude Dallas, a loner, part-time trapper and a full-time poacher, as so well described by Cort Conley in his entertaining book, *Idaho Loners*, gunned down two Idaho Fish and Game Wardens, Bill Pogue and Conley Elms, with his .357 magnum. The wardens had caught Dallas red-handed with poached carcasses and pelts around the camp.

Both wardens were armed but never stood a chance. To many it looked like a clear cut case of cold-blooded murder, except to an Idaho jury, who acquitted Dallas on the grounds of self-defense. He was then convicted of a lesser charge, and sent to prison, which he subsequently escaped from and was on the lam for months. He finally was recaptured and sent back to prison but had obviously been assisted by lots of folks while on the lam.

He became for some the romantic kind of out-law he himself had dreamed of as a young man while reading western novels like Zane Grey's *Riders of the Purple Sage*. He was not a native Idahoan having been born in the upper Shenandoah Valley of Virginia into a family that moved frequently through the south and other states.

Jack Olsen captured it all in his fine book, *Give a Boy a Gun*. There are ambiguities and complexities to this entire issue of gun ownership and gun rights. And there are no simple answers to the many challenging questions it gives rise to in people's minds. Olsen's book is still one of the best examinations of these issues and well worth the time to read.

Dallas was released from prison in 2005 and has since been living quietly in Grouse Creek, Utah.

That Idaho has been stigmatized by this tragic story is incontestable.

So where to from here? Can anything more be done to protect innocent lives without trampling on the rights of the millions of legitimate, law-abiding gun owners?

I think so. Here are some suggestions that merit discussion and debate:

1. More funding for the treatment of mental illnesses. Those committing heinous crimes using weapons like semi-automatic rifles and pistols are clearly off their rockers. We as a society have to do a better job of identifying these types and getting them into counseling before they become psychotic killers with nothing to lose.

2. Incentivize reporting to authorities when one comes across another's deranged threat. In almost all cases these mass-killers have signaled their intentions by postings on personal Facebook pages, or calls to friends or threats to enemies. I call it "rat on a rat," and people should get a reward for doing so.

3. Utilize more preventive detention. Police can hold folks without a charge for up to 72 hours. Anyone threatening mass killings or shooting a highly visible public person, if police can be made aware of it, should be visited by the appropriate law enforcement agency, informed that he or she will be placed under a police watch, and any activity remotely related to threats against other persons will result in arrest and sentencing to prison.

4. Background checks are the *sine qua non* when it comes to protecting the public from a nut case attending a gun show and walking away with a weapon. While there is no real evidence supporting those that claim this is how nut jobs get their weapons, common sense should tell one that the three-day waiting period should be applied across the board on all gun sales. Despite what one reads many weekend gun shows do conduct background checks on purchasers of weapons.

5. Support your local police chief or county sheriff. If those sworn to protect me tell me that the bad guys should not have access to exploding shells, I believe them. Moreover they deserve our full support.

These all strike me as reasonable, achievable goals. But therein lays the dilemma and the challenge: they are reasonable and achievable, but this debate is too often shaped by raw emotions and fears. It's an atmosphere in which ideology and zealotry hold sway, and where reason and common sense fear to tread.

10 ■ Nobody Calls Me Senator

Senator Edwards Kennedy (left) and senatorial candidate Bud Davis. Photo by Barry Kough.

In the last chapter of his 1972 book, *Nobody Calls Me Doctor*, William E. "Bud" Davis, the then affable, charming, charismatic president of Idaho State University, tells an apocryphal story of how I hornswoggled him into running for the United States Senate.

I "lured" him up to the Senate Press Gallery and, since the Senate was not in session, out to the gallery seats where the press sat to watch Senate proceedings. Davis recalls me pointing out where Idaho Senator Len B. Jordan sat, a chair being vacated because the Senator had announced he was not running for re-election.

Davis alleges I told him the seat could be his if he wanted it. He even says he protested strongly, but then acquiesced to my request that I send a little item to my five Idaho newspaper clients, including his hometown paper, Pocatello's *Idaho State Journal*, saying he had been in D.C. and was thinking about a possible bid for the Senate.

On his way back to Pocatello, Davis says he called home from the Salt Lake City airport to check in with wife Polly but was informed by son Doug that Polly wasn't speaking to him. Davis says she was distressed that he had all but announced for the Senate race without consulting with her which she first learned when the *Journal* bannered the story across its front page.

This all took place in early November of 1971. The story makes for good reading, but it is revisionist history. I found the original column which my clients ran on November 10, 1971, and it is clear I was just confirming what had already been decided.

The lead paragraph is as accurate today as it was when first written:

"Idaho State University President William E. "Bud" Davis is doing more than just casting a cursory glance at the 1972 Democratic Senatorial nomination. He is weighing his assets and debits, and doing some serious thinking."

The column quotes Davis saying "It would of course be a great privilege to be a U.S. Senator, and now does appear to be a time to make a bid, if I'm so inclined."

Davis admits having discussed the prospect with at least ten other folks as well as his wife, Polly, and with Governor Cecil Andrus – all of whom encouraged him to make the race. In looking at the pluses and the minuses, he acknowledged he might have to resign the ISU presidency or ask the Idaho State Board of Education (ISBOE) for a leave of absence (which he did and was granted), and there might be a negative hit at ISU's budget by the legislature (there wasn't).

While not a statewide name, he pointed out he gave 200 speeches a year around the state, which had to have given him some name familiarity. He conceded lack of political experience and a probable lack of adequate funding, but said he had ways to overcome those issues.

Davis had already concluded he was going to rely on young people, high school as well as college, to be the bulwark of his campaign. He opined that lack of political experience in the current political environment would be as a plus. He also guessed his probable general election opponent would be First District Congressman Jim McClure.

More to the point, Davis knew it would be a contested primary, with Attorney General Tony Park a likely candidate; a Harvard-educated, Boise attorney, Byron Johnson; and, a female candidate out of the women's movement, Rose Bowman, from Boise. He saw this as fortuitous knowing that three candidates out of Ada County would divide up their base vote.

If all three stayed in the race (as they did), Davis thought he would win the nomination. He relished the primary and looked forward to walking away with the nomination. While he had yet to put together a campaign organization, he recognized he had less than a year to get it altogether and pull it off.

The other amusing, tell-tale sign was that later that evening we met in downtown D.C. for an after work drink – then cabbed over to the Shoreham Hotel where one Mark Russell, the viciously satiric comic held forth. Bud was clearly hooked as he scrambled to scribble political lines he thought (and many other lines as well) were absolutely dynamite. He wanted to borrow some to salt through his stump speech when on the campaign trail.

In many respects Bud Davis' run for the U.S. Senate was an historic endeavor. Only one other Democrat would win a Senate race after 1972, and that would be incumbent Senator Frank Church, who won his fourth and last term in 1974 riding the coat-tails of the incredibly popular Cecil Andrus as well as having the luxury of a fairly weak opponent in Bob Smith.

For all practical purposes, the Idaho Senate seats started down the path of becoming the private purview of the Republican Party following Jim McClure's victory over Davis. The Democrats were able to mount only two other worthy charges after Church's narrow defeat in 1980 by Congressman Steve Symms. Governor John Evans ran a respectable race against Symms in 1986 but nonetheless lost, and Congressman Richard Stallings ran a respectable race against Boise Mayor Dirk Kempthorne for the Symms seat in 1992, but also lost.

The Davis campaign was different though in that it was fundamentally a shoe-string endeavor fueled by the constant influx of numerous young people who volunteered for a variety of different tasks without pay. This idealism attracted support and was infectious; creating almost a sense of inevitability that Davis was going to pull off the upset.

The campaign never did have gobs of money. In fact campaign manager James E. "Jay" Shelledy later estimated they ran a credible campaign on about $250,000 whereas Jim McClure spent over one million dollars in winning the seat.

The campaign started of course with the candidate himself. While it is safe to say Davis did not just wake up one morning and see a future U. S. Senator in the mirror while shaving, he never has revealed exactly when he decided to give it a try. Surely, though, as he looked to the west and saw the Ada County threesome start preparing, he took the measure of each and none intimidated him.

There's an old political saying that the office seeks the man, not the man the office. It's nice to believe that but is seldom true. Most successful politicians have carefully calculated and planned their candidacy far ahead of when it becomes publicly known. Such was the case with Bud Davis.

Davis also knew that no less a judge of good horse flesh than Governor Cecil Andrus himself in 1970 had encouraged him to think about running for governor against incumbent Don Samuelson. Then state Senator Cecil Andrus initially thought Democrats would need a "fresh face" to win in 1970, and had offered to step aside if Davis would make the race.

Besides Andrus, among the ten people Davis must have talked with about a possible U.S. Senate bid were Pocatello jeweler Mel Morgan who would have to raise the money, Pocatello banker Bob

Montgomery, ISU outside legal counsel Herman McDevitt, former state Senator and ISU ACTION program director Perry Swisher, personal assistant Dwight Jensen, Bannock County labor leader Bob Lenaghen, former second district congressman Ralph Harding, former state Senator Diane Bilyeu, current state Senator Chick Bilyeu, and Blackfoot businessman Lynn Broadhead.

All of these folks possessed sharp political minds. All could see that Davis, as the only non-Ada County candidate, could easily take the southeast, south central and north Idaho Democratic vote and win while still conceding the split Treasure Valley to one of the others.

Davis did a superb job of letting speculation build as to whether he would actually jump into the race. My column of November 10th was bannered in the *Journal* and also prominently played in the *Lewiston Morning Tribune*. Since Bannock County and Nez Perce County were two of the strongly Democrat counties in Idaho it created a buzz among many of the faithful and kept some from prematurely committing to Attorney General Park or Byron Johnson until they knew for sure whether Davis would be in the race.

On November 15th I sent a short note to Davis saying I hoped the column had not caused him or his family any undue embarrassment. He wrote right back on November 18th and reconfirmed both the thrust of the column and that he was and had been giving the race serious consideration.

In the letter he jokingly wrote about causing himself further trouble in Ada County because Idaho State had defeated Boise State, 21 to 17, causing the Broncos to lose a share of the Big Sky championship and instead handing the title to the University of Idaho.

He also referenced the challenge in funding such a race and said he was still in the "investigative phase." Tellingly, though, he also indicated that, as I had suggested, he would be calling Jay Shelledy to discuss his availability.

In another twist of irony, on November 19, 1971, I received Jim McClure's letter clarifying comments he had given me for a previous column when we discussed "release time." (See Chapter 4) The issue was the source of much heartburn for the first district congressman during the Republican primary contest for the Jordan Senate seat.

Bud Davis, at 42 years of age, was, and still is, one of those rare people with the gift of inspiring confidence. He radiates that sense of "here's a man who can get a job done, and done well." Part of his charm is a self-deprecating humor; part is a gift for telling a story; part is an ability to communicate in a way that makes everyone listening think he is talking directly to them.

Bud Davis. Photo by Barry Kough.

Davis exudes quiet leadership. A former Marine officer, a pressed-into-duty-temporary-head football coach at the University of Colorado, a former dean of men and an executive vice president in his early 30s, Davis had been wooed away from the University of Wyoming and became Idaho State's president at the young age of 35 in 1965.

He came to ISU as a problem solver, one who could make decisions. He was and is a history buff, especially the Civil War. He collected thousands of small replica soldiers and battle pieces from the Civil War era as well as other eras of military history.

Serendipitously, I had helped his "image" grow two years earlier.

On a warm spring day in April of 1970, 38 students staged a sit-in in his office. Getting a call at the *Journal,* where I was working as the politics and education reporter, I grabbed a camera and rushed to the campus. There I took a picture that the *Journal's* photo editor put on the Associated Press wire and it went national. Newspapers across the country, not to mention Idaho, ran it, often on the front page.

The picture showed a calm President Davis, leaning against a desk in his outer office, puffing on his ever-present pipe amidst a sea of students who had to be wondering when they were going to get busted. Davis bluntly said to them he was not going to order the CIA to stop recruiting on campus nor was he going to get rid of ROTC or stop the military from recruiting. Identifying all 38, he immediately suspended them.

Davis decided to outwait them. Instinctively, Davis understood that protesters thrive off of the publicity generated when they are seized and arrested. He was not about to give them the photo-op they were seeking. After several hours, students began to get up and leave. No police were called. No heads busted. The state saw, as did the nation, a president standing up to the "punks and the hippies" and his standing took another leap upward.

To meet Bud Davis still is to like him instantly. Throw into the mix Polly, his lovely, devoted spouse, along with their beautiful children and it was a dynamite mix. Republicans across Idaho immediately started saying that if the Democrats nominated Davis he would be the toughest one to defeat.

Another factor helping Davis was speculation among Democratic insiders whether State Representative Vernon Ravenscroft from Tuttle would enter the race. Some pundits thought he ought to run either for the Senate or for the congressional seat in the second district in order to capitalize on his name familiarity from his 1970 run for governor.

Ravenscroft would be viewed as the true conservative by voters, which would still be a winning formula for Davis in the primary, with Davis being viewed as the moderate and the three Ada county candidates as the liberals. Still, Davis waited.

Ten days after my column appeared in the *Tribune* an editorial by Bill Hall appeared in the Sunday edition. Its headline said it all: "Davis Should Go For the Senate."

Saying Davis was one of the most promising potential candidates to come along in years, Hall urged the ISU president to throw his hat into the ring. "This is a creative man of quality in the tradition of Church and Jordan," Hall wrote.

On December 5th the Dean of Idaho political editors and writers, the *Idaho Statesman's* John Corlett, wrote a long piece on Davis and his possible candidacy. Corlett especially took note of Ravenscroft's possible impact but speculated correctly that debt from his gubernatorial campaign would keep him out. Corlett also correctly predicted the final field for the August primary, guessing that none of the three Ada County candidates would drop out.

Ravenscroft played his Hamlet-like game until early April of 1972, when he took himself out of the Senate contest but still did not tip his hand as to what he might do. When he finally did decide where he would head, it was a shocker. He announced he was switching to the Republican Party after having been a life-long Democrat. In the process, he left long-time friend and supporter, Joe McCarter, of Corral, holding a note on a substantial part of Vernon's debt. He never did repay McCarter.

On January 2, 1972, in another column Corlett noted, "As for Davis he has moved about the state carefully meeting the "right" people and the "right" Democratic pros and has convinced them that he will be a candidate, albeit he will be unable to formally announce until after the 1972 Legislature adjourns."

The delay would allow Davis to argue ISU's budget before the Joint Finance and Appropriations Committee of the Legislature. It also allowed him to continue to speak around the state while lining up supporters.

Finally, though he had made no staff hires yet, and his finance chair, Mel Morgan, had not yet raised the modest $30,000 he thought the campaign would need for the primary, Davis appeared ready to announce.

The *Idaho State Journal* on Sunday, March 26, 1972 carried an article by Gary Lofgren saying Davis had made up his mind to run and would formally announce in early April. It was more like late mid-April with Davis announcing his candidacy on April 20, 1972, in the auditorium of Edd Bailey Hall on ISU's campus.

What Davis said over 50 years ago resonates still today. He said the over-riding issue in the campaign would be addressing people's lack of confidence in their government. H promised to bring real leadership towards meeting challenges confronting Idaho and the nation.

"There is a powerful need for leadership with reverence for the people, a need for men and women who are both responsive and responsible," he said.

Recognizing he would need a core group of volunteers drawn from the ranks of high school and college students, and that opposition to the war in Vietnam was still a galvanizing issue for them, he debunked those who said the election cycle of 1972 would not have the war as an issue.

"It is tragic that in a campaign four years ago we were talking about whether or not to stop the bombing, and now on the eve of another election we are still talking about stopping the bombing," Davis pointed out. He said he would support efforts to limit the power of the president to prosecute the war and tacitly endorsed efforts by Idaho's senior senator, Frank Church, to do just that through the Church/Case and Cooper/Church amendments to the defense department budget.

He laid out strong support for more funding for education, said he would seek an inventory of all the natural resources of the country with an eye towards developing a list of special places to be set aside and protected; and, expressed strong support for the nation's and state's labor movements.

He volunteered that neither Senator Church nor Governor Andrus would make any endorsement before the results of the primary.

Almost clairvoyantly he started framing the stark differences that existed between him and first district congressman Jim McClure.

While Davis could and did call on academic friends on campus and supportive students to help in these early stages, he still had neither paid staff nor any professional campaign manager. This lack of a professional early on was soon going to contribute to the campaign's incubating fatal error – the signing of the Cesar Chavez petition on a lettuce boycott.

Sometime in February, I received a call from Bud at our apartment in Gaithersburg, Maryland. The message was "Chris, you got me into this race. Now you have a moral obligation to help me win it. I want you either to run the entire campaign or oversee the communications program and be the campaign press secretary, which will include traveling with me around the state."

Admittedly I was tempted. I had already, however, turned down a similar offer from Andrus' chief of staff, Eddie Williams, who was running for the first district congressional seat being abandoned by McClure to make his run for the Senate. I'd told Ed that I'd only been in D.C. a little over a year, and that it made little sense for me to come home, help him win and then turn right around and move back to D.C.

That same rationale applied still and led me likewise to decline Davis' offer as well. I did, however, repeat to Davis my earlier recommendation from the previous November. I suggested again he reach out and grab Jay Shelledy, who at a minimum could do an excellent job serving as campaign press secretary. Shelledy was then working as a reporter with the Associated Press in Boise.

I had known Shelledy since the summer of 1968 when we attended Gonzaga's summer session and took a special 10-credit course in education which enabled me to qualify for an Idaho provisional teaching certificate. It also enabled Shelledy to recommend me in August of 1968 to the Kootenai School District board of trustees, where he already taught and coached.

He recommended I be hired to fill a vacancy in their 8th and 9th grade classes and that I also could be the junior varsity basketball coach. The board accepted his recommendation. Shelledy and I have remained friends ever since, though there have been twists and turns on the trails we have walked.

Davis mulled things over then contacted Shelledy. They hit it off, and by early May, Shelledy was the first paid campaign staffer. From the first day he was the "de facto" campaign manager as well as communications manager because he was the only person who traveled with the candidate and the only person around Davis willing to make quick decisions.

Though intuitively smart, Shelledy would be the first to tell anyone he was an amateur and the campaign could have used at least one seasoned professional to assist them in negotiating their way through the thicket. Considering the lack of a seasoned hand, that they did as well as they did is remarkable.

A question that may be asked is would the outcome have been any different if I had accepted Davis' offer? The answer is no.

While I did not lack for confidence, I as yet had no real campaign experience myself. Nor did I possess Shelledy's talent for creating "news" events or staging photo-ops. Nor was I single and it is doubtful I could have given the effort the amount of time Shelledy was able to give.

While Jay can be colorful and controversial, as well as acerbic and cutting, he is one of the most gifted natural teachers I have ever met. I doubt I could have done half as well as he did along with Davis in the critical category of inspiring young people to believe in their cause and to keep working.

Following the announcement, Davis jumped in his car and headed for north Idaho to broaden his name recognition and expand his contacts. He knew that to win the primary he had to do well in his "backyard" (southeastern and south central Idaho), try to break even with the Ada County candidates in southwestern Idaho and then swamp the opposition when they all crossed the Salmon River at Riggins, entering the Pacific time zone and the panhandle containing the ten northern counties – all up for grabs.

On June 14th he opened a campaign office on Main Street in downtown Lewiston and named Lewiston High School teacher Ron Harlow as his Nez Perce County coordinator. The next day Davis and Shelledy hit Jay's old stomping grounds around Plummer, St. Maries, and Harrison before heading on to Coeur d'Alene.

Shelledy targeted several teachers, coaches, and referees he knew and hoped would be available to generate a turnout for the August primary. In Plummer, for example, Shelledy introduced long-time teacher and coach Warren Shepherd to Davis. In Post Falls, Shelledy found teacher John House, who had previously refereed both basketball and football games with him. At stops like Rose Lake he introduced Davis to gyppo-logger families like the Chatfields whose children he had taught while at Kootenai. Always they were passing out a basic brochure with the union "bug" that gave a biography on Davis and where he stood on the key issues.

Shelledy had also spent a summer working on Lake Coeur d'Alene as a Marine deputy sheriff, so as they traveled he knew many of the law enforcement folks in the northern counties (some of whom got to know Jay because of his penchant for speeding on U.S. Highway 95).

Between the teachers and the law officers, as well as Davis' charisma and charm, they were easily winning the battle for the Democratic votes in the ten northern counties.

Shelledy estimates today that at least half the students involved in the campaign came from high schools (Including Bishop Kelly, where he taught a journalism class.). "I would say we had a total of 100 who could be counted on continuously. At different times there would be different people. Probably 1,000 to 2,000 different Idahoans actually got out and did something at least once," Shelledy said, and dubbed this group Bud's "Youth Brigade."

The two congressional district coordinators, Brian Lamb in the first CD, and Jay O'Connor in the second CD, were college students. Other students playing prominent roles included Dale White, son of former Congressman Comp White, Jr., in Clark Fork; Kevin Roche, at the University of Idaho; Paul Boyd, from Boise, who became the campaign press secretary; and, two other fine Bishop Kelly students, Steve Smith and Kay Hummel.

By late June the campaign was starting to hum despite the still incubating seed of destruction that had already been planted at the Democratic State convention held in Sun Valley in mid-June.

Shelledy and Davis both report the same thing. Yes, Davis made a mistake in signing the lettuce boycott petition, something Governor Cecil Andrus flatly refused to do (but they were not aware of that at the time). Both insist the only reason Davis signed was that one of the signatures on the petition higher up was that of Senator Frank Church. Additionally, Nampa Mayor Ernie Starr's "John Hancock" was on the copy Church is supposed to have signed.

"The only reason Bud signed was because he saw Senator Church's signature a few lines higher up," Shelledy flat states. The only problem is that was the only copy that had a Church signature and no copies were made of it. Most political historians speculate Verda Barnes, Church's savvy chief of staff, somehow cabbaged onto that one copy and destroyed it. For Davis that was bad luck #1.

Bad luck #2 was that McClure's savvy and veteran campaign manager, Jim Goller, quickly learned about Davis signing the lettuce boycott and was able to secure a copy. The first reference to the deed in print was an article shortly after the convention by young Dave Espo writing for the *Twin Falls Times-News*. Sam Day, the editor and the publisher of *The Intermountain Observer*, a Boise weekly, also mentioned the signing of the petition in a column before the August primary.

Espo has gone on to better things: For the past 15 years he has been the Associated Press' primary political writer covering the Presidency and the U.S. Senate for the wire service out of the nation's capital.

As the August primary date approached the McClure campaign began referring to Davis having signed the lettuce boycott, but they added a more incendiary charge, saying this meant Davis would support a potato boycott! It was a classic "false syllogism." Despite emphatic denials from Davis, it began to take hold among independent farmers in Davis' southeastern Idaho base.

It was pure balderdash, but politics is all about creating positive perceptions about your campaign and negative perceptions about your opponent's.

Shelledy knew the campaign had made a mistake that was going to bite them, but not until he studied the numbers after the general election did it become clear to him that the false advertising undertaken by an allegedly independent group of farmers hitting hard at the potato analogy had probably cost Davis the win.

During July the two continued campaigning hard, passing out thousands of Davis brochures, shaking hands, appearing anywhere and everywhere two or three people might be assembled. Shelledy, who had an aptitude for figuring out gimmicks that would attract media coverage, was having a field day.

He had Davis descend over a mile down deep inside a mine while in Shoshone County, which rewarded Davis in August by bringing him within a whisker of winning the county. In Idaho County, Shelledy had the Davis' take a "break" from the campaign and float through some of the Salmon River's rapids near Riggins.

Davis losing at the log roll in northern Idaho. Photo courtesy of Chris Carlson.

His "media attractor" in Priest River, though, topped them all. He entered Davis in a log-rolling contest against a 17-year-old girl. Davis never stood a chance and was dumped in a nano-second. The crowd loved it, however, and Davis subsequently narrowly carried Bonner County. That Davis was a good sport about it all surely helped him.

It was also in July when the campaign sanctioned another "raise the Davis profile" promotion – the thousand mile bike ride from Bonners Ferry to Bear Lake. Four recent graduates of Bishop Kelly led by Bill Petersen undertook the venture and in a disciplined manner stopped at stores and news outlets along the entire way to tout the virtues of Davis' candidacy. It was priceless PR and much free publicity.

On Friday, August 4th, just three days before the August 8th primary, the state's largest newspaper, *The Idaho Statesman*, ran a flattering profile of the Davis campaign written by veteran reporter and editor Mindy Cameron. She duly noted the campus atmosphere that permeated the campaign, realizing many were volunteers not yet given any particular assignments. Any one though could see numerous volunteers ready to hit neighborhoods all over with the last minute appeal brochure put together by the communications staff.

Cameron also noted the "coaching fraternity," pointing out that campaign coordinator Pat Ebright – a former Boise State quarterback – was also a high school football coach, and that Dave Lachiondo and Jay Shelledy also shared high school coaching credentials. Of course the candidate, Bud Davis, was the biggest and best coaching figure around the campaign having been a head football coach at both a high school in Greeley (Colorado) and for one fateful year as the interim coach for a University of Colorado football team devastated by a football betting scandal that resulted in more than half the team and its coach being fired.

The most interesting note of the campaign though came in the largely unnoticed federal filing candidates have to make with the Federal Election Commission. The third and final pre-primary report showed Bud Davis had come from out of nowhere in a mere matter of months to be the probable favorite going into the primary; and, he had done it on a budget of $23,377 which he reported in expenses. Income to date was $24,244.

That they had done so much so soon on so little was remarkable. Now they had to step up and do combat with a sophisticated, well-financed juggernaut assembled by Jim Goller for his good friend Jim McClure.

Davis' confidence he would win on primary night was contagious, and as the election results came in, the team visibly relaxed as voters rewarded the Davis work ethic and its strategy. The strategy of dominating in his own back yard (southeast Idaho), quietly doing well in south central Idaho in counties like Twin Falls, breaking even in the total vote in southwestern Idaho and then taking seven of the ten northern counties catapulted Davis to victory.

Results on the morning of August 9th indicated Davis had won by a 6,347-vote margin over his closest opponent, Attorney General Tony Park. Davis carried thirty of the state's forty-four counties with Park taking eight counties and Byron Johnson taking six.

Davis' home county of Bannock obviously loved him. He emerged with almost a 4,000 vote margin over Johnson. Nearby Bingham County (Blackfoot) also gave him an easy victory. Indeed, he easily won most of the heavy LDS counties in the southeast part of the state.

He carried Caribou with a 300-vote margin over Tony Park. He doubled Park in Butte County, clobbered both Park and Johnson in Jefferson County, and walked away with a solid plurality in Oneida, Power, Minidoka, Fremont, Cassia, Franklin, and Teton counties. Only in Bonneville did he lose to Johnson, and then by less than 400 votes.

In the greater Treasure Valley, he ran a couple thousand votes behind Johnson and Park but edged out Rose Bowman. And when the votes from the north started to roll in it was clear he was indeed going to be the nominee.

Davis more than doubled Park in the timber dependent county of Benewah; edged him by 61 votes in Bonner county; won easily in the Canadian border county of Boundary; won Clearwater County by 200 votes; and, won by more than 600 votes in Nez Perce County. In the then Democratic stronghold of Kootenai County, it was a toss-up with Davis pulling in 1,134 votes to Johnson's 1,376 and Park's 1,582. Davis rebounded though in Latah County, winning it by more than 600 votes. He lost Idaho County to Park by 113 votes and Shoshone County by 87 votes.

When they had counted all the votes Davis polled 23,953 votes (almost $1 per vote) to Tony Park's 17,636, Byron Johnson's 15,526 and Rose Bowman's 9,327. Ominously for the fall campaign the total Republican vote of 129,013 doubled the total Democratic vote of 66,442 votes.

In his remarks (crafted with Shelledy's assistance) late in the evening of August 8th "accepting" his party's nomination, Davis displayed an off-the- cuff eloquence that would lead any critic to admit he was indeed capable of inspiring legions of loyal troops to man the battlements for him.

Davis said his victory "was the direct result of a coalition of long-haired, short-haired, silver-haired, curly-haired and non-haired. It was a campaign of dedicated workers who make it possible for me to do something about the present state of affairs in the nation. It was a stunning alliance with an awesome voice that will maroon the hesitant and inspire the brave. We will stand together and direct this powerful voice in a swift and determined move to restore pride in our nation's government. And we will be heard. ..."

The Republican winner was indeed First District Congressman Jim McClure, who also doubled Davis' total vote. McClure tallied 46,522 votes to Davis' 23,953. It was clear Davis had one heck'uv' a mountain to climb still if he hoped to sit in the Senate.

He and Shelledy promptly made two smart moves.

They walked across the street to their opponents' campaign headquarters and hired Rose Bowman to run their fall campaign in Ada County, Gay Davis from the Johnson campaign to beef up their outreach program and Ginny Ison from the Park campaign to coordinate their campaign scheduling and provide additional sound counsel.

Davis and titular campaign chairman, Lynn Broadhead, then got on a plane and headed to Washington, D.C. to see if they could shake the money tree, line up more labor support, and convince the Democratic Senatorial Campaign Committee they had a shot at winning if they could get the help of Democratic icons such as Hubert Humphrey, Ted Kennedy, Warren Magnuson and Senate Majority Leader Mike Mansfield, all of whom ended up coming to Idaho to campaign for Davis.

Meanwhile, the juggernaut Goller had put together was moving relentlessly forward. Unlike Davis, who had started from scratch with just one year until the general election, Goller had been preparing for over two years. He guessed in early 1970 that Len Jordan would not run for another term and that probably in the late summer of 1971 would make it official. Goller told McClure he was going to start preparing.

Except for the legendary Republican lobbyist, Lloyd Adams, Jim Goller was without an equal in the state. He was a masterful campaign strategist, one who had a wide network of contacts throughout the state. He was good at staying in contact with this network as well as mining it for valuable tidbits of information. A devout Republican, for years he had a printing business in downtown Boise that had the contract to print the legislature's daily journal.

A regular for coffee and often lunch at Moon's Café, just a short block away from Congressman McClure's Boise office in the downtown's old Post Office Building, he found Moon's was a good place to pick up rumors as well as bits and pieces of useful intelligence which, unlike most political pundits, he was capable of connecting disparate dots of and quickly reading the emerging picture.

He kept his ears open and generally was pretty close mouthed. A taciturn individual by nature, when he spoke most folks listened carefully. He had been the architect of all of McClure's campaigns and he knew the importance of early planning, polling, and fund-raising.

When Senator Len Jordan surprised most everyone in Idaho and announced late in the August 1971 recess that he would not be running for another term, Goller ironically had to argue with McClure, who was in Alaska on a committee field trip at the time, about the logic of his at least announcing that he was thinking of seeking the seat.

Goller wanted McClure to issue a "placeholder" to freeze any money and or workers going to other possible candidates who might otherwise be with them. McClure felt he should take his time deciding and perhaps even run a poll. In the end, Goller put out a semi-authorized statement in Boise in McClure's name.

Even though Goller moved quickly his fears were realized as McClure's statement was followed soon after by declarations of outright candidacy from former Bannock County state Senator Bill Bergeson and former three-term Governor Robert Smylie. Expressions of possible interest in seeking the seat were quickly issued by former second district Congressman George Hansen and former Governor Don Samuelson.

The crowded Republican field seemed to be set when Kendrick political novice Glen Wegner, who held both a law degree and a medical doctor's degree, announced his candidacy. In the end there were four Republicans in the primary race just as there were four Democrats.

Governor Samuelson decided not to risk his sinecure as the Region 10 Director of the Federal Department of Transportation and Bill Bergeson was tragically killed in a head-on collision on I-84 by a driver going in the wrong direction.

Both McClure and George Hansen made their formal announcements of candidacy in November of 1971. Goller was confident McClure had a stronger base of support in the first district than did Hansen in the second district, a seat which George had basically abandoned in 1967 in his losing effort to take Frank Church's senate seat in 1968.

Goller's confidence came from a poll he had which showed McClure defeating Hansen in the Magic Valley and the counties surrounding Twin Falls. Nonetheless, McClure continued to worry that he and Hansen would split the conservative Republican vote allowing Smylie to eke out a primary win. This worry led to two separate meetings between the two strongest candidates in which McClure and Goller tried to convince Hansen to drop out.

The first took place in Pocatello at the Bannock Hotel. The second took place a couple months later at Boise's Hotel Boise.

At the first meeting in Pocatello, Goller and McClure offered Hansen a deal whereby each candidate would agree to abide by the results of a statewide poll that would tell who was the strongest candidate. He felt Hansen might bite because Goller suggested using well-known Republican and Mormon pollster, Dick Wirthlin. Among Wirthlin's major clients was one Richard Nixon.

Hansen, knowing in his heart he was better at campaigning than McClure or just about any other politician in Idaho, spurned the proposal. Likewise, Bill Bergeson, before his fatal auto accident, turned down a similar offer from Goller.

Hansen alluded to this effort to squeeze him out several times during the primary campaign. He said nothing, however, about the second meeting until interviewed by a *LA Times* reporter doing a story on the general election race between McClure and Davis that appeared a week before the November polls.

In the *Times* article, which received little play in Idaho, Hansen charged that in a second meeting with McClure and Goller the two had brought along the government affairs poo-bahs of the state's major corporations, all of whom were backing McClure.

The firms represented were Idaho Power, Simplot, Boise-Cascade and construction giant Morrison-Knudsen. In other words, Hansen was looking across the table at some formidable players like Logan Lanham and Larry Mills. At this meeting there was a *quid pro quo* offered, Hansen said. If Hansen dropped out, all the players in the room would commit to support him as the Republican choice to take on Governor Cecil D. Andrus in 1974. The implication was the heretofore probable nominee, Lt. Governor Jack Murphy, would be forced to drop his expected bid.

Recognizing even then that Andrus would be tough to beat, and having far more interest in being a senator than being governor, Hansen declined this deal also.

When asked by the *Times* about the proposed deal, McClure made no apologies, candidly admitting having tried to get Hansen to drop out. He told the *Times* his fear of splitting the conservative vote was more than ample justification for the endeavor.

In late September of 1971 I wrote a column based on a D.C. interview with McClure. He was preparing to announce formally. The dead give away was his willingness to share the "numbers" analysis Goller had done for him.

In the interview, McClure said he had studied the voting abstract on the 1970 election results of the second CD and he liked what he saw. He pointed out that though Governor Don Samuelson had lost the statewide vote to Cecil Andrus, in the second district Samuelson beat Andrus, 53,865 votes to Andrus' 52,802.

McClure further pointed out in his district he ran ahead of Andrus, garnering 77,515 votes to Andrus' 75,000. McClure said these numbers told him a conservative would win statewide even if the opponent were someone as formidable as Andrus. It also reassured him that his strength in the first district was stronger than Hansen's in the second district.

McClure used the interview to send several messages to his primary opponents such as Hansen. The messages were, he had the financing, he had the campaign team, he was the GOP's strongest candidate, and Hansen had had his chance in 1968 and lost. He said he was looking for a red light to tell him to stop but as of the interview he had not seen any. Nor did he ever see one.

He did allude briefly to the fact that multiple-person primaries did not always produce the strongest candidate, that it was possible three conservatives could so divide the field that a weak moderate like Smylie might slip through. He exuded confidence, however, and only later did pundits and others find out how really worried he was.

Part of Goller's primary campaign strategy was to demonstrate McClure's fund-raising prowess with the hard core conservative base. To accomplish this, Goller brought into the campaign the original practitioner of direct-mail fund-raising, Richard Viguerie. In 1972, Viguerie had not quite yet elevated the direct mail pitch to the fine art form it is today, nor was he well known.

By the close of the decade he would be well known in all political circles, and, indeed, his various pitches were of inestimable value to Congressman Steve Symms when the cherubic apple farmer upset Senator Frank Church in 1980. Goller's tying up Viguerie also kept him out of the hands of Hansen's backers. (In a later conversation with me, Goller on background questioned how much Viguerie brought into the campaign, pointing out the high cost of the direct mail results with a smaller net than one would have thought.)

The overall primary plan for McClure was to keep George Hansen primarily penned in his own territory, trying to further solidify his base, to go one-on-one with Mormon leaders in eastern Idaho to convince them of McClure's conservative credentials, to use Smylie as a foil to assist fund-raising and to tie up Viguerie.

Goller also focused on the plan's tactical components, which called for good county coordinators to be given specific targets, to engage those who signed petitions to become volunteers passing out brochures and slapping on bumper stickers, and to recruit more volunteers.

Hansen thought too there would be a "religious affiliation pride" that would cause his LDS brethren to deliver an historic turnout. Goller mockingly called it Hansen's "southern strategy" for it kept Hansen from spending much time in north Idaho. It proved to be a costly mistake on Hansen's part.

The morning of August 9th greeted McClure with the news he had won the primary by 11,000 votes over Hansen. McClure decisively carried the first district including big wins in Kootenai and Nez Perce counties; held his own in many of the second district's LDS counties; and, took much of the Magic Valley as predicted. Hansen's "southern strategy" failed to deliver as big an LDS margin as he hoped to see.

Hansen was not a gracious loser, either. McClure heard from both Smylie and Wegner right away, both conveying gracious thoughts and offering to help in the general election. McClure never did receive a call from Hansen, though Hansen did endorse McClure at a major fund-raising event for the GOP in Blackfoot later in October.

Observers there say he gave a stem-winder for McClure, but others argue Hansen was more interested with impressing the Nixon Cabinet's Secretary for Housing and Urban Development, George Romney, as well as the D.C. party brass in attendance.

That it was still a half-hearted endorsement became clear when a week after the Blackfoot GOP fund-raiser Hansen leveled the charge about the second meeting in which McClure and corporate pooh-bahs had tried to force him out. He again charged the McClure effort of toadying to the select few and trying to thwart the right of the many Republicans across the state to make their will known through the primary.

Hansen's grousing about McClure being tied to the corporate interests in fact played right into Davis' charge that McClure represented the special interests, not the public interest. It was a charge that put McClure at times on the defensive.

One issue arching over many others was the escalating war in Viet Nam and the public's growing disenchantment with America's seeming inability to win. Davis came out strongly against escalating the conflict through increased bombing and then by the general election time was against the conflict, period.

The Bud Davis for Senate campaign received an unexpected and surprising boost a week before the election when a long and laudatory editorial endorsing the Davis candidacy appeared in the state's largest newspaper, the *Idaho Statesman*. In a strong, well-thought out and clearly written editorial the newspaper explained why Davis would be a better senator for Idaho.

The editorial cited Davis' balanced approach to issues, his record on the environment, his opposition to the Viet Nam war, and his ability to inspire. All in all, the Davis team could not have written a better one themselves.

With regard to McClure, the paper's editors dismissed him as a tool of the special interests, repeated George Hansen's charge regarding being foisted on the voters by four powerful Idaho corporations, cited his opposition to the seven-year moratorium on dam-building on the Middle Snake, something both Church and Jordan supported; and, his failure to fully disclose his campaign contributions. It all made them highly suspicious regarding the type of senator he would be.

Davis garnered numerous other editorials supporting his candidacy, including The *Lewiston Morning Tribune* and *the Idaho State Journal*.

The war in Southeast Asia, however, was a two-edged sword for while it helped galvanize young people to volunteer for Davis as a way to work against the war; it also inexorably tied Davis to the presidential crusade of George McGovern, the Democratic candidate for president. To say that McGovern was not popular in Idaho is an understatement.

The McGovern candidacy was an albatross around the neck of the Davis campaign, and would remain so.

The amount of money being expended in the general election soon became an issue that placed McClure on the defensive. When asked about how much he was spending, McClure badly low-balled his number and then charged Davis with spending as much if not more.

This prompted the *Tribune* to retain me to research the Federal Election Reports to obtain the actual numbers being filed. Even Goller laughed out loud when called to respond to reports that showed McClure spending three to four times as much as he was publicly estimating.

Goller candidly admitted McClure had no real idea and should have checked with him before responding to news media inquiries.

The net effect of this, as well as questions about McClure's independence from moneyed interests, was that by October 1st independent polls showed Davis gaining ground and McClure losing ground. Shelledy later said that in early October he had seen one poll showing Davis with a 22 point lead over McClure.

Shelledy makes a strong case that this lead directly to the formation of the independent committee of farmers and their intensive radio and statewide full page ad campaign repeating the scurrilous charge of Davis supporting a potato boycott.

This was one of two things that changed the campaign dynamic and broke Davis' momentum. The first of three debates was held and most all observers concluded Davis' avuncular style did not play well on television. He appeared unprepared for McClure's pointed attacks and McClure's reasonable sounding responses. Though Davis more than held his own and accredited himself well in the second and third debates, he could not overcome that first impression.

The more damaging, though, was the potato boycott charge. The "independent committee," made up largely of Idaho Republican farmers and water masters across southern Idaho, ran the full page ads in papers all around the state several times in the last two weeks. The intensity of the effort indicated how desperate the McClure campaign was to break Davis' building momentum.

It was absurd but of course effective and deadly. Despite Shelledy and Davis re-issuing his flat denial and going after those who would use innuendo and falsehoods to advance their candidacy, the b.s. charge was enough to cause Davis' support in southeast Idaho, especially with the farm community, to erode quickly.

As noted, campaigns often turn on perceptions, or misperceptions, people want to believe about candidates rather than the real facts. Shelledy will always feel that the false potato boycott ads dealt a fatal blow to their campaign. Goller thought otherwise, telling McClure biographer Bill Smallwood, "Look at the numbers. Davis won in 11 counties; McClure won in 33 counties. McClure won by 21,000 votes."

Goller went on to say, "Yeah, the potato boycott ad may have persuaded some voters, but remember the press had reported this at some length and continued to do so throughout the campaign. To tell you the truth I was never really worried. I felt all along that McClure was going to win. ... McClure had solid support. He worked hard and ran a good campaign. I think it would be distorting history to leave the impression McClure won because of a few negative ads. That kind of thinking makes me a little irritated."

At the end of Election Day, November 7, 1972, Davis pulled in 140,913 votes – not enough to overcome McClure's 161,804 votes.

In many respects, though, it was a remarkable if not stunning performance by a neophyte candidate in his first run for any political office. Having started slightly less than a year before election day, Davis came from virtually nowhere to within a respectable margin of an upset against a veteran Republican officeholder.

Two numbers tell the story: Davis garnered 61,000 votes more than George McGovern's 80,826 votes for president. Davis also added 117,000 votes to his primary total of 24,000 votes.

McClure, by contrast, ran behind Richard Nixon's total of 199,384 votes by 38,000 votes. In other words 38,000 folks who cast their ballot for Richard Nixon then crossed over to vote for Bud Davis – a remarkable cross-over.

As befits the man he is, Davis issued a gracious concession statement on election night and also called McClure to offer his congratulations.

Shelledy's contention that a little gray hair, an experienced hand on the helm earlier could have made a huge difference seems incontestable, but it is doubtful an experienced campaign manager would have anticipated Davis being asked to sign the Cesar Chavez petition and been prescient enough to tell Davis not to sign no matter what, and no matter even if Frank Church's name was on the petition.

In reviewing the campaign contribution filings 40 years later, it is clear the traditional sources of major funding for Democrats – the unions, the Hollywood "wine and cheese" liberals, the Jewish financial community, the major environmental groups, and the national party, never saw the phenomena of Bud Davis coming down the track like a diesel locomotive.

Labor initially invested heavily in Byron Johnson in the primary and the national party went for Tony Park while women's organizations went for Rose Bowman. If all had rallied immediately behind Davis it could have made a difference.

Davis, though, was a classic outsider candidate, without strong ties to the long-time party workers and the traditional base of the Democratic Party. One searches the contribution lists in vain for the names of the usual contributors to Democratic candidates in Idaho. Few of the names of those who usually contributed to Church's campaigns or to Andrus' appear on the pages.

When it came to the actual number of donors, those giving to McClure far outnumbered those who gave to Davis.

Though it was probably too little, too late, the Democratic Senatorial Campaign Committee did detail one of their top media advisors, David Sawyer, to come to Idaho to work with the young Ben Godard and Ric Glaub who were handling Davis' dollar-constrained television and radio ad program.

The party also sent some true heavyweights in to make appearances on behalf of Davis – again, too little too late.

Forty plus years later that Davis in less than a year did so much so well on so little is downright stunning. His campaign raised in total about $250,000 and spent $240,000. McClure, by contrast, raised and spent over $1,000,000.

Could more money have made a difference? Certainly. Could it have pushed Davis over the top? Maybe, but we will never know.

When all is said and done, with the 20/20 hindsight of history, Jim McClure turned out to be a fine U.S. Senator, one of the best this state ever produced. Bud Davis would agree with that statement. Another aspect of their 1972 contest that stands out in hindsight is the genuine mutual respect the candidates held for each other.

They fought hard, but the differences remained philosophical, not personal. There was no effort to demonize the opponent, to charge that the other was not just wrong, but in fact was evil.

On more than one occasion Davis would say without prompting "the guy who beat me was my friend – before, during, and after the campaign." That attitude made it easy for the State Board of Education to restore Davis to the presidency of Idaho State University following the election with no fear there would be lingering adverse politics that would unfairly victimize the Pocatello institution.

Davis to his great credit understood what an incredible learning experience the campaign was both for him, Polly and the family. He drew the correct lessons from it understanding intuitively that it would make him a better university president, and, more importantly, a better communicator.

Years later, reflecting on the race, he wrote, "I can testify that the running for high public office is an education and I learned and savored the importance of meeting and knowing students, public school faculty and staff, parents, city officials, media hounds thirsting for a juicy story – *en toto* the whole shift and shebang of the constituents who make good education available and affordable, and who in later years will be visiting us in hospitals or nursing homes or attending our funerals."

He added, "In running for office, I met and worked with or against men and women with lofty dreams and ambitions – sometime lonely candidates or volunteer workers who pounded the pavements and waded through the cow manure to meet the people, to shake their hands and know them better.

"If a man indeed grows and learns through a tough campaign, he never loses. I hold to the theory that a man is the sum total of all his experiences, and I savor the memories of having been in the big arena of politics. The lessons I learned from that experience have served me well as I, in turn, have strived to serve them well as a university president or chancellor."

This writer will always believe that Bud Davis would have become a truly great U.S. Senator.

Besides his intelligence and wit, his genuine charm and his sense of a calling to public service, just what was it that brought the Idaho State University president from his post to almost to being a United States senator in less than one year?

The answer lies in something Davis wrote four years earlier in *Idaho Yesterdays* about one of his heroes, the powerful and influential Republican lobbyist from Rexburg, W. Lloyd Adams. Also an attorney, Adams was legendary in his ability to influence political outcomes across the state, his masterful use of the telephone to stay behind the scenes, the rarity in which he was seen or photographed. As the saying goes in politics, he was rarely finger-printed.

In describing Adams, Davis was also unwittingly describing himself:

"His, too, is a trained intelligence. His life is testimony to the fact that by no means is all of education acquired by formal study; that man learns by all of his experience, and, of this, formal study is only a part. This is particularly true of the knowledge of men gained through dealing with men and leading to that valuable and mysterious quality which transcends formulas or expositions and which we call common sense. (Bud Davis) is imbued with this common sense. He believes that opportunity lies about us, that it is present in every human contact. If a man has an intense urge to learn and the will to rise, the acquisition of knowledge is perennial and cumulative. Opportunity and learning do not belong to youth alone, but create strength and yield satisfaction as long as life shall last."

There is one other attribute that Bud Davis possesses in abundance. Maybe it is because he was once an officer in the U.S. Marine Corps. For lack of a better way of expressing it, let me just say Bud Davis radiates a sense of integrity and a deep sense of honor. In 1997, in a lecture at the U.S. Naval Academy, former education secretary William J. Bennett captured what Bud Davis lives and has lived:

"Honor never grows old, and honor rejoices the heart of age. It does so because honor is, finally, about defending those noble and worthy things that deserve defending, even if it comes at a high cost. In our time, that may mean social disapproval, public scorn, hardship, persecution, or as always, even death itself. The question remains:

What is worth defending? What is worth dying for? What is worth living for?"

Just as there are "unofficial" colonels in Kentucky, there ought to be unofficial senators in Idaho; and, Senator William E. "Bud" Davis would be the first and foremost.

11 ■ The Sensible Monkey Wrench

Dworshak Dam near Orofino. Photo by Brian Mosher.

Ed Chaney has been correct all along. So has my Columbia classmate, Pat Ford. From their first appearances before the Northwest Power Planning Council in 1981, through all the intervening years in interviews, articles, lawsuits, and speeches, each has consistently said that the best science says and will always say that the only real solution to restoring native salmon and steelhead runs to their former state, as required by the Northwest Power Planning Act, is to breach the four lower Snake River dams.

They were, are, and always will be absolutely correct; it is only a matter of time before the Federal District Court produces a judge who reaches the inevitability of their conclusion. And it is not just what the science says, it is also what economics say.

Furthermore, to those critics who, like former Idaho Governor Cecil Andrus, say it is ridiculous to even discuss dam breaching because Congress will never appropriate the hundreds of millions of dollars necessary to breach and remove the dams, there is an easy answer. Congress does not have to appropriate the necessary dollars. All it has to do is authorize the activity and direct that it be the priority expenditure for several years for the funds that come from revenues generated by the power sales the Bonneville Power Administration garners annually.

The region's ratepayers would be taking on the obligation, not the nation's taxpayers.

In other words, instead of spending the $7.35 billion on various tasks related to salmon and steelhead recovery, as the BPA did between 2001 and 2011, it can spend a minimum 10% of that amount, or perhaps 20%, $735 million to $1.47 billion, to take out the four dams and still be money ahead in terms of reducing the amount of funds they could pay to the Treasury for debt repayment.

The Pacific Northwest Electric Power Planning and Conservation Act, otherwise known as Public Law 96-501, was signed into law by President Jimmy Carter on December 5, 1980. The Act explicitly elevated fishery enhancement to an equal status along with power planning needs and the resources necessary to meet those needs.

Under the purposes for the Act contained in Section 2, number 6 states:

"... to protect, mitigate and enhance the fish and wildlife, including related spawning grounds and habitat, of the Columbia River and its tributaries, particularly anadromous fish which are of significant importance to the social and economic well-being of the Pacific Northwest and the Nation and which are dependent on suitable environmental conditions substantially obtainable from the management and operation of the Federal Columbia River Power System and other power generating facilities on the Columbia River and its tributaries."

Section 4, which addresses the creation of the Planning Council, specifically directs the Council in subsection (h) to make timely recommendations with supporting data from studies that will provide information and facts to take on measures "to protect, mitigate, and enhance fish and wildlife affected by operation (of the dams), and fish and wildlife R&D which will provide **improved passage**, and **enhance survival of anadromous fish at and between the region's hydroelectric dams.**"

An important distinction for Chaney and Ford and those supporting their viewpoint is that this law, coupled with the powerful Endangered Species Act, means the Council and BPA are to protect and enhance the runs of *wild* anadromous salmon and steelhead.

Supporters of the status quo and of leaving the dams in place like to point out that in terms of sheer numbers of the various runs of returning salmon and steelhead, the count is up and still rising. This is of course due to the large amount of supplementing the runs with hatchery-raised fingerlings and smolts.

Chaney points out that one should only examine the numbers of wild fish, which continue to steadily decline. In his view, this means that despite the over $8 billion spent both directly and indirectly by BPA since the turn of the century, the Council plan has failed miserably, as has the Council.

Like me, Chaney supports the abolition of the current Council in its current format and the creation of a new, Interior Secretary-chosen Council which will be given the mandate to try to disprove the case for dam breaching, rather than trying to prove the negative.

I am also obligated to make it clear that my old boss, the former governor and secretary of the Interior, does not support or endorse my view that the dams should be breached as it is the only way the wild runs can be protected and enhanced. He still strongly supports his "fish flush" plan as a way of replicating the "before the dams were built" sweep to the sea that smolt underwent during the spring run-off.

Just when someone developed a gleam in their eye that Lewiston could become the furthest inland seaport in the nation, I'm not sure. On the face of it, one has to concede it is an arrogant, nature-defying task. However, one should never underestimate the U.S. Army Corps of Engineers. They love challenges and taming rivers with dams is one of their favorite activities.

One suspects they will never rest until they have built dams on virtually every major navigable river in the nation. And creating a seaport 500 miles inland after all would only require five dams with locks on the Lower Snake River. And, oh yes, they'd put in fish ladders for salmon and steelhead migrating upstream, and channel smolts away from the turbines with fish screens that would herd the smolts to causeways on the downstream rush to the ocean. No sweat.

Over a number of years, the Corps contractors, under the direction of Army personnel in their Walla Walla District office, constructed on a steady pace the Ice Habor, Lower Monumental, Little Goose and Lower Granite dams, the last one dedicated in April of 1973.

Plans had also called for a dam upstream of Lewiston at Asotin, to be called Asotin Dam. Its purpose was to catch and contain the vast amount of sediment coming down the Snake and Salmon River systems. That sediment build-up in and around Lewiston, as well as behind the dams, is an issue that today grates with the Corps since they feel they had a plan that would have taken care of the matter, but politics interfered.

The *New Yorker* magazine writer, John McPhee, captures quite well the Corps' "can do" attitude in his fine book, *The Control of Nature*. In the book he describes the Corps decades' long fight with the Mississippi River which appears to have a mind of its own regarding its preferred channel to the Gulf of Mexico. One gets the feeling that "controlling" the Snake and the Columbia is viewed by the engineers in Walla Walla as a piece of cake

McPhee also quotes a Tulane Law Professor, Oliver Houck, who talks about the arrogance and the *hauteur* of mankind. He lays out the three best examples: "The greatest arrogance was the stealing of the sun; the second is running a river backward. The third is trying to hold the Mississippi in place."

If Professor Houck were to visit the northwest, it is a safe bet he would suggest making Lewiston an inland seaport would be number four on that list.

The best service McPhee provides in his essay on the Corps and its fight to conquer the mighty Mississippi is his insight into the Corps understanding and mastery of public relations. As an agency of government they are second to none.

Much of the McPhee essay recounts a trip aboard a fancily refurbished tug down the Mississippi River and through Atchafalaya aboard what can best be described as a large, floating "town hall meeting." The general commanding the Corps district wines, dines, charms and spins the many Corps constituencies as they migrate down the river, stopping at key communities to let local political leadership on and off.

There are of course major economic conflicting interests just as there are in the northwest. Some want more water, some want less. Interests range from crawfish fisherman to farmers to industrial plants to sport fisherman, to cities and parishes dependent for survival on Corps-constructed levees.

One can just imagine the Corps arriving before the Orofino Chamber of Commerce in the late 50s to sell the citizens of Clearwater County on the merits of constructing the huge Dworshak Dam on the Clearwater's North Fork just before it merges with the main stem.

With slick slides and brochure promises of incredibly enhanced tourist trade and recreationalists who will come from all over to fish, water ski and boat on the huge reservoir that will be created behind the dam they sold the locals on a bright future.

Little mention was made of the hundreds of thousands of acres of prime timberland and elk habitat that would be inundated, or the loss of the cutthroat fishery not to mention salmon and steelhead runs up the North Fork.

And for what? Dworshak Dam is a mere re-regulating dam with only some small generators in several of the penstocks. The purpose of this monstrosity is to provide added flow when needed to maximize throughput of water at the dams downstream to boost the power production when needed; or, when the market demands more power, for the air conditioners in southern California and Arizona.

Looking up the face of this dam, second in height only to the Hoover Dam on the Colorado River along the Nevada/Arizona border, one notices an unusual (to the layman) amount of leakage. All dams leak one is told and then assured it is nothing to worry about.

Having watched film of the Bureau of Reclamation's Teton Dam in southeastern Idaho, and its catastrophic collapse, one is not reassured. If anything less than the Divine hand accomplishes the work, mistakes can and will be made. Humans have made marvelous progress over eons, but have yet to master engineering perfection all the time.

There can be design flaws. There can be construction flaws. There can be both.

One of the key arguments by the Northwest Resource Information Center, of which Ed Chaney is a founding member, is that the four dams on the Lower Snake have design flaws, especially as they relate to fish and smolt migration that self-evidentially prove they do not facilitate fish passage.

Chaney calls it "an epic ongoing betrayal of the public trust." In particular, Chaney and Ford believe the law as reflected by and through the Northwest Power Planning Act and the Endangered Species law requires the restoration of the wild runs of salmon and steelhead. They insist these runs represent a distinct and separate gene pool that is declining, but that the decline is masked by the salting of the runs with millions of hatchery raised salmon and steelhead smolts.

On the face of it, their contention the dams continue to damage and facilitate decline appears incontestable. Courts appear also to agree with them as they have successfully petitioned to have most of the so-called "Bi-ops" developed by the Corps, the Department of Environmental Quality, the US Fish and Wildlife Service, the NOAA and BPA invalidated.

Breaching the dams is therefore the only measure not tried yet to restore and enhance the runs. From an environmental and biological point of view they are correct.

What seals the deal, however, are the economic arguments for breaching the dams of which there are three. There is only one good economic argument made by wheat farmers for keeping the dams in place.

There are 31 federal dams on the Columbia and Snake Rivers which produce 60 percent of the region's hydroelectricity. The power produced by the four lower Snake dams is about one percent of the overall production. BPA of course sells and distributes this power.

Due to the several laws guiding BPA's management of this "federal base system," the agency also funds and manages a fishery enhancement program whose goal is, as the law requires, protecting, mitigating and enhancing the runs.

In March, 2013, I asked the agency's public communications office to provide me with an estimate of how much money they have expended to meet the law's requirement for the 11-year period of 2002 through 2012.

I wanted the number to include direct programs – the hundreds of fish and wildlife projects across the region including restoring habitat, managing hatcheries, land acquisitions, predator control (paying fisherman to catch whitefish, for example), and research.

Also, the number should include the reimbursable, the monies they reimburse to the Army Corps and the Bureau of Reclamation for a portion of the costs of operating and maintaining fish passage improvements at their respective dams, and for the operation and maintenance costs of fish hatcheries.

The number should also include the capital repayment obligations and a number reflecting replacement power purchases to replace revenues lost when spills are required to facilitate fish passage. Finally, a number to reflect "lost opportunity" costs – the value of energy that could have been generated and sold had it passed through turbines. To the BPA's great credit, embarrassing as the number is, they produced all I requested as one can see from the attached chart that is part of the "Fact Sheet" the BPA sent me.

As noted earlier, the total number is a staggering $7.35 billion, or an average of $677 million a year, with little, if any, progress being made in enhancing and protecting the wild runs.

Subtract the breaching costs from that figure and cease funding all of the fruitless efforts underway and the region's ratepayers would be billions ahead shortly.

The next unsound economical entity is the Port of Lewiston itself. Sold by its boosters that it was going to be the catalyst of an economic rebirth for Lewiston, it has been nothing of the sort. Boosters of the port sold Nez Perce County voters a bill of goods, saying that a local-option sales tax would be short-lived and retired.

Fifty years later the tax is still on the books. The years the port has made money can be counted on the fingers of one hand. Even the much bally-hooed super large equipment headed for Alberta's tar sands, some of which is still being stowed at the port, has not generated enough cash to put the port's operation in the black.

Face it – the Port of Lewiston is a heavily subsidized operation that will never pay for itself. The citizens of Lewiston and Nez Perce County would be far better off shutting it down and supporting dam breaching as their preferred path back to real prosperity.

Another reason that should galvanize support for dam breaching is the likelihood of a ten-year flood event inundating Lewiston's downtown core. In large part due to the rapid buildup of silt in and around the confluence of the Clearwater and Snake rivers, water is already well above the street level in the downtown.

The levees constructed by the Army Corps were designed (there's that engineering word again) to have a seven- to eight-foot margin above the anticipated highest level of the water. Today it is much closer to a two- to three-foot margin.

Meteorologists and other government agency forecasters, when pressed, will admit that a ten-year flood event, such as heavy snow in the mountains followed by a surge in temperature with a commensurate heavy rain that could bring most of the mountain moisture cascading down the Clearwater could easily inundate the city.

Lewiston City officials will also concede their ability to remove that amount of water is virtually nonexistent. For all practical purposes, the water would be trapped on the inside and it might take weeks to remove it by various siphoning methods. The damages would be in the hundreds of millions of dollars and insurance would not begin to cover the rebuilding cost.

This is not a case of if; it is rather a matter of when.

The Corps response is to propose a massive dredging program for the next fifty years. They produced a large EIS on the issue entitled the Lower Snake River Sediment Management Plan. Public comment on it closed on March 26, 2013.

Walla Walla District Commander Lt. Col. Andrew Kelly conceded to *Idaho Statesman* environmental reporter Rocky Barker in a January 28, 2013 interview that the environmental aspects of dredging will always be a challenge but it is nonetheless the preferred option.

By law the Corps is required to maintain a channel behind Lower Granite dam, just downstream from the confluence of the Snake and Clearwater Rivers, that is 14 feet deep and 250 feet wide to facilitate barge access to the Port of Lewiston.

It's not happening, folks.

Needless to say, the rapid accumulation of river-borne sediment will significantly add to the cost and the subsidies necessary to keep the port open and to operate the dams. Just how much is a key question and the subject of several on-going lawsuits that have been filed in the salmon vs. dams debate.

Kooskia resident and environmental activist Linwood Laughy calls the Corps dredging EIS a $16 million big-government plan for another $30 million in dredging costs over the next decade according to Barker's report. Laughy further estimates the ten-year cost of the taxpayer subsidy necessary to keep the port of Lewiston open would be $39 million – and the sedimentation accumulation would still continue.

He believes each fully loaded barge leaving the infrequently used Port of Lewiston leaves with a taxpayer subsidy of $19,000 reflecting the dredging and sediment management activities. To date no one has refuted his numbers.

With that in mind, one has to ask if shipping of Palouse wheat out of any of the Lower Snake ports (and there are several) is really more economical than shipping the grain by rail. Farmers in the area have long contended that it is cheaper for them to ship by barge than by rail despite the fact that both BNSF (Burlington Northern & Santa Fe) and Union Pacific have lines that serve the area.

If the lower Snake dams were breached, one can speculate there would be an immediate competition between the two rail lines for the wheat shipping traffic that in all probability would match the previous low barging costs. Farmers, however, don't believe this.

They believe the two railroads would conspire and collude to fix an agreed upon high price and in effect they would be held hostage. Essentially, this is their counterargument:

First, they cite a Corps study which highlighted that without the river system, at least 30 cents/bushel would be added to the grower's costs. When that study was done, wheat was $2.84 – so thirty cents in that environment was quite costly. Thirty cents against $7/bushel wheat in 2013 is less so, but still significant.

The difficult part to quantify wheat farmers say is this: they believe the cost of rail is only kept competitive by the presence of the competition from the barge system. Without the competition – the entire PNW becomes a "captive shipper" situation like Montana.

Washington and Idaho wheat farmers say their interaction with Montana growers ALWAYS includes a conversation about rail rates, and the feeling the Montanans have of being tremendously overcharged. Of course there is a long history of adversity in Montana between growers and the Burlington Northern that goes back several generations.

To further highlight the lack of competition: even though the UP line travels through the area, Union Pacific moves no Washington wheat, according to Brett Blankenship, a Washtucna area wheat farmer and the former president of the Washington Wheat Growers Association. BNSF has a monopoly.

Blankenship is currently rising through the chairs of the National Wheat Growers and though he comes from a long line of Republicans, he has been canny enough to cultivate U.S. Senator Patty Murray, now chair of the Senate Budget Committee and a strong ally of his. He flat believes any legislation authorizing lower Snake River dam breaching would pass only over her dead body and it is hard to argue the point.

Blankenship also says the average annual value of wheat to the state is over $600 million.

Turning to the whole Northwest, he says the cost issue is magnified. The areas where much of the nation's wheat is produced are often not served by rail at all – or at best, nominally. Southern Idaho has rail issues, as they are far afield from the river system, and often ship wheat toward Salt Lake rather than Portland. The Camas Prairie, Palouse, Walla Walla, and lower Columbia Basin are the prime wheat areas, and all have easy access to the river system.

As federal involvement decreases in production agriculture, anything that adds costs or risk to the producer's equation is very serious, Blankenship states.

He also points out the Columbia-Snake River system is the most carbon friendly mode of transport. Without the barges, trucks will be used much more intensely, not only using more diesel and tires, but pounding rural roads even more. He says his costs to transport would have an added 20 to 30 cents to get to Portland, but also an added 20 to 30 cents just to haul the grain to a facility 70 miles away, rather than 20. Barges themselves are much more efficient on carbon that even rail, he adds.

To summarize the majority viewpoint of most northwest state farmers, they believe the positives of having a river system that reaches hundreds of miles inland as far as Lewiston, is a national treasure. There is added value also since product travels both ways. This is vitally important in an international market such as wheat.

Blankenship says farmers know the system has not been without problems, but they believe technology should be able to continue to address the problems. They say an honest, balanced assessment of the dams vs. fish issue would conclude that progress is occurring. Unfortunately, farmers believe many people are unaware of the steps that have been taken at the dams to address fish passage. To most farmers the idea that tearing out four such dam superstructures would somehow magically restore the river to the way it was before Lewis and Clark traveled through is naive at best.

Blankenship says farmers also believe it is highly hypocritical to just remove the lower Snake dams. If dams are so bad for fish, even those with fish ladders, why leave any of them in place? One could argue that they should all go, or why bother?

Blankenship argues that we would better utilize our political and economic assets by making the system as fish-friendly as possible, and preserve the value of the transportation and hydro system. That outcome would be much more beneficial than the current "keep them or take them" discussion.

Palouse farmers also appear to be hedging their bets. The Pacific Grain Growers Co-op at McCoy, a few miles east of Rosalia, Washington, is investing in a massive expansion of their rail grain-shipping station to accommodate 110-car trains that could carry the vast majority of their product to West Coast ports at Portland, Tacoma, Seattle or even Vancouver, B.C.

Blankenship believes the McCoy project is a case of one group of farmers wanting to stay competitive with another group; in this case those backing the McCoy expansion want to be in the same class as the Ritzville Warehouse.

He concedes that the northern Palouse wheat farmers have a pretty long truck haul to Lewiston or Almota, so looking for options is the right issue for them to work on. "One always wants options," he says.

He adds the reason for building capacity to load 110-car units comes back to the problems with the railroad. BNSF is not at all interested in anything less than 110 cars, and maybe even more. None of the grain companies have ever had that capacity until Ritzville built theirs ten years ago.

In his view, those supporting the McCoy expansion "have not solved the captivity issues, and may even have made them more extreme by becoming dependent on a "short line" rail, just to have access to BNSF main line."

These growers also produce products other than wheat, he says, which have not moved by barge. So getting better rates to move peas and lentils and garbanzos is reasonable.

Many of the larger growers in the region bypass the local co-ops by using the river terminals. So this is a play to attempt to get some of the players back "in the fold."

Blankenship also has doubts on the profitability or the necessity, but knows the co-ops are forging ahead. Loading trains this close to Portland has always seemed to him to be a marginal enterprise. "And it will have to compete with rail 'bandwidth' against coal moving through the area. That can raise the concern regarding railcar availability – but the railroad dismisses that concern outright. Depends on who one trusts."

If they were building the facility in Lewiston, then he might call it a hedge – but building in a landlocked place that's not even on a main line seems to imply other reasons.

The facility will have no impact on people in his situation. "Without the river, I haul clear to Pasco, or uphill to Ritzville, or sell grain to feedlots; none very attractive. So, at present, I don't think the facility will have much effect on river volume. Many of those bushels may be going by smaller train cargoes already," he states.

So perhaps the McCoy facility is not the hedge one would think, but it clearly will provide an alternative if the dams are breached. At what price, is the key unanswerable question. Additionally, there are many who believe the Port of Portland is rapidly losing out to the Port of Tacoma as the primary overseas wheat shipping port.

Unfortunately, sound as Blankenship's arguments are and his logic is, it will not meet the tests Federal judges are consistently saying are contained within the Northwest Power Planning Act and the Endangered Species Act. Virtually the only option left to comply with the law appears to be breaching and it is just a matter of time – unless of course those that want to save the dams can muster the political support to amend the Power Act and the ESA law. Such a prospect is highly unlikely.

So as a region let's face up to the inevitable and get on with breaching the four dams.

Of course nothing is simple. Everything is complex and there is no reason not to think that the law of unintended consequences could assert itself, as it often does. It is a virtual certainty that breaching would be considered a major federal action which means an Environmental Impact Statement would have to be drawn up, options developed, public hearings held, and then a preferred option selected.

Furthermore, once the preferred option is chosen it is another virtual certainty that one of the interest groups would file suit and the matter litigated for years.

Additionally, an assessment of cost will be made regardless of whether the funds or breaching comes from the BPA ratepayers or from the taxpayer. The Corps is currently working on an historic undertaking on the Olympic Peninsula – the removal of two dams on the Elwha River near Port Angeles. According to the Corps it will take three to five years and cost about $325 million.

A pure guess is that the breaching of the four lower Snake River dams would be somewhere between $500 million and $1.5 billion. This is a huge chunk of change, but still represents less than 20% of the costs incurred by BPA over the first decade of this century trying to enhance the native salmon and steelhead runs.

In this period of diminishing federal resources as the nation tries to get a handle on its deficit spending challenge, however, the cost benefits derived from adopting the last, best chance for real fishery enhancement are overwhelmingly compelling.

Add to that the cost avoidance of the flooding out of Lewiston and the elimination of shipping subsidies and breaching is a no-brainer.

12 ■ "They Also Serve. . . .

"First friend" congressional candidate Ed Williams (left), Senator Edward Kennedy (right). Photo by Barry Kough.

The full quote from the 17th century English poet, John Milton (1608-1674; author of *Paradise Lost*), is "They also serve who only stand and wait." It's from another of his writings, *On His Blindness*, made poignant by the poet's own blindness.

It's a reminder that most are supporting cast on the stage of life to a few star players whose light outshines others and who are more noted by historians. That said, their roles, seemingly insignificant, are necessary to fill out the drama. Every star needs a supporting cast to help them stand out in life's movable parade.

These thoughts were prompted following a discussion with two of the four "note worthies" from the Idaho State Senate freshman class of 1961. This class, with seasoning and maturity, four years later led Idaho into modernity by debating, then adopting and sending to the voters for ratification the first ever sales tax designed to better fund public education and meet the primary purpose stated by Idaho's Constitution.

Fifty years later, two of the "notables," who played critical roles in the sales tax debate and its passage, are still alive with sharp memories: former four-term Governor Cecil D. Andrus, who in 1961 was elected to the Senate as a Democrat from Clearwater County, and former Majority Leader Bill Roden, a Republican from Ada County.

Curious about whom were the other less well-known members of that class, I asked each what he might recall of these supporting players.

Each began by recalling two conservative members, who became "note worthies," but opposed adopting the sales tax: State Senator Jim McClure (Payette County), and Bonner County State Senator Don Samuelson. McClure carved out a long career as a congressman and a U.S. senator, while Samuelson served one term as governor, defeating Andrus in 1966 and then losing a rematch in 1970.

In today's political environment it is stunning to realize in the 1960s progressive Republicans like Pocatello's Perry Swisher led the charge for adopting a sales tax dedicated to properly funding public education. Roden cites another member of that class, Watt Prather, from Boundary

County as being the real thinker for the "Rat Pack," a nickname given to Roden and his supporters who worked closely with Swisher.

Co-chair with McClure of the "Economy Bloc" (senators of both parties who opposed the sales tax) was Bill Dee (Idaho County). Dee would always make a motion to cut every budget regardless of need by 5%, Andrus recalled. Likewise both Andrus and Roden remembered Senator Joe Ausich (Custer County) who boasted he never voted for any appropriation bill.

Andrus has not forgotten State Senator Cy Chase (Benewah County) who supported Dee for Minority Leader in 1963 over Cece, who lost by one vote. Always a good vote-counter, one could tell Andrus was saying without saying that Cy had double-crossed him. Later Chase became minority leader, a position from which every day he and Roden would engage in verbal combat over the issue of the day.

Andrus and Roden fondly recalled Cecil Sandberg, a mortician (Bingham County). Solid and steady, he was especially good when the legislature had to redistrict itself. Andrus noted though that Sandberg was quick to get caskets exempted from any sales tax – just the beginning of a series of exemptions that over the years has gutted the sales tax's ability to achieve its intended purpose.

Other members of that class were: Ray Burge (Power County), Rollie Campbell (Valley County), Vince Nally (Gem County), Hal Wallington (Blaine County), and J.E. Yensen (Boise County). They all played some role which, while history may not have recorded it, still was a part in the play.

This started me thinking about the hundreds if not thousands of folks across Idaho who in one form or another gave of their time, talent and treasure to Cecil Andrus. They saw in him a rising star with talent, ability, sincerity, and honesty that they could trust to do what he said he would do.

This positing of the public trust reflects a sacred bond between the elected and the electors. Good political officeholders know this is sacred and would rather die than let their constituents down. Hence, one can hear the religious-like overtones when good officeholders say they have responded to a calling to serve.

One of the great joys of the 40 plus years I have been associated with Cecil Andrus in the public and private sectors has been the opportunity to meet and work with hundreds of decent people from all walks of life.

If we all are the sum of our experiences, both good and bad, so are we the sum of the many people we meet who impact in various ways, large and small, our lives. It is fair to say an excellent officeholder draws strength from the folks he or she meets.

The diversity is constantly astounding. Hobbies, interests, educational pursuits, beliefs, and personalities reinforce the message that each and every one is unique, endowed not only with inalienable rights but also a God-given talent of some sort. Every one faces a variety of challenges and undergoes forging on the hearth of experience. It becomes so clear that every one has an interesting story to tell.

As one interacts with this constantly changing parade of diverse people it becomes more evident that it takes an exceptional talent to inspire and move people in a certain direction, to inform, educate, and instill a sense of trust necessary to lead successfully towards the greatest good for the greatest number.

Among the most cherished of traits that emerges from this symbiotic relationship between leaders and the led, that grows between good friends sharing similar values and goals, is that of loyalty. The ability to garner loyalty lasting a lifetime from folks who posited their faith and trust is the only explanation for Andrus' unique grip on the Idaho electorate spanning generations.

Even after having been out of office twenty years he remains well-liked. For many, when one says "the Governor," there's only one person who comes to mind.

A beneficial aspect from writing the book on my experiences having worked with and for Governor Andrus over 40 years was and still is the incredible number of people who come up to me with their own Andrus story. The stories are always heart-warming, often reflecting occasions when the Governor helped someone solve a problem or face a challenge.

A common theme is, "Cece helped me or a family member." Or, "Cece is a problem-solver, and he even remembers my name (So true – the best I've ever seen – and he never forgets a face; sometimes a name but never a face.)."

Andrus is one of those rare people who in the phrase of the poet, Rudyard Kipling, can walk with kings but not lose the common touch. He knows every man puts on his pants one leg at a time. He knows we all are a mixture of good and bad, that sometimes the noble side of our nature leads to extraordinary sacrifice while at other times the egotistical side can lead to incredibly self-serving rationalizations for immoral conduct that reflects the greedy, selfish side of our nature.

From him I have learned not to be hasty in my judgments, to learn what drives a person, to recognize the yin/yang of everyone, to cherish and guard the rare relationship and privilege of true friendship, to value loyalty, and to walk humbly before my fellow man and my Creator.

Loyalty is the value ranked highest by Andrus. He reciprocates that loyalty also. Some say his tendency to fire a "direct hire" that has surprised him by letting bad news appear in the media before telling him is not the hallmark of reverse loyalty. I would argue otherwise: To not tell him "bad news" before it hit the press or to make a mistake and then try to shift blame or worse, lie about it, were to him breaches of loyalty an executive could not and should not tolerate.

Andrus is the first to tell anyone his success is due to these hundreds of people who dedicated time, talent, and treasure to put him into high office and to help keep him there. He is especially generous in dishing out praise to the fine staffs he assembled during both his first and second stints as governor as well as his four years as interior secretary.

That is true, but his eye for talent, his ability to mentor and help subordinates grow, were just a few of his many unseen and largely unappreciated talents.

He inspired a loyal following across the general public as well as across his administrations – the agency heads comprising the cabinet as well as the personal staff and the hard working public employees in state government including teachers.

He engendered trust and respect not only because he was a great problem-solver, but because he respected voters and their right to set direction and policy as well as remove one's crown.

At the risk of leaving worthy people off an arbitrary and completely subjective list, I have drawn up a list of a few of the hundreds who labored in relative anonymity for the good, great former governor and interior secretary. These are people I knew and the impressions are mine. There are easily several hundred more names I could add. I mean no disrespect nor do I wish to appear to diminish equally wonderful contributions by the unmentioned and loyal many.

In selecting these folks in no particular order I hope to provide insight into the diverse individuals who came together to work for the state or the nation because of the extraordinary leader Andrus was. These brief sketches should provide insight into the man I know was the greatest governor the state ever produced or will ever produce.

I often think about the obscure, rarely noticed, anonymous, unsung heroes, such as the Basque grounds-keeping employee who tended the Capitol flowers and went by the nickname of "Friday." His name was **Severiano Legarrata**. His Basque friends called him "Fraile" and we non-Basque types thought they were calling him "Friday," and so that's how we addressed him. He could barely speak English, but Andrus would often stop and chat with him for five minutes about the flowers when arriving at the office early on weekday mornings.

The look of "pride" in Friday's eyes at the governor stopping to admire his handiwork was heart-warming. Somehow one instantly knew that Friday would charge through a brick wall if the governor asked him, especially after Andrus saved his job.

In the first few months of the first year of the first Andrus administration the governor noted the good work Friday was performing nurturing and caring for the Capitol grounds and in particular the flower beds. On several occasions he would stop to chat with Friday who candidly did not speak very much English.

Somehow, and Cece always had amazing traplines into all of the state agencies, Andrus learned that Friday was slated to be fired primarily it seemed to Cece not because of poor work habits – to the contrary he was a hard and excellent worker by all accounts – but because of his inability to communicate in English very well.

Andrus summoned Friday's supervisor to his office. Behind a closed door he told the supervisor that he did indeed have the authority to fire Friday. However, Andrus explained he had the authority to fire the supervisor. If Friday was fired, then Andrus told the supervisor to be ready to follow Friday out the door because he would be fired also.

The supervisor explained quickly he understood the message and that neither of them would be going out the door.

A few years later an event was held on the Capitol steps for the visiting president of the Basque homeland. Andrus spotted Friday in the crowd, motioned him to the front and introduced Friday to the Basque president. Andrus watched with pride and pleasure as the two conversed in Basque for a few minutes. He made Friday's day, but Friday also made Cece's day.

Friday also gave a very special gift to Idaho that few know about. Among his "charges" he was nurturing a sapling that came from the Basque city of Guernica, the bombing of which by the Germans before World War II was immortalized in the famous painting by Picasso.

One night the Capitol grounds were vandalized and the "Tree of Guernica" damaged beyond salvaging. It was replaced quietly by another sapling from Guernica that Friday had at his home. During the Capitol remodeling it was moved over and placed next to the Pete Cenarrusa Building where the mature tree stands today.

Personally, I had a soft spot for **John Thomas** who worked in the ground floor coffee shop of the Capitol. Johnny had MS, or a similar affliction, which caused him to walk and talk a bit differently. It seemed his nose was constantly running and often his shirt-tail was sticking out.

John Thomas loved Cecil Andrus and he loved politics. He listened constantly to the radio and often he would hear something on the news and would fly up the stairs and down the marble corridor into my office to make sure I'd heard it. Nine times out of ten, I hadn't; and, I was always grateful he wanted to make sure I was on top of breaking news.

More than once his "breaking news" message allowed me to give due deliberation to preparing a response from the governor once the media wanted his reaction. This was back in the days when there was no internet, no 24-hour news cycle, no YouTube and clips going viral in a matter of seconds.

Being on top of the news was damned important, and I'll forever be grateful to John Thomas for helping me to stay informed. He also picked up an amazing amount of gossip while standing behind the counter or wiping off tables. People constantly misjudged him, thinking he was some sort of mentally handicapped person who wouldn't begin to understand what they were saying. They were so wrong. Beneath the exterior was one sharp, absorptive mind. Too many folks judged the book by the cover.

So they would say the stupidest, self-incriminating things while talking about their strategies and the legislators they were working – all of which John would dutifully report to me. More often than not I would then stroll into the governor's office and let drop the pearl of information Johnny had overheard. Sometimes I would even give him credit.

Jean Taylor was the liberal conscience of the Andrus staff in the early 70s. The wife of a distinguished Nampa physician, she was the chief scheduler and often the first voice one would hear when calling the office as she also had charge of the front desk. Unabashedly liberal, she often would remind the many Catholic men on the personal staff that women were to be treated as equals and we were all there to serve the public, especially the poor and disenfranchised.

She especially appreciated that Andrus not only was often the first person in the office, he also would make the first pot of coffee for the incoming crew. This leading by example was Andrus' way of saying there was to be no stereotyping by roles. When Andrus had his legislative liaison run the Equal Rights Amendment up in the waning hours of the anxious-to-depart 1973 Legislature, and it passed by voice vote, his stock rose even higher with all the female staff.

Pat Vaughan was one of the best departmental liaisons Andrus had. It was the Andrus style of managing to have a small executive staff with approximately ten people reporting directly to him at the Monday morning staff meeting. Five were in charge of keeping track of several agencies and carrying Andrus' instructions when he was unable to do so. Make no mistake, Andrus was an extremely hands-on manager but he still needed staff to filter the important from the less important.

The other five direct reports were the chief of staff, the deputy chief of staff, the press secretary, the legal counsel, and his personal secretary. One thing Andrus never did in assembling his staff was inquire as to one's religious affiliation. As a result, by pure chance nine of the ten were bead-carrying Roman Catholics, and the tenth, his personal secretary, Zuriel Brown, was LDS.

Andrus started jokingly referring to the "chain gang" coming to work in the morning because of all the Rosaries jangling in pockets. In a gesture much appreciated by all the "mackerel snappers" on his staff, Andrus brought back with him Rosaries blessed by Pope Paul VI, after a visit with the Pontiff while returning from a trade mission to Iran.

He later said the two most impressive men he ever met during his entire career in politics were Egyptian President Anwar Sadat and His Holiness, Paul VI.

Vaughan was one of the Catholic mafia with an absolutely unflappable manner sprinkled with a great sense of humor. A devoted family man, he and his wife, Cecelia, were proud of their daughters as well as their son, Pat. Jr. He won an appointment to the military academy, graduated with honors but did not make it career. Pat, Jr. today is the Latah County assessor.

Joe Nagel was another one of the talented liaisons. Andrus though installed him as head of two different agencies – Health and Welfare during his first stint as governor; and, during his second, as head of Environmental Quality. Incredibly sharp, he had a knack for solving thorny issues and Andrus developed great respect for his administrative skills. A low-key manner and a sense of humor served him well also.

A native of Chicago who studied for the priesthood, he came west with his teacher spouse and started public service in one of the health and welfare agencies serving the poor. He rose quickly, for as Andrus liked to say, in Idaho cream rises to the top quickly.

Andrus added to Nagel's duties that of emissary to the National Governor's Association and his personal staff for the NGA while he served as chairman. When Andrus went to Interior, he gave Nagel the important portfolio of liaison with all the nation's governors. Whether Republican or Democrat, every governor Nagel dealt with felt they were heard and treated fairly.

While Andrus had many fine and capable administrators running the various departments during his terms as governor, when pressed for who was the best of the best, he would always cite Nagel and **Yvonne Ferrell**, who during Andrus' second stint as governor took over a moribund Department of Parks and transformed it into a dynamic, well-run, highly professional agency. Yvonne was instrumental in completing the state's acquisition and appropriate development of the Harriman State Park.

Zuriel Brown was Andrus' personal secretary during his first six years as governor. As the only Mormon on his personal staff, she made sure we all were aware of the importance of the LDS on the Idaho political landscape. She was perhaps the best "forger" of the Andrus signature before the advent of the "sig-mac" machine. Her skills were employed when the governor had a mass mailing to send out. Knowing that most folks could tell the difference between a real signature and an artificial one, he had the office always strive to send letters out of the office bearing a real signature.

R.J. Bruning, was a veteran newspaper editor and publisher from Wallace who put out the *North Idaho Press*. An expert on mining and mining law, he was close to Harry Magnuson, one of the most influential people in north Idaho by virtue of his extensive real estate holdings, banks, and newspapers he owned, as well as stock holdings in various mining ventures. Bruning was a Republican who supported Don Samuelson and editorialized against Andrus because of his opposition to Asarco's proposed mine at the base of Castle Peak.

Andrus shrewdly brought him onto the staff because of his "gray hair" to off-balance the numerous "kids" on the staff. Besides agency liaison work he became a traveling ambassador for the governor, constantly driving around the state to speak at Rotary and Kiwanis clubs about the governor's programs. A chain-smoking, hard working, aggressive advocate with a great sense of humor, he was another of the Shoshone County and Catholic mafia surrounding the governor.

He also went to D.C. with the new Interior secretary to do invaluable work as a deputy assistant secretary for Energy and Minerals. He and his wife, Florence, were the parents of John Bruning, a former member of the Coeur d'Alene City Council and a founding member of the Kootenai Environmental Alliance as well as a strong supporter of the governor.

Bill Murphy was a former member of the Idaho House from Shoshone County and an accountant by training. Murphy first joined the Andrus team as legislative liaison and then became one of several chiefs of staff. Another member of the "gray hair" set, and another Catholic, Murphy bore a quiet demeanor and spoke softly. He clashed often with John Hough and me on various policy and communication matters, but he commanded our respect.

When Andrus was tapped as Interior secretary, Lt. Governor John Evans, upon his elevation to the governorship, selected Murphy to be his lieutenant governor. However, when he sought election to a full four-year term in 1978 Murphy was defeated by future Republican governor Phil Batt.

John Hough was the Andrus campaign press secretary in 1970 and then Andrus' first press secretary after his successful election as governor. A graduate of Gonzaga University and a former television news director at KLEW-TV in Lewiston, Hough was one of Andrus' most talented staff members. Full of creative ideas for keeping Andrus' profile high with the media, he also clashed frequently with several of the veteran reporters covering the Statehouse.

He was becoming more interested in natural resource policy, however. Andrus, sensing that Hough's too frequent clashes with the media was soon going to be counter-productive, moved John to the administrative side of the office to be deputy chief of staff and his natural resources advisor. To Hough's credit he first suggested that he move out of the press role and that I be approached about taking the position.

Hough then played a key role in advising Andrus on numerous issues from creation of the Birds of Prey to the Hells Canyon and Sawtooth national recreation areas, to wild and scenic river status for the St. Joe, to protecting Chamberlain Basin from logging, to orchestrating the governor's opposition to Idaho Power's proposed coal-fired Pioneer Power plant. He became Andrus' last chief of staff before the move to Interior, and chose, rather than to go to D.C. as chief of staff at the Interior Department, to remain in the West as the Western Field Director.

After three years in that post Hough went to the private sector as the government affairs director for multi-national corporate giant IT&T. Now semi-retired and living on Bainbridge Island, he remains close to the governor and they usually spend a week fishing together for salmon in Puget Sound each summer. John's wife, Ellen, is close to Carol Andrus with whom she has played bridge for many years.

While Andrus always had competent chiefs of staff, the best of the best was **Marc Johnson**, a native of Nebraska and a graduate of South Dakota State's fine journalism program. Johnson first came to Idaho as a television reporter for KBCI-TV having been hired in 1972 by the then news director, Lamar Crosby. Arriving on the day that Lamar was fired, he found himself working for Pauli Crooke, a challenging experience to say the least.

Gravitating to policy and political issues, Johnson found himself working for Idaho's public television network and hosting during the legislative session a daily "Statehouse Reports" while also doing some freelance writing. Andrus spotted him early and when he mounted his return to office campaign in 1985 tapped Johnson to be his campaign press secretary.

After the return to office Johnson became the press secretary who because of his native smarts and competence developed an expanding portfolio within the office. He ghosted many of Andrus' speeches and was elevated to chief of staff in the fourth Andrus term where he performed superbly.

A natural historian, his perspective always served Andrus well not the least of which in his insistence that Andrus carefully read H.B. 625, the heartless, anti-abortion bill passed by the Idaho legislature. Andrus, though pro-life, saw what Johnson wanted him to see and courageously vetoed the politically written bill.

Johnson moved to the Boise office of The Gallatin Group in the last year of the last term. His experience and wise counsel soon saw him prospering as a consultant of the regional public affairs firm that he also served as president of for a few years. He was instrumental in helping Andrus set up the Andrus Center for Public Policy as an important way of preserving and protecting the Andrus legacy. Today he is semi-retired and working on a biography of Montana Senator Burton K. Wheeler. He still serves as president of the Andrus Center. He and his wife, Dr. Pat Johnson, a former top executive at Boise's St. Luke's Hospital, reside in Oregon during the summer and Tucson during the winter, but still stay close to Andrus and to Idaho affairs.

Andrus not surprisingly had a knack for attracting and keeping talented office secretaries who processed the mail in and out in a timely manner, always answered the phone by the second ring with a cheerful voice, and helped the staff assistants and departmental liaisons resolve the numerous requests and problems that pour into a gubernatorial office. They saw that the critically important "thank you's" were sent to anyone who extended courtesies to the governor and kept a steady stream of congratulatory notes going out to Idahoans with noteworthy achievements gleaned from the daily and weekly newspapers that were constantly scanned as well.

They ensured a steady flow of communication materials, background white papers, press releases, question and answer sheets, weekly columns from the governor that went to the state's weekly newspapers and information packets as well as tapes that were sent to radio stations. Andrus' office was among the first to send "b-roll film" to television stations for background usage.

Among this pool of talented folks were **Marilyn Crutcher, Wanda Kaye, Vera Noyce** and **Phyllis Lord** to whom I was particularly indebted for her smooth handling of my voluminous correspondence and her diligence in making sure I always got back to members of the press within the same day that they called. Phyllis and husband, Robert, also were stalwart volunteer workers in all of Andrus' campaigns, as was their son, Steve, and daughter-in-law, Julie, during Andrus' second stint at governor.

Billie Jepsen was the governor's extraordinarily competent executive secretary, chief scheduler and guardian of the gate when Andrus was Secretary of the Interior. She zealously guarded Andrus' private time. Her job was made easier by the fact that Andrus did not play the D.C. game of having his secretary call someone else' secretary and then see who understood the pecking order and would come on the phone first. Andrus placed almost all of his own calls.

Clareene Wharry was another extraordinarily talented executive secretary, scheduler and jack-of-all-trades for Andrus in his post-gubernatorial life. For years she was the heart and soul of the Andrus Center for Public Policy, single-handedly taking care of the myriad of details relating to agendas, speakers, dinners, and press interviews for the numerous conferences sponsored by the Center. She also oversaw the books and assisted with the continual fund-raising in order to keep the Center up and running.

The Andrus Center is now housed at Boise State with constitutional scholar **David Adler** serving as the executive director and the Cecil D. Andrus Professor of Public Policy.

Gary Catron was another key staff liaison for Andrus. A former teacher, previously he was a top aide to Senator Len B. Jordan. A native of Payette (and therefore a big fan of Minnesota Twins slugger Harmon Killebrew, also from Payette) and a Stanford graduate, Andrus tapped Catron to run his legislative liaison office while at Interior. That Andrus got along so well with members of Congress is in no small degree due to the skills with which they were handled by Catron and his team.

There is an item in the archives of the weekly newspaper published for years in Payette that still brings a smile to my face. Catron, the then student body president at Payette High School, is commending his fellow students for having the wisdom to vote in favor of dropping the word "comrade" from the high school's fight song.

Idaho's rabid, right wing Republican senator, "Little Joe from Idaho" as Herman Welker was called, must have smiled since Payette was his home town.

Darrel V. Manning and **Wayne Mittleider** were two of the governor's best "can do" trouble shooters, though one was more of an out front person while the other operated more behind the scenes. Manning, a former legislator from Pocatello, had served in the House while Andrus was in the Senate. Once Andrus was governor, he made Manning his Director of Aeronautics before moving him up to the critical post of Director of the State Department of Transportation. Manning not only served Andrus well, he has served each of the succeeding governors well also. He retired on December 31st, 2011, to much deserved acclaim.

Mittleider handled some of the more delicate personal and social tasks the governor needed help with. These ranged from advancing the governor's highly successful trade mission to Iran, to seeing that Andrus' family safely was moved across the country to Washington, D.C., to organizing and running the highly acclaimed Governor's Cup at Sun Valley and Elkhorn. This program, begun by Andrus, has raised hundreds of thousands of dollars from various contributing corporations for scholarship money to help keep Idaho's best and brightest going to college in-state.

Mittleider and his wife, Patty, also provided key assistance to Harmon Killebrew in putting together the annual Danny Thompson Memorial Cup at Sun Valley to raise funds to fight the form of cancer that took Thompson's life. Besides handling these delicate tasks he also ran the Department of Administration's communications bureau for a time and additionally was the executive director of the Idaho Housing Financing Authority for a number of years. He is one of a handful of "surrogate sons" the governor has adopted along the way.

The day Andrus hired **Jim Bax** away from the U.S. Department of Health and Welfare, where he was an Assistant Secretary, to run the Idaho Department of Health and Welfare, he knew the time would come when he would have to fire him. Bax knew it also. He was brought in to reorganize an agency in sore need of streamlining. A talented administrator, he was one of those personalities who love the limelight, enjoy sparring with the media and eventually become controversial and the kind of lighting rod no governor can keep. He made things interesting, garnered an incredible amount of federal funds for Idaho's department because of his knowledge and contacts in D.C., and was entertaining along the way. He and Andrus remain friends to this day.

Andrus replaced Bax after three years of increasing controversy with the calm demeanor and steady hand of Joe Nagel. To this day Bax will tell anyone who asks that of the 100 some governors he has worked for directly or as a consultant, including Arkansas' Bill Clinton, Andrus is hands down the best he ever was associated with.

Brad Stoddard is one of the few folks from Andrus' second stint as governor that I am listing, in part because I discovered him while he was working for Andrus' comeback campaign as the Kootenai County chairman in 1986. As 1990 drew near with Andrus' permission I recruited Stoddard to temporarily abandon his law firm partnership with former Kootenai County State Senator Jay Ray Cox, uproot his wife and sons and move to Boise to run the 1990 statewide Andrus gubernatorial campaign. He did so without complaint and did a masterful job of running the governor's last campaign, a run away win over state Senator Roger Fairchild almost as big as the historic victory in 1974 over Jack Murphy.

Stoddard then returned to the practice of law in Coeur d'Alene and has become a successful, sought-after attorney and an expert on workman's compensation law. He and spouse Catrin have raised three fine sons. He has eschewed involvement in politics ever since Andrus left office, saying that he worked for the best and has had no interest in working for anyone less than the best.

Merle Parsley and his wife, Judi, will always hold a special place in the governor's heart. A school teacher and a Kennedy Democrat active in his youth in the almost non-existent North Dakota Democratic Party, he was a member of the Idaho House for one term (1965-1966) and then ran for and won the Bonner County Senate seat vacated by Don Samuelson in 1966 in his successful quest for the governorship. Parsley served in the Senate for one term, 1966 to 1968.

An incredible bundle of energy, and an irrepressible sense of humor, quick with a quip, one of those people with a constant God-given twinkle in his eye, to know him was to love him. He was an early supporter of Andrus' 1970 quest and held several positions in state government during the 24 years the D's held the chair, the last of which was heading up the State Insurance Fund.

He and Andrus would hunt together and occasionally fish together, and the banter between them was marvelous to listen in on. Andrus would recall staying with Merle while campaigning in 1970, and that the log home's guest bedroom he was put in had cracks between the logs two inches wide which let the cold wind whistle through and practically freeze him.

Merle would cackle and then get off a line about how he was glad to now be living in Hope (Idaho) but he expected to die in Hell (yes, there is an unofficial bump on an Idaho road called Hell, Idaho!). When campaign time rolled around, we would assign a sizable moving truck to Merle, jam it full of yard signs and larger campaign signs, and send him off to drive north on Highway 95, the main route connecting north Idaho with south Idaho.

A week or two later anyone driving north would think there wasn't a farmer or homeowner along 95 that didn't support Andrus. Merle had a way of getting even the black-hearted Republicans to put up Andrus signs in their fields abutting 95.

Catholic to the core, Judi and he, with nine kids they were extremely proud of, obviously practiced "Vatican roulette." On occasion this led to the Governor asking Mrs. Parsley if she would like him to take care of her apparently insatiable husband. He of course was also Irish, could be wonderfully sentimental at times, and on occasion temperamental and subject to a bout of depression.

Loving him like a brother, the governor had to "reel him back in" a time or two, as did I. We both dearly miss him.

Two key counties that always delivered for the governor were Bannock and Nez Perce, the latter of which Andrus represented in the state senate for one term before his election as governor. Each town had a hard core coterie of folks who always worked tirelessly for Andrus' election and remain to this day precious friends though unfortunately too many have already departed this good earth.

Topping the list in Pocatello were **Chick** and **Diane Bilyeu**, who between them held the State Senate seat for almost 30 years. When not serving at the legislature, Chick, who passed away in 2007, was a speech professor at Idaho State and Diane served in several elected county positions. Idaho State's outside legal counsel, **Herman McDevitt**, brother to former Supreme Court Justice Chuck McDevitt, was another Andrus stalwart and advisor who the governor talked to frequently and always called upon when in Pocatello. An avid hunter he often weighed in on various state fish and game matters. He too passed away prematurely a few years back.

Bannock County long-time labor leader **Bob Lenaghen** always helped to deliver union endorsements for Andrus and served his administrations in several capacities including the Public Utilities Commission; his last post was executive director of Idaho's NWPPC office. Pocatello banker **Bob Montgomery** served as treasurer and chief fund-raiser for several of the Andrus gubernatorial runs. Persistent and tough, few could say no to his requests for donations. No list would be complete without mentioning the dedicated support of **Ian** and **Charlene Martindale**, as well as super campaign field worker **Steve Lee** who has probably worked in almost every Andrus campaign regardless of where he was living at the time.

Joining this core group of Bannock County supporters during Andrus' second stint was County Commissioner **Tom Katsilometes** and his wife, **Bessie**.

Topping the list of stalwarts from Nez Perce County was teacher, coach and former state Representative **Ed Williams** who became Andrus' first chief of staff. Tragically, as mentioned in Chapter 1, he drowned in a boating accident in Hells Canyon in 1973. Andrus loved him like a brother and still stays in touch with Ed's widow, Bobbi, and their children.

The heart and soul of almost all of Andrus' campaigns in the "north country" was long-time state Senator **Mike Mitchell**, who owned a successful Coors Beer distributorship. He later served as another Andrus chief of staff. He and his wife Arlene are two of Cece and Carol's closest friends.

Lewiston Tribune publisher emeritus **Butch Alford** is another confidante and close advisor over the years, as was the late **Harry Wall**, a Democratic national committeeman for years, and **Wynne Blake**, an outside counselor to Potlatch Corporation. My Columbia classmate from the class of 1968, **John Tait**, also worked tirelessly for the governor and other Democratic candidates, as did the **Paffile brothers, Don** and **Sonny**.

Another core group of supporters came out of Latah County: radio station owner and state Senator **John Mix**; University of Idaho professor of government and Andrus' first budget director, **Syd Duncombe**; **Gordon Law**, a communications instructor and the godfather of Idaho public television; County Commissioner **Vera White**; and, motel owners **Jap** and **Lillian Inscore**.

Special mention should be made of **Marty Peterson**, a former member of Senator Frank Church's staff who came back to Idaho to help in Andrus' 1970 campaign. He served Andrus ably and well in a number of capacities including working in the budget office and assisting with the Capital for a Day program. He capped his time with Andrus when the governor selected him to undertake the difficult task of organizing the Idaho Centennial of Statehood in 1990. Working with Centennial Commission chairman, Wallace millionaire and investor, **Harry F. Magnuson**, the two pulled off an incredibly successful Centennial that all Idahoans took justifiable pride in.

Marty has also been the executive director of the Association of Idaho Counties, the long-time vice president for government affairs for the University of Idaho and as of this writing is the executive director of the James A. and Louise McClure Public Policy Institute at the University of Idaho.

There is an old saying derived from a slight mis-stating of the Biblical verse to the effect that a prophet is not honored in his own land. The message generally is taken to mean that one's neighbors know one best and those that really know and live with the few that are elevated generally don't have a lot of good things to say. Familiarity can often breed contempt, not to mention envy.

Judging from election results out of Clearwater County, such was not the case with Cecil Andrus. In the 1966 Democratic primary for governor he tallied 1,187 votes to Charles Herndon's 317 votes and Bill Dee's 275 votes. In the 1966 general election he tallied 1,833 votes to Don Samuelson's 574, Perry Swisher's 264 and Phil Jungert's 275.

Four years later in the 1970 Democratic gubernatorial primary he tallied 1,130 votes to Vern Ravenscroft's 471 and Lloyd Walker's 112 votes. In the general election in 1970 he swamped Samuelson in Clearwater County with 2,299 votes to Samuelson's 636 votes. In contrast, Samuelson just narrowly won his home county of Bonner, garnering 3,181 votes to Andrus' 3,099.

In the record-breaking election of 1974 Andrus carried Clearwater County with 2,348 votes to Jack Murphy's 294. In the comeback election of 1986 even though Andrus had not lived in Clearwater County since 1966 the folks still considered him the hometown boy and he garnered 2,514 votes to David Leroy's 980.

In his final race for the governorship in 1990 he carried the old home county with 2,175 votes to Roger Fairchild's 726. Clearly this prophet was honored in his home land.

Besides his neighbors knowing and liking Cece, he forged life-long partnerships with folks who remained his friends through the proverbial "thick and thin," folks like the **Ponozzo brothers, Les** and **Don**, State Senator **Marguerite McLaughlin** and her husband, **Bruce**, **Bill Crutcher's family**, the **Bennett brothers, Dick** and **Frank**, lumber mill owner **Don Konkol**, and **Bill** and **Bo Shields**, to name just a few.

Another gratifying aspect of these solid relationships was the multi-generational aspect – the children of many of his friends were captivated by the same charisma that captured their parents. Two excellent examples are Idaho Public Television's Joan Cartan and former state Senator Jim Hansen.

Joan is the daughter of long-time friend and key Idaho Falls worker **Gloria Cartan** and Jim is the son of former Second District Congressman **Orval Hansen.**

Moving to Boise in 1970 opened up a vast array of additional folks in the Treasure Valley who while they may not have known Andrus personally had still voted for him after the embarrassing four years of Don Samuelson. Once these folks met and saw him a legion of new loyalists joined the Andrus fan club.

A few of the many included **Carol Humphries, Skip Oppenheimer, Doug Oppenheimer, Art** and **Jane Oppenheimer, Joe Albertson, Joe Scott, State Senator H. Dean Summers, Jim Bruce, Bob Krueger, Georgia Davidson, Roy** and **Al Eiguren, Carl** and **Gisela Burke, Dick Cade, Joe Welch, Neil Sampson, Bob Wise, David Alvord, Dave Frazier, Sal Celeski, Keith Higginson, Wally Hedrick** (one of several surrogate sons), **J.R. Simplot, Ralph Comstock, Bob McFarland, Jimmy Kerns, Myrna Sasser, Betty Richardson, Pat Ford, Rick Johnson, Conley Ward, Jeff Fereday, Ken** and **Marsha Pursley, Larry** and **Chris LaRocco, George Klein, Dr. John Marks, Tim Olson, Suzie Budge,** and **Matt Mullaney.**

I'll leave it to my former Gallatin Group colleague, Marc Johnson, to draw up a similar list of those who were instrumental to the success of Andrus' second stint as governor. As both the press secretary and then the chief of staff he can much better characterize and capture the core group then – folks like **Clancy Standridge, Alice Koskella, Kevin Fenderson, Andy Brunelle, John Carter, Julie Cheever, Scott Peyron, Pam Parks, Jody Taylor, and Chuck Moss.**

Then of course Andrus had an exceptional team helping him while serving as the Secretary of the Interior in the Administration of Jimmy Carter. An old friend from Shoshone County, **Leo Krultiz**, became the solicitor for the department, Andrus having drafted Krulitz away from the Cummins Engine Company. From that same firm Andrus also quietly wooed away **Jim Joseph** to become his number #2, the Under Secretary of the Interior. From the pool of talented Georgians he recruited **Chuck Parrish** to serve as chief of staff. **Jay Hakes** and **Holly Miller** were two other key Georgians that mingled well with the Andrus mafia from Idaho.

Barbara Heller was brought in to oversee and make some modest but environmentally more protective changes to Interior's off-shore leasing program. To head up his special office on Alaska lands Andrus recruited **Cynthia Wilson** and then put former Idaho Statesman reporter **Gerry Gilliland** in the department's Alaska office.

When Parrish departed Andrus brought in **Steve Freudenthal** from Wyoming, the brother of future Wyoming Governor Dave Freudenthal. Key Interior assistant secretaries were Alaskan **Guy Martin** for Land and Water, **Bob Herbst** for Fish, Wildlife and Parks and **Joan Davenport** at Energy and Minerals. In the key position of Assistant Secretary for Policy, Budget, and Administration, Andrus put long trusted aide **Larry Meierotto.**

Two key deputies without whom I would not have been nearly as successful were **Harmon Kallman**, my deputy in the Office of Public Affairs and **Dave McCraney,** my deputy when I served as the Western Field director.

As Andrus so nicely said in his political biography written with the help of Seattle *Post-Intelligencer* columnist Joel Connelly:

"There are hundreds of others. Each has a special place in my heart, the kind of place possible only when people share great affection and common purpose. I've often said the very best thing about a life in politics, and this may be particularly true in the West, are lifelong friendships."

I started this chapter with a quote from John Milton. Let me close with a quote from one of John Donne's (1573 to 1631) most famous writings, taken from one of his devotionals, Meditation 17:

"No man is an island/Each is a piece of the continent/A part of the main./If a clod be washed away by the sea/Europe is the less./ As well as if a promontory were/As well as if a manor of thine own/Or of thine friend's were./Each man's death diminishes me/ For I am involved in mankind./Therefore send not to know/For whom the bell tolls/It tolls for thee."

This is oh so true for someone like Governor Andrus or me. Trying to grow old gracefully and handling the challenges of aging is tough enough without the almost weekly news and ensuing sorrow that another fellow rider on the trail has passed on to the Big Roundup. A piece of our heart goes with them.

Many of those listed above have already taken on the last journey. We could attend a funeral a week, for the downside of knowing so many is indeed losing so many. It is understandable we have both become more discriminating out of the simple necessity to provide our own hearts a modicum of protection.

I know though that I am just that much better for having known and worked with so many. Most feel like I do – truly privileged to have had a bit part in the on-going play that is Idaho and to have supported its greatest governor to date in his starring role.

Governor Andrus and I both share a strong belief in an Afterlife, and we both believe in what our respective churches call "the communion of Saints." And we both hope part of the heavenly reward is the joy in "seeing" again so many who gave so much to assist the good, great governor in moving our beloved state forward.

13 ■ "I could not stop for Death . . ."

Brad Stoddard (left) and Chris Carlson at a favorite camping site in Hells Canyon. Photo by Marcia Carlson.

Most people will not recognize the opening line of Emily Dickinson's famous poem because most people, like the voice in the poem, do not like to think about the end of their life. Despite death being all over the news, for most it is something that happens to other folks and many go on acting like they will live forever.

Funeral directors with their pre-planning services are still amazed at how many do not plan, leaving a grieving spouse and family to try to divine what the deceased would have wanted.

With the first wave of baby boomers starting to hit retirement age, however, many families are starting to have to deal with the many difficult questions regarding aging parents who have prolonged their lives far beyond the average life span of *their* parents, in part by taking full advantage of incredible strides in modern medicine that unfortunately have increased the cost of medical care incredibly.

As a bead-carrying Roman Catholic I have tried to deal intelligently, humanely, and compassionately with what my Church emphasizes: the sanctity of life from conception to natural death. But does life begin at conception or is it rather at the point of fetal viability and the ability of the child in the womb to survive outside of the womb?

And shouldn't there be exceptions for rape, incest, and life of the mother, especially in the first 16 weeks? After that, though, except where it is an issue of the mother's life, isn't abortion clearly infanticide?

And just what is natural death? I support the concept and fought vigorously against the state of Washington adopting a physician-assisted suicide law, but a solid majority of Washingtonians voted for it.

During the campaign though I heard from many people for whom a relative's pain was unbearable to watch, let alone to be the one suffering. Yes, palliative care can supposedly take care of all the pain, but many don't like the idea of being so doped up they leave this life unaware they are leaving. Clearly, too, many people simply could not afford the drugs to ease the pain.

I also picked up a series of stories where a compassionate hospice nurse might have given an extra heavy dose of morphine which put an end perhaps prematurely to one who was within days of dying anyway. But isn't that murder and an example of someone playing God?

Some people would look you in the eye and simply say: "Ask me no questions and I'll tell you no lies."

None of these questions are really new, but someone brave enough to tackle them publicly is rare. Yet Idaho's Senator Frank Church took both the beginning of life and the end of life issues head on. Using the pulpit of his chairmanship of the Committee on Aging , he did the groundwork that led directly to getting Medicare and Medicaid expanded to cover the costs of hospice.

Millions of Americans will forever be grateful to him.

In the summer of 1972, Idaho, like much of the rest of the nation, was beginning to focus on the issue of liberalizing laws governing abortion. Idaho, like many states, banned abortion except in instances where it was necessary to save the life of the mother, or the pregnancy resulted from rape or incest.

There was no "pro-life" movement yet. The Catholic families around Greencreek (in Idaho County)--the Uhlencotts, the Wassmuths, the Nuxolls – were not yet galvanized, nor organized. At the time the thrust of the law clearly leaned towards recognizing the fetus in the womb was, if not a person yet legally, a human being waiting for the birth into the world and "personhood."

A drum beat for liberalizing had begun, though, driven largely by activists in the increasingly growing women's rights movement which felt strongly that a woman's body and its reproductive capabilities were hers alone and everyone else should get the heck away. The claim was based on a constitutional right to privacy.

Many activists in the women's movement were aware of a case called *Roe v Wade* that had been heard by the United States Supreme Court in December 1971 and was scheduled for re-hearing in October of 1972. Women in northern Idaho only had to look across the state line to Spokane for inspiration.

The inland northwest's then leading newspaper, *The Spokesman-Review*, despite a well earned reputation as the editorial mouthpiece for all things conservative, was surprisingly supportive of abortion rights and had applauded a liberalizing state statute in Washington. The paradox was easily explained if one was familiar with Allison Cowles, the late wife of William H. "Bill" Cowles III, the then young heir to the throne of the Cowles family's extensive publishing empire.

Thus it came as no surprise that a plank was added to the state Democratic platform when Idaho's Democrats held their June 1972 state convention in Sun Valley. Knowing this was going to be, at least in the short term, a divisive issue, from my desk at the A. Robert Smith News Bureau in Washington D.C., I called Idaho Governor Cecil D. Andrus to set up an interview while Andrus was in the nation's capitol for an upcoming Federation of Rocky Mountain States meeting.

I also placed a call to Cleve Corlett, press secretary to the senior senator from Idaho, Frank Church, and asked to talk with the senator about his position on the plank. I had every reason to expect to talk as usual directly to the Senator, for not only did the *Lewiston Morning Tribune* and the *Idaho State Journal* carry my weekly offerings from D.C., so did three other newspapers in southern Idaho.

Much to my surprise, the senator would not talk to me and instead issued a statement to be read through Corlett. Andrus, on the other hand, sat for an interview during his visit to the nation's capitol.

The result was a column that questioned the senator's stance, captured Andrus's usual candor, and in an eerily prescient way forecast this would indeed be a divisive issue for years to come.

The column was entitled **CHURCH STRADDLES THE ABORTION PLANK** and ran on July 1, 1972, in the *Lewiston Tribune*.

Today many of Senator Church's admirers would be surprised to see that he invoked "states' rights." The key paragraph of the written statement Corlett gave me read:

"The question of abortion is in the hands of the individual state governments where I believe it should be left. Any legislative proposal affecting personal matters, such as abortion should be debated and decided by the Idaho Legislature or by direct vote of the people... The platform of the Idaho Democratic Party is directed at local statutes inasmuch as there are no generally applicable federal laws on abortion. I will oppose any attempt to legislate on this manner at the federal level"

Andrus, during his interview, repeated his long-held position against abortion on demand. However, he then touched on the issue of whether he might have to veto a liberalizing law if passed by the Idaho legislature. This, with the 20/20 hindsight of history, is ironic in that the veto he ended up casting almost 20 years later was to an incredibly restrictive proposal, the infamous H.B. 625.

That bill, drafted by those in the national pro-life movement, was designed to peel away Supreme Court Justice Sandra Day O'Conner from the 5-4 Court majority supportive of *Roe vs. Wade* with its carefully crafted language allowing abortions only in the first trimester and only for rape, incest or life of the mother. In the instance of rape under H.B. 625 a woman would have had to report it to the police within seven days of the occurrence. The proposed bill also called for harsh penalties for any doctor performing an abortion beyond its narrow definitions.

The exact quote from the July 1, 1972 column was: "*Idaho's Governor, however, would not go so far as to state he would veto any liberalized abortion bill passed by a Legislature, though the possibility does exist. He apparently believes even a Democratic controlled state legislature would not pass a liberalized abortion bill.*"

I speculated as to why the senior senator was straddling the fence. Even in 1972, Church's stance was puzzling. Initially, it led to speculation that he was quietly maneuvering to become the running mate of the presumptive presidential nominee, South Dakota Senator George McGovern.

"*His current fence straddling may be explained in Church's new status as a McGovern delegate to the Democratic Convention in Miami Beach, for his position is consistent with that expressed by McGovern. A participant in the Sun Valley convention speculated Church is fence straddling on the abortion issue because he does not wish to antagonize his fellow McGovern delegates, most of whom endorse the liberalized abortion plank.*"

The *Roe v Wade* ruling did not initially cause a split along party lines as there were prominent Republicans, such as Senator Bob Packwood of Oregon, who championed women's rights. Slowly, though, each party evolved to the point where one's views on abortion became a litmus test as to whether one was a good Democrat and supportive of the ruling or a good Republican and supportive of the ruling's repeal.

What stands out initially is Church sounding like a southern Democrat from Georgia or South Carolina and essentially saying this is a matter best left to each state to decide, not a federal issue. Invoking states rights by a liberal like Church was counterintuitive. The Supreme Court, of course, was saying that it is a federal issue, that the commerce clause is present and a woman could not be discriminated against access to abortion by one state providing it and another not.

Church then moved with alacrity following the court's ruling on *Roe v. Wade*, and quickly authored, and then guided through the Senate, the first conscience clause legislation which allowed Catholic hospitals and other religious medical providers to exempt themselves from any federal mandates with regards to abortion.

Washington Roundup
a report to the people of Idaho from:
Senator Frank Church

Washington, D.C.   April, 1973

The Senator's Chair

James Huntsman, a fifth-grade student from Gooding, was given the opportunity to try out Senator Frank Church's chair for size during a recent visit to the nation's capital. James is the son of Mr. and Mrs. James L. Huntsman of Gooding.

JOBS LOST, MILLS CLOSE

Timber Crisis Grows in Idaho

Senate Passes, 92-1, Church's Legislation To Protect LDS, Catholic Hospitals From Having to Perform Abortions

With only one dissenting vote, the Senate has approved legislation authored by Senator Frank Church to prevent the Fed-

IDAHO CALENDAR

A crisis threatens Idaho's lumber industry.

Several mills have already closed; jobs have been lost, and many more are in jeopardy, according to Senator Frank Church.

Alarmed at the impending economic consequences, Church has met with Forest Service Chief John McGuire to outline Idaho's concern. The Senator is also sponsoring legislation to help solve the prob-

Andrus has in the years since he vetoed H.B. 625 in 1990, pointed out that supporters never once talked to him or ran their draft bill by him. They mistakenly assumed he would sign whatever came before him. Once Andrus read the bill carefully, and saw that there was virtually no compassion in it, such as the previously mentioned victim of rape having to file a report with the police within seven days, he had to veto it.

The Idaho Legislature, knowing a turkey when they saw one, deliberately waited until the end of session to pass the bill and send it to Andrus. They were long gone when he nixed it. To their surprise, the bill generated a huge cross-party response. Not only did many Republican women oppose the bill, most independents did. Large marches around the Statehouse were organized, as were candlelight vigils.

Uncharacteristically, Andrus also took most of the time the law allowed before vetoing it. He saw it as a rare chance for people to better acquaint themselves with the issues from an emotional and moral standpoints. He called it one of life's "teaching moments."

The Republican Party awoke the day after the election not only looking at a tie in the state Senate, but significant Democratic gains in the House. When a less restrictive but nonetheless still intrusive bill, S.B. 1387, came up in 2012, a similar outpouring of opposition caused the Republican leadership in the house to suggest the Senate not hold a hearing on the bill. In today's "viral age," where *YouTube* and *Twitter* send items world-wide almost instantly, the bill's sponsor, Boise Senator Chuck Winder, was turned into a laughing stock for the inarticulate way he tried to explain his bill.

The passage of time has clearly not lessened passions surrounding the subject. Andrus's veto also has grown into one of the hallmarks of his four terms as governor. It made him a modern-day hero to many in the women's movement.

The irony of course is his personal views never changed. He considers himself to be a pro-life Democrat in that he opposes abortion on demand, and believes it is only justifiable before fetal viability when the mother's life is at stake or in cases of rape or incest. He recognizes, though, the inherent logic in Bill Clinton's formula that abortion ought to be safe, legal, and rare.

So why did Frank Church straddle the fence? One can take a principled stand either way. What voters do not like is the appearance of flip flopping, one of the many challenges that vexed – and probably damned – former Massachusetts Governor Mitt Romney's run for the presidency in 2012.

With the passage of time, I have concluded Church was not fence straddling out of deference to his fellow pro-choice delegates to the Democratic convention in Miami Beach. Rather, he was indeed harboring hope that the South Dakota Senator George McGovern would turn to him as a logical running mate.

Such a hope flew in the face of both being from small states and representing the same constituencies.

Not knowing for sure just exactly where McGovern would be on the then emerging issue led him in an abundance of caution to straddle the fence. He did not want to give the presumptive Democratic nominee a reason not to ask him to join the ticket.

McGovern's choice of Missouri Senator Thomas Eagleton was a disaster. Eagleton's admission that he had been treated for depression was enough, given the press-driven furor regarding mental illness, to prompt Eagleton to pull out of the race. With the advantage of hindsight, McGovern would have been far better served to have picked Church than the disastrous selection of the Missouri senator. His replacement, Sargent Shriver, was not exactly a step up, either.

Jumping now from the issues of beginning life I move to those dealing with the end.

As I referenced earlier, I chaired the 2008 campaign against Initiative-1000 in the state of Washington. I was a Spokane resident at the time having founded the region-wide public affairs firm, The Gallatin Group, and serving as the Spokane office managing partner for a number of years.

The initiative legalized with almost no safeguards one's access to Physician Assisted Suicide (PAS). It passed by a 58 percent to 42 percent margin.

"Death with Dignity" is a euphemism for the sad and tragic act of deliberately ending one's life. The renamed Hemlock Society called itself *Compassion and Choices*. No matter how one painted this pig, however, it advocates people killing themselves before their time. Thus, I was surprised to come across a clip 40 years later in which Senator Church was using the language of a group whose mission I despised.

The clip referenced a hearing Senator Church was conducting a mere six weeks after the column on abortion – the two being so close it left me wondering why he would straddle one but probe the other. The following column appeared in the *Lewiston Tribune* on August 14, 1972.

Washington- " Death With Dignity" or "Euthanasia"

Depending on one's point of view, Idaho Senator Frank Church (D) last week opened an exploratory inquiry into the public issues related to the above subject. In his opening statement before the Senate Special Committee on Aging, which he chairs, Church tacitly acknowledges that the hearings are sure to spark controversy.

Church emphasized several clarifying points. "One is that the committee has no preconceived conclusions, nor are we floating trial balloons on proposals for governmental action"

"Second, this inquiry is not a hearing on euthanasia," Church said, indicating he feels there is a great difference between 'death with dignity' and 'mercy deaths.' "This hearing has nothing to do with euthanasia."

Despite the Idaho senator's intentions, those opposed to 'death with dignity' are sure to brand the hearings with the tag 'euthanasia.'

Church also acknowledged the hearings will by their nature deal with ethical and even spiritual questions, but pointed out the committee, "must, of equal necessity, deal primarily with public issues. We will not invade issues that should remain the exclusive domain of family, clergy and physician"

The 48 year old senator reiterated, "We want to take no action that will in any way suggest that we regard any person as expendable, whether that person is one year old or one hundred years old"

Church told the committee they must face the fact that the "right to die" issue has the greatest impact on the elderly population and that chronic and terminal illness will continue to increase as the population of elderly Americans increases.

Acknowledging the function of the hearings was to define the issues involved in the controversial questions, Church nevertheless said an outline could be provided.

He said the outline should begin with the fact that at least 80 percent of the population now dies in institutions such as hospitals and nursing homes in marked contrast to the early decades of this century when most Americans died at home or in the residences of relatives.

Church pointed that to some it now appears modern medical talent sometimes crushes the dignity and comfort of a patient while working to save their life. Citing Dr. Elizabeth Kubler-Ross, author of "On Death and Dying," Church said, "Her basic point is that the patient may be treated like a thing, rather than a person. Decisions are frequently made without their opinion, even on major questions on treatment. He becomes, as the book says, an object of great concern and financial investment"

According to Senator Church, Dr. Kubler-Ross' indictment has special meaning for members of Congress because in recent years Congress has taken many actions directly related to the types of institutions available to most Americans.

As examples he cited charges that Medicare puts too much emphasis on the institutionalization of patients, thereby increasing the costs. With reference to Medicaid and reimbursement of long term care, Church said that too often the committee has been told that federal funds are used simply for minimal maintenance of chronically ill patients, when they could possibly be served by other means at lower cost.

Church said the basic fundamental question the committee would deal with was, "When is an illness truly so hopeless that no fight should be made against it?"

He pointed out the answer will vary from patient to patient, family to family, physician to physician. He said the differences of opinion sum up the sensitivity and the importance of the hearings which will now begin."

He added, "Clearly, there are no easy answers. But there should be public discussion and greater public understanding of issues related to death and dying in the United States today. Unwillingness to face such issues is probably rooted in our reluctance to think about our own mortality. But life can have more meaning if we make the end of it as worthy as the span of it. We are here today with that purpose in mind"

The committee and audience later gained an insight into the Idaho Senator's compassionate concern for "death with dignity" when he once again made reference to a fact that makes him a rare American: Frank Church was cured of cancer in 1949 while a student at Stanford.

Church displayed a remarkable sensitivity to the complexity of the issues involved and does a marvelous job of cutting off the elements at both ends of the political spectrum to underscore how important it is insured and non-insured elderly pay attention to this issue.

It is almost as if Church is playing the role of Paul Revere, urging citizens to be alert to excessive government intrusion on a massive scale into this issue. He seemed acutely aware there is a gray area where one can wade into a swamp and come close to endorsing PAS as a rational answer and certainly a potential cost saving matter. He sensed the slippery slope.

His acute sensitivity to the complexities led him to the view that the state should be kept out of this intensely personal matter and he all but said leave it to the individuals to decide with the help of family, doctors and clergy.

There's poignancy to his remarks, in particular because the senator's cancer did return and led to his premature death at age 59 in 1984. According to *Father and Son*, the wonderful book his son, Forrest, wrote, the senator as he lay dying chose not to take most of the drugs to lessen the pain. He wanted to be in full possession of his faculties at the end.

Forrest spoke and wrote eloquently on his own impending death from cancer a few years ago while serving as pastor at New York City's Riverside Cathedral. Neither father nor son made a case for doctors to ease them out of this life prematurely. Their actions at life's end speak louder than any attempt to divine where each might have come out on the issue of PAS.

Neither would the senator be surprised to see the issue arise particularly as the cost of health care has skyrocketed. Always aware of the cost side of the equation, Church knew that 60% of all the dollars spent on medical care in one's lifetime occurs in the last six months of life. This suggests, the senator pointed out, that too many people are fearful of their own mortality to really rationally address the end of life issues facing them.

Ultimately, these hearings led two years later to Church and Utah's Senator Frank Moss introducing a bill that would authorize the federal government to cover through Medicare and Medicaid the costs of hospice care (Some costs though are means-tested), much as had been outlined by Dr. Kubler-Ross in her committee testimony.

It took eight years of pounding away, but in 1982, two years after Church had left the Senate, Congress authorized that hospice care costs be covered It is an incredible legacy of Frank Church, one of which few are aware today.

Not surprisingly, the 2012 Idaho Legislature saw pro-life forces introducing and passing through the Senate a bill most doctors viewed as unnecessary according to a poll by the Idaho State Bar. The bill was designed to ensure a patient's wishes would be followed on end of life care. A foray into Idaho by *Compassion and Choice* in 2011 had been rebuffed by the conservative Idaho House.

Idaho's Legislature though slow seems to be learning not to touch some issues. The 2012 session ended without the House having taken up the Senate's invasive "ultrasound" legislation, which would have required a woman to view an ultra-sound of the child in her womb, but Pro-Life Idaho leaders indicated they would reintroduce the bill in the 2013 session. They announced this knowing the lead Senate sponsor, Chuck Winder of Boise, who was burned by negative media nationally and internationally, also was saying that before the bill was back there would be major changes to it. "Once burned, twice shy," is the expression.

The debate on life issues almost always devolves into and is framed as a "right to choose" issue. Lost in the selfishness of those who want to pass along their suffering to their loved ones by prematurely passing from this world is the irrationality of getting the state involved.

Lost also is the increased risk of elder abuse and the fact that someone else can make the choice for you in part due to almost non-existent safeguards in both the Oregon and Washington assisted suicide laws.

Among the arguments I have used against the PAS phenomena is one in which I empathize that we are all in this together, that none of us is truly a solitary island though many of us like to think we are.

Another quote some are familiar with comes from the previously mentioned (See Chapter 12) 16th century English poet, John Donne, *"No man is an island entire unto himself, but each is part of the main."* The meditation ends with a line made famous as the title to an Ernest Hemingway novel, *"There fore ask not for whom the bell tolls, it tolls for thee."*

The point is we are all part of the family of humankind and every person's death diminishes us. Because most (but not all) people think we are all in this together, we instinctively feel a breach of trust, a breaking of faith, when someone commits suicide. The person has passed their pain onto surviving family members, and we wonder, even if we're not directly related, what can bring one to feel so burdened as to take the option from which there is no recourse.

In the interest of full disclosure I have to point out my strong feelings on this subject of the suicide passing his or her pain onto their survivors derives in no small part from the suicide of my father in 1961 when I was 14. For years afterwards I can bear witness to the on-going grief, the endless pain my mother and siblings all carried in their hearts.

By nature, we strive to live, to breathe, and to be. Instinctively, we subscribe to the first law of the social compact. We come together to protect life. Most societies and cultures pass laws to keep the strong from preying on the weak, to ensure the aged, infirm, very young and the developmental and physically disabled are protected. It is true there are some still primitive nomadic cultures that will kill a baby born with a deformity or dispatch an aged and infirm elder who cannot keep up when a village has to move locations or they have to flee an enemy. They are the exception, however.

Protection of life has been a paramount value for hundreds of years. One of the hallmarks of American society is we value life for itself and do not measure it in terms of one's economic value or ability to contribute to societal productivity.

At least that is the way it has been until recently, when a pernicious movement has begun to erode that absolute value of the sanctity of life from conception to natural death.

I have found over the years that my personal story is often one of my more potent arguments.

As one diagnosed with a rare terminal cancer in November of 2005 and given six months to live by several doctors, I would have qualified under the initiative to avail myself of PAS. Instinctively though, I knew that for me such a course of action was wrong. There are few absolutes in this world, few things clearly black and white instead of shades of grey, but the sanctity of life, its incalculable value, and the natural desire to fight and live are one.

To the surprise of my doctors, not only have I fought cancer to a standstill, but in doing so I've been able to see my grandchildren grow and continue to share the joys and sorrows of normal family life. For a state to be in the business of incentivizing me to consider opting out prematurely is just insanity redefined as sanity.

Almost always, when speaking at campaign events in 2008, I closed by quoting one of the co-founders of the *Hemlock Society*, a man who incidentally has been accused of browbeating his first wife into committing suicide as the answer to her health challenges.

Derek Humphrey, one of the movement's few honest proponents, has said on several occasions that physician assisted suicide and euthanasia "will inevitably prevail in our society because they make economic sense."

If you believe that somehow there is a consensus definition as to what constitutes "quality of life" and what is an acceptable definition of "dignity," if you can trust government to compassionately establish criteria, and if you believe that life is defined in economic terms, then endorse tacitly or implicitly the selfishness of assisted suicide.

It is a slippery slope, however. I believe it to be morally, ethically, historically and legally wrong. It is a breach of faith with one's fellow human beings and it screams out that you think you are an island.

On March 21, 2012, I took another stab at this issue of life:

Been rolling "life matters" through my mind of late. I always do at this time of year because March marks the third anniversary of the implementation of Washington's physician assisted suicide law. I was among the leaders in the fight against Initative 1000 which allows doctor assisted suicide especially if one is deemed to have less than six months to live.

Though I consider myself strongly pro-life, I do recognize and believe the law should allow exceptional circumstances. One may talk principle, but if it is his or her daughter's life at stake they almost inevitably have a different view.

Life begins at conception: All one's possibilities are present in the embryonic child. There is a constitutional right to life and society has a responsibility to protect it, especially the weak, the infirm, the disabled, and the innocent.

One, however, also has a right to privacy. Despite the tragedy, in cases where the life of the mother is at stake, a woman's right to make that decision in consultation with her doctor trumps the child in the womb's right to life and society's interest in the child. It is simple self-defense and classically sanctioned by St. Augustine. You may take a life to save your own or those of others. There are few dads in the real world that are not glad the law recognizes their daughter's right to make that call.

Additionally, in cases of rape or incest, most dads are glad daughters have a right to choose, innocent though the child in the womb may be. It neither makes one happy or sad where I end up.

So how does society then, handle equally valid constitutional rights in conflict?

The answer is: Not well.

Protecting life should be and most often is an absolute value for society – the first law of the social contract. However, in reality, it is only an ideal because society in practice acts differently.

We sanction the right of a woman to kill her child in the womb, especially in the first 20 weeks before probable "fetal viability," but also after those first 20 weeks under the guise of it being within her reproductive freedom. We sanction the state to take the life of criminals convicted of heinous crimes. We sanction an individual to be able to prematurely kill themselves, and don't let suicide be listed on the death certificate. We sanction killer missile hits on American citizens outside this country, without the benefit of a trial, if we believe they are engaged in terrorism.

We are especially inconsistent with our views on abortion not being matched by our views on the death penalty.

All these, no matter how one dresses them up are legal murder.

The conclusion is inescapable: there are matters which defy being neatly defined in legislation. Have you ever noticed how the more carefully one tries to define all possible contingencies, the higher the probability of unintended consequences and exceptions arising? The Catholic Church for example, even has a "hierarchy of life" matrix.

Society should state as a goal but understand it is an ideal, the protection of life from conception to natural death. Society should also recognize it cannot legislate morality nor should it plunge ever deeper into trying to make moral distinctions regarding medical matters.

Individuals, families, and their doctors are the ones best involved in such personal matters.

Some things are best left unsaid, undefined and outside the political arena.

The passage of time and the seeming inability to find common ground on almost any aspect of the so called debate over life issues is disconcerting to one who believes in the importance of comity in society. Nor ought we allow emotional issues to become so contentious they cause us to view a differing viewpoint as evil. This is what is happening.

Compounding this, of course, is the internet social media phenomenon that enables one to find like minded people of the most aberrant views anywhere in the world. While the internet may be seen as a blessing for bringing us more together, it strikes me it also divides us like no other phenomenon as a vehicle that has in many cases further exacerbated the things that divide us.

The one issue that has prompted a shift in my views on abortion and life was the advent of the so called "morning after pill." Science and medicine at last brought the issue squarely away from fetal viability and, in effect, drilled down to the core issue of conception being the exact moment life begins.

The Catholic Church held that taking the morning-after pill was still tantamount to an abortion and rigidly holds the view that the embryo in the womb had been murdered. Weighing against that is the fact the body often prompts miscarriages of its own if the fetus is plagued with serious defects. Sometimes though, it carries to term a child with a strong heart but no brain, such as hydrocephalic babies. Does society truly want to play God in these instances or should it be content to leave such personal decisions to the individuals directly involved and their families, clergy and doctors?

And what if a rape victim believes she has conceived immediately and is in such a state of panic that a doctor refusing to prescribe her the morning after pill will be enough to put her over the edge into suicide? Does anyone let alone the doctor and pharmacist involved, want to play God in this instance also?

Nothing creates more conflict, controversy, and tragedy than a face-off between constitutional rights. Should the conflict itself not be a possible signal that this is an area where things are best left unsaid, undefined and outside of politics?

In historical terms and within the context of Idaho politics are there any conclusions or lessons one can draw from the some 40 year debate still raging on abortion and life issues? I think so.

Lesson 1) **Do not touch intensely personal issues**

Despite a strong slice of the state that says it's pro-life, the truth appears to be that the stronger support for a pure pro-life resides with primarily Republican men. Even these men, if the fathers of daughters, waffle if asked how they would feel if it was their own daughter's life, or their daughter who had been raped.

Idahoans abhor abortion on demand, but recognize the complexity of the issue and the exceptions. Truth be told, Bill Clinton captured the view of the majority of American's, and Idahoans, especially women, when he said abortion ought to be "safe, legal, and rare"

The two times Republicans in the Idaho Legislature have grabbed onto this divisive social issue, they have been badly burned in the next election.

Lesson 2) **Stick to your principles and be consistent**

The voter will cut one slack if he or she is consistent and does not appear to want it both ways. Nor will they punish an office seeker who shies away from hot-button social issues and remains focused on issues like education and job creation.

Lesson 3) **The issue is more than abortion or physician assisted suicide.**

It is one's attitude towards the whole gamut of life issues from conception to natural death. Of increasing importance is how it is dovetailing into the broader issue of health care costs.

Life issues and one's views towards their differing manifestations, especially at different times in the natural span of one's life, can be revealing about what one really thinks.

While we all want to think that protecting life is a basic absolute, our actions often belie this belief and secular society's culture of death continues.

Lesson 4) **We all should prepare for our own death.**

Sounds simple but few of us are. It goes beyond just taking care of one's will and filling out the pre-planning form a funeral home gives you. Each of us should talk with our loved ones about the end, what we have done to prepare, what we believe lies beyond if we are believers in the Afterlife, what we hope will happen for our children and grandchildren, what we think our legacy is or will be. Talking about death will in fact be comforting for all.

When all is said and done my message to my loved one especially, but also any who have taken the time to read these thoughts from Medimont is simply this: Trust God always; and in all ways.

APPENDIX A: Power Council Members

Idaho

Chris Carlson	April 8, 1981-January 1984 (Left late in 1981)
Robert Saxvik	April 8, 1981-January 1984
	January 1984-January 1987
	January 1987-January 1990
	January 1990-January 1993
	January 1993-replaced by Gov. Batt, Dec. 1994
W. Larry Mills	November 4, 1981-January 1984
	January 1984-January 1987
James A. Goller	February 1, 1987-January 1992
	January 1992-January 1995 (Resigned November 1992)
Jay Webb	February 1, 1993-January 15, 1995 (Resigned December 2, 1994)
Andy Brunelle	December 2, 1994-Dec. 31, 1994
Todd Maddock	January 15, 1995-January 15, 1998 (Finished Andy Brunelle's term)
	January 15, 1997-January 15, 2000
Mike Field	January 15, 1995-January 15, 1998
	January 15, 1998-May 13, 2001
Jim Kempton	January 1, 2001-January 31, 2003
	January 15, 2003-January 15, 2006
	January 15, 2006-January 15, 2009
Judi Danielson	May 14, 2001-January 31, 2004
W. Bill Booth	January 15, 2007-January 15, 2010
	January 15, 2010-January 15, 2013
James Yost	October 16, 2007-January 15, 2009
	January 16, 2009- January 15, 2015

Montana

Keith L. Colbo	April 1981-January 1984
	(Terms are at the pleasure of the governor)
Gerald Mueller	April 1981-January 1987
Morris Brusett	January 1985-January 1989

George Turman   January 1987-January 1989
John Brenden   January 1989-December1992
Stan Grace   January 1989-Sept. 2001
John Etchart   January 1993-December2000
Leo Giacometto   January 2001-March 2002
Ed Bartlett   October 2001-December2004
John Hines   March 2002-December 2004
Bruce Measure   January 2005 (reappointed in
Rhonda Whiting   January 2005 (reappointed in March 2009)
                     (resigned in January 2013)
Pat Smith   January 2013
Jennifer Anders   March 2013

Oregon
Leroy Hemmingway   April 14, 1987-January 15, 1983
                     January 15, 1983-January 15, 1986
Herb Schwab   April 13, 1981-January 15, 1984 (Left in 1982)
Alfred Hampson   February 1, 1982-January 15, 1984
Don Godard   January 16, 1984-January 15, 1987
Robert Duncan   January 16, 1984-January 15, 1989 (Left mid-1988)
Norma Paulus   February 4, 1987-January 15, 1990
Ted Hallock   June 17, 1988-January 15, 1989
                     January 16, 1989-January 15, 1992
                     January 15, 1992-January 15, 1995
                     (Replaced by Gov. Roberts with a term ending
                     December19, 1994)
Angus Duncan   January 16, 1990-January 15, 1993
                     January 16, 1993-January 15, 1996
                     (Resigned in Sept. 1995)
Joyce Cohen   December19, 1994-January 15, 1998
John Brogoitti   Sept. 16, 1995-January 15, 1996
                     January 16, 1996-January 15, 1999
                     January 16, 2000-January 15, 2002
Eric Bloch   April 10, 1998 (June 15)-January 15, 2001
                     January 16, 2001-January 1, 2003
                     (Left January 2003)
Gene Derfler   November 8, 2002-January 15, 2005
Melinda Eden   January 1, 2003
                     January 2004-January 2007
                     January 2007-January 2010
Joan Dukes   January 15, 2005-January 15, 2008
                     January 15, 2008-January 15, 2011
                     (Left July 31, 2012)
Bill Bradbury   January 3, 2011-January 15, 2014
Henry Lorenzen   August 1, 2012-January 15, 2015

Washington

Daniel J. Evans	April 26, 1981-January 15, 1984
	January 15, 1984-January 15, 1987
	(Left September 1983)
Charles Collins	April 26, 1981-January 15, 1984
	January 15, 1984-January 15, 1987
	(Left January 1986)
Kai N. Lee	October 1983-January 15, 1987
	January 16, 1987-January 15, 1990
	(Left November 20, 1987)
Tom Trulove	January 31, 1986-January 15, 1989
	January 9, 1989-January 15, 1992
	January 15, 1992-January 15, 1995
	(Replaced by Gov. Lowry, February 28, 1994)
R. Ted Bottiger	Nov. 2, 1987-January 15, 1990
	January 15, 1990-January 15, 1993
	January 15, 1993-January 15, 1996
	(Retired January 1995)
Ken Casavant	February 28, 1994-January 15, 1995
	January 15, 1995-January 15, 1998
	(Served until June 30, 1998)
Mike Kreidler	January 15, 1995-January 15, 1996
	January 15, 1996-January 15, 1999
Tom Karier	July 1, 1998-January 15, 2001
	January 16, 2001-January 15, 2004
	January 15, 2004-January 15, 2007
	January 16, 2007-January 15, 2010
	January 16, 2010-January 15, 2013
Frank L. Cassidy, Jr.	August 3, 1998-January 15, 1999
	January 16, 1999-January 15, 2002
	January 16, 2002-January 15, 2005
	January 16, 2005-January 15, 2008
Richard K. Wallace	January 15, 2008-July 1, 2011

APPENDIX B: Election Results: 1972 and 1974

Courtesy of the Idaho Secretary of State's office.

1972 Primary — U.S. Senate

Counties	Rep Hansen	Rep McClure	Rep Smylie	Rep Wegner	Dem Bowman	Dem Davis	Dem Johnson	Dem Park
ADA	4,340	11,882	7,037	6,528	1,654	1,424	3,297	2,941
ADAMS	49	329	78	71	42	72	89	109
BANNOCK	2,654	690	1,076	1,008	1,090	5,737	1,943	1,422
BEAR LAKE	835	158	288	22	99	447	132	220
BENEWAH	70	423	89	37	75	300	49	123
BINGHAM	2,080	761	631	987	301	1,167	515	769
BLAINE	261	233	174	342	184	230	163	362
BOISE	60	311	116	95	22	47	40	66
BONNER	251	1,462	263	284	250	756	343	705
BONNEVILLE	4,070	1,796	1,408	2,050	267	967	1,379	713
BOUNDARY	55	412	62	54	168	502	185	117
BUTTE	240	133	93	130	34	153	70	65
CAMAS	95	115	38	45	7	13	17	29
CANYON	2,052	7,353	2,352	4,150	298	487	888	821
CARIBOU	792	259	322	60	49	381	64	83
CASSIA	1,519	763	289	292	75	304	146	171
CLARK	92	102	52	33	6	11	10	17
CLEARWATER	29	130	69	48	354	671	235	476
CUSTER	179	274	57	75	39	119	69	81
ELMORE	298	726	241	265	126	287	193	500
FRANKLIN	960	468	337	27	24	330	42	41

FREMONT	1,215	262	218	168	45	426	168	158
GEM	253	892	288	703	139	195	167	288
GOODING	728	694	294	339	78	191	72	184
IDAHO	234	760	303	132	356	599	287	712
JEFFERSON	1,727	322	255	396	45	307	220	129
JEROME	1,051	821	284	508	27	176	48	119
KOOTENAI	381	2,516	462	196	825	1,134	1,376	1,582
LATAH	218	974	839	671	529	1,105	623	656
LEMHI	768	371	231	113	66	139	191	81
LEWIS	56	193	110	57	174	234	132	221
LINCOLN	351	190	99	157	14	52	30	83
MADISON	1,400	456	362	182	36	672	179	135
MINIDOKA	1,083	592	259	296	85	345	112	237
NEZ PERCE	318	595	1,074	739	637	1,305	646	791
ONEIDA	238	91	30	13	42	309	31	95
OWYHEE	173	631	111	232	40	73	51	125
PAYETTE	238	1,963	245	393	50	92	133	245
POWER	424	107	198	167	51	245	63	98
SHOSHONE	48	1,042	116	50	520	902	554	990
TETON	439	48	48	32	20	112	41	36
TWIN FALLS	2,786	2,962	1,151	2,071	232	682	306	434
VALLEY	69	393	242	170	61	108	86	124
WASHINGTON	233	867	206	194	91	145	141	282
TOTAL	35,412	46,522	22,497	24,582	9,327	23,953	15,526	17,636

1972 General   U.S. President

Counties	Rep Nixon	Dem McGovern	Amer Schmitz	P&F Spock	SW Jenness
ADA	36,665	12,687	4,727	184	48
ADAMS	963	293	162	3	0
BANNOCK	12,856	7,840	1,348	78	69
BEAR LAKE	2,213	716	251	3	2
BENEWAH	1,494	1,062	129	3	2
BINGHAM	6,886	2,476	1,312	22	9
BLAINE	2,113	1,240	97	12	3
BOISE	676	256	86	2	0
BONNER	4,405	2,599	632	19	10
BONNEVILLE	13,134	4,199	4,073	44	16
BOUNDARY	1,587	860	218	9	4
BUTTE	788	387	220	1	0
CAMAS	344	95	24	0	0
CANYON	18,383	5,630	2,769	54	21
CARIBOU	2,069	614	274	1	0
CASSIA	4,576	1,080	473	18	15
CLARK	339	64	52	0	1
CLEARWATER	1,590	1,412	112	14	10
CUSTER	989	274	166	3	0
ELMORE	3,078	1,153	382	10	2
FRANKLIN	2,787	611	490	5	0
FREMONT	2,621	819	825	4	1
GEM	2,717	1,069	637	6	2
GOODING	3,124	1,030	256	5	2
IDAHO	3,235	1,622	330	7	7
JEFFERSON	2,983	715	1,406	5	1
JEROME	3,661	888	316	8	1
KOOTENAI	9,958	5,162	1,076	33	9
LATAH	6,043	4,548	268	46	13
LEMHI	1,812	526	578	5	2
LEWIS	961	635	85	3	3
LINCOLN	1,120	313	66	6	1

MADISON	3,606	710	889	8	3
MINIDOKA	4,097	1,423	430	11	6
NEZ PERCE	6,232	5,081	433	143	52
ONEIDA	1,204	402	77	1	1
OWYHEE	1,630	463	229	0	2
PAYETTE	3,577	1,113	565	15	2
POWER	1,405	625	142	8	0
SHOSHONE	3,868	3,020	286	26	7
TETON	932	298	129	0	0
TWIN FALLS	13,075	3,344	1,127	62	65
VALLEY	1,324	537	280	7	3
WASHINGTON	2,264	935	442	9	2
TOTAL	**199,384**	**80,826**	**28,869**	**903**	**397**

	U.S. Senate		1st District		2nd District		
Rep	Dem	Amer	Rep	Dem	Rep	Dem	Amer
McClure	Davis	Stoddard	Symms	Williams	Hansen	Ludlow	Thiebert
28,628	25,184	873	24,691	16,430	8,171	4,383	297
880	517	12	856	488			
7,047	14,726	398			12,347	8,227	525
1,653	1,434	74			2,266	738	79
1,221	1,413	41	1,281	1,196			
5,131	5,262	483			7,322	2,989	402
1,504	1,859	28			2,029	1,174	36
607	398	6	601	366			
4,329	3,217	141	3,878	3,282			
11,316	9,569	759			15,032	5,201	1,241
1,545	1,084	40	1,318	1,166			
609	769	33			856	484	36
284	171	7			338	108	6
16,555	9,728	365	17,396	9,224			
1,728	1,074	90			2,096	652	86
3,982	2,042	168			4,782	1,104	211
301	143	12			330	86	17
1,101	2,026	53	1,025	2,098			
909	448	43			838	411	59
2,391	2,150	80			2,937	1,317	112
2,573	1,169	57			2,885	720	68
2,378	1,641	240			2,938	919	276
2,327	1,990	75	2,312	2,011			
2,514	1,757	86			2,919	1,122	94
2,650	2,426	33	2,631	2,296			
2,814	1,944	283			3,569	1,044	353
3,136	1,505	132			3,552	1,070	138
9,225	6,430	351	8,655	6,248			
3,985	6,926	93	4,536	6,253			
1,545	969	352			1,829	720	218
706	976	9	662	974			

939	512	28			1,030	367	29
3,106	1,905	253			4,066	845	300
3,393	2,344	134			4,105	1,382	144
3,740	8,058	134	3,885	7,942			
963	674	17			1,192	400	23
1,504	745	42	1,633	640			
3,440	1,699	81	3,338	1,653			
1,001	1,162	25			1,450	644	30
3,485	3,641	32	3,242	3,620			
754	566	28			983	320	27
10,758	6,201	576			12,675	3,654	753
1,080	965	42	1,164	867			
2,067	1,494	76	2,166	1,352			
161,804	**140,913**	**6,885**	**85,270**	**68,106**	**102,537**	**40,081**	**5,560**

1974 Primary			U.S. Senate			
	Dem	Dem	Rep	Rep	Rep	Amer
Counties	Church	Olson	Bolstridge	Smith	Winder	Stoddard
ADA	6,157	731	925	8,984	3,667	39
ADAMS	199	43	24	179	42	1
BANNOCK	7,041	1,694	142	1,649	443	12
BEAR LAKE	562	56	76	369	263	3
BENEWAH	787	205	11	105	39	0
BINGHAM	1,571	146	169	1,765	579	6
BLAINE	472	45	36	361	100	0
BOISE	166	27	18	194	54	0
BONNER	2,585	392	85	662	248	14
BONNEVILLE	2,521	292	451	5,821	1,317	19
BOUNDARY	656	142	12	206	39	0
BUTTE	305	38	17	267	45	0
CAMAS	63	3	10	118	25	0
CANYON	2,880	356	581	4,748	1,357	15
CARIBOU	418	61	68	463	228	1
CASSIA	546	70	74	1,245	463	15
CLARK	41	0	15	147	35	0
CLEARWATER	1,045	143	12	147	41	1
CUSTER	197	90	26	320	28	4
ELMORE	1,125	167	40	494	143	0
FRANKLIN	506	73	36	732	123	0
FREMONT	899	143	48	877	100	1
GEM	602	95	51	556	196	3
GOODING	579	70	55	842	163	1
IDAHO	1,377	478	18	502	75	0
JEFFERSON	714	116	88	1,224	247	1
JEROME	435	51	66	1,036	223	1

KOOTENAI	4,078	800	122	820	285	4
LATAH	2,276	252	80	712	247	6
LEMHI	194	62	89	940	174	20
LEWIS	557	109	6	99	21	1
LINCOLN	187	29	44	356	74	2
MADISON	1,554	312	57	878	188	8
MINIDOKA	653	71	57	939	230	3
NEZ PERCE	2,874	425	53	778	199	7
ONEIDA	496	60	22	115	128	0
OWYHEE	338	38	27	359	111	0
PAYETTE	533	55	52	718	161	0
POWER	310	24	41	205	129	2
SHOSHONE	2,512	598	39	281	90	1
TETON	208	18	24	306	65	1
TWIN FALLS	1,186	136	394	3,258	807	5
VALLEY	397	77	27	253	84	0
WASHINGTON	857	111	43	523	130	0
TOTAL	**53,659**	**8,904**	**4,331**	**45,553**	**13,406**	**197**

MEDIMONT REFLECTIONS ■ 253

	Governor				Lieutenant Governor			
Dem	Rep	Dem	Dem	Dem	Rep	Rep	Rep
Andrus	Murphy	Evans	Rigby	Solberg	Harwood	Kading	Ravenscroft
6,805	11,062	3,440	1,653	1,030	1,841	6,175	7,052
228	220	75	78	51	35	79	152
8,187	2,006	5,453	2,589	490	416	458	1,507
567	716	309	222	28	170	54	551
866	161	371	287	179	42	25	93
1,673	2,084	660	847	141	484	417	1,833
495	483	242	134	68	41	166	429
183	249	83	62	19	39	94	162
2,752	1,030	887	832	701	213	117	721
2,711	6,976	758	1,719	245	1,853	2,151	4,171
712	226	319	186	149	45	34	148
323	314	90	192	39	65	83	195
66	110	23	28	10	17	21	139
3,175	5,031	1,735	717	496	2,366	1,710	2,662
432	755	236	166	35	199	92	559
586	1,642	291	217	58	300	415	1,190
40	210	12	28	3	61	40	144
1,131	172	423	156	533	27	63	123
238	350	104	131	30	50	45	300
1,249	626	622	361	137	94	255	383
528	809	233	244	52	255	108	515
976	974	78	954	33	156	177	753
669	713	344	175	100	114	230	500
614	948	261	214	81	155	123	964
1,667	525	213	164	1,479	68	162	356
770	1,500	93	677	55	718	184	838
471	1,165	215	171	61	156	165	1,110
4,406	1,223	1,714	1,064	1,479	279	252	736

2,387	954	860	395	1,018	114	362	614	
229	1,120	75	106	43	172	249	876	
601	118	89	46	521	15	39	80	
207	419	64	87	31	32	73	438	
1,712	1,072	80	1,793	29	240	191	718	
694	1,044	322	261	90	172	209	902	
3,102	888	1,203	480	1,350	176	388	506	
484	243	518	39	5	80	48	139	
363	439	143	135	41	88	129	294	
571	858	245	139	117	170	276	518	
321	360	232	66	21	72	83	293	
2,767	426	1,133	1,094	552	84	108	229	
204	366	19	185	11	82	55	270	
1,236	3,421	470	344	249	760	930	3,422	
440	320	222	99	76	74	128	204	
940	622	350	286	161	122	176	429	
58,778	**54,950**	**25,309**	**19,823**	**12,097**	**12,712**	**17,339**	**38,218**	

1974 General				U.S. Representative			
	U.S. Senate			1st District		2nd District	
	Rep	Dem	Amer	Rep	Dem	Rep	Dem
Counties	Smith	Church	Stoddard	Symms	Cox	G. Hansen	Hanson
ADA	20,357	26,439	779	21,878	14,092	5,120	5,550
ADAMS	597	613	21	805	376		
BANNOCK	5,869	12,111	318			8,734	9,266
BEAR LAKE	1,150	1,395	49			1,573	950
BENEWAH	802	1,511	19	1,365	856		
BINGHAM	3,398	5,484	250			4,880	4,062
BLAINE	803	1,615	31			995	1,147
BOISE	529	721	15	777	405		
BONNER	2,241	4,350	121	3,350	3,064		
BONNEVILLE	7,539	9,215	335			8,544	8,177
BOUNDARY	1,022	1,302	21	1,361	927		
BUTTE	473	703	15			485	630
CAMAS	175	227	5			231	149
CANYON	11,614	10,428	263	15,096	7,005		
CARIBOU	1,095	1,205	64			1,397	838
CASSIA	2,893	2,212	229			3,552	1,688
CLARK	168	183	8			205	137
CLEARWATER	577	2,039	51	1,132	1,493		
CUSTER	711	428	22			575	504
ELMORE	1,169	2,311	45			1,397	1,723
FRANKLIN	1,794	1,441	100			2,137	1,098
FREMONT	1,649	1,832	37			2,030	1,254
GEM	1,722	2,046	61	2,274	1,444		
GOODING	1,899	1,803	61			1,912	1,480
IDAHO	1,970	2,276	56	2,498	1,690		
JEFFERSON	2,359	1,901	103			2,611	1,394
JEROME	2,252	1,693	63			2,298	1,283
KOOTENAI	4,741	7,952	104	7,042	5,578		
LATAH	2,157	6,438	121	3,775	4,787		

LEMHI	1,150	905	222			1,311	838
LEWIS	439	914	26	658	642		
LINCOLN	696	628	29			731	505
MADISON	2,178	2,463	103			3,048	1,620
MINIDOKA	2,280	2,392	144			2,747	1,983
NEZ PERCE	2,558	6,928	158	4,147	5,331		
ONEIDA	671	734	38			736	653
OWYHEE	926	994	21	1,347	537		
PAYETTE	1,846	2,114	66	2,552	1,333		
POWER	601	1,271	32			941	798
SHOSHONE	1,534	3,662	47	2,328	2,742		
TETON	527	623	17			734	386
TWIN FALLS	7,794	6,778	303			8,350	5,486
VALLEY	772	1,053	23	1,108	637		
WASHINGTON	1,375	1,807	39	1,911	1,062		
TOTAL	**109,072**	**145,140**	**4,635**	**75,404**	**54,001**	**67,274**	**53,599**

Acknowledgments

Writing a book of essays on issues I'd either covered as a reporter or worked on as a staff member, and incorporating thoughts on other dynamic and interesting political personalities I encountered along the way proved to be more difficult than I originally imagined. My first thought had been to take some of the early columns I'd written from D.C. and update them by saying where the issues were now some 40 years later.

It was not that simple, however. Most matters still remaining on the docket, had to be approached cautiously and with the broad perspective 40 years in the arena can bring. Certainly there was a tendency 40 years ago to want to see things in black and white, good guys vs. bad guys, and the desire to succinctly explain complex matters, leading me to oversimplify.

With the perspective of experience and time the truth of A. Bartlett Giamatti's saying I have framed above the desk in my study/library resonates ever more strongly:

"As I think back and look forward, I see how nothing is straightforward, nothing is unambiguous. Salvation does not come through simplicities, either of sentiment or system. The gray, grainy complex nature of existence and the ragged edges of our lives as we lead them defy hunger for a neat, bordered existence and for spirits unsullied by doubt or despair."

It should come as no surprise either that the first person I must acknowledge and thank is of course the man who gave me the opportunity to experience and grow exponentially, the one who invited me to take a run at public service working with him to achieve some worthy goals. That I somehow had enough smarts to hitch my star to his will always remain a mystery to me, but next to marrying my wife it was and still is the smartest move I ever made.

Thanks, Cece, for inviting me along and tolerating my slow learning curve.

As with the previous book, I want to thank Dan Hammes, the publisher of the *St. Maries Gazette-Record*, for letting me share his weekly platform, the editorial page of his excellent weekly newspaper. Having a print outlet for one's views does somehow seem to legitimize one more than just having pontifications appear in a personal blog.

Hammes' cheerful challenge to my views keeps me thinking and helps to keep me honest. I deeply appreciate his support and friendship. Two members of his staff were also of indispensable help and I want to thank them for so much time and effort: Kaisie Brede and Jamie Sloper. Kaisie helped integrate the numerous photos and produce the digital text while Jamie once again came up with a fine cover design. Thanks too to reporters Mary Orr and Summer Crosby.

Special thanks should also go to A.L. "Butch" Alford, Jr., the retired publisher emeritus of the *Lewiston Tribune*. The *Trib* was the first Idaho daily newspaper to see value in a column from Washington, D.C. Butch has been a friend ever since and was glad to lobby his son, the *Trib*'s publisher today, Nathan Alford, and the editorial page editor, Marty Trillhaase, to start reprinting my column from St. Maries. I will always be grateful for his support, friendship, and wise counsel.

Special thanks to longtime *Tribune* photographer Barry Kough, who granted us full access to his many fine photos, and whose work added greatly to this project. Other photographers who should be thanked include David Frazier, Steve Lee and Marcia Carlson, as well as the College of Idaho.

Jay Shelledy once again did me the courtesy of reviewing the text and providing numerous invaluable editing tips, most of which I accepted. His counsel on the wisdom of including or dropping a couple of sections was also well-taken. Thanks also to my former partner at The Gallatin Group, Marc Johnson, for his review of the text and some useful observations on text and context.

Special mention should also be made of my wheat farmer friend from Washtucna, Brett Blankenship, with whom I had a vigorous debate regarding the chapter on dam breaching. I thank him for being such a worthy foil. Special thanks also to Marty Peterson, a long-time friend going back to the early days of both our associations with Governor Andrus. A fine student of Idaho history, he was the source of several anecdotes and provided excellent input into several chapters.

I wish also to acknowledge and thank for his encouragement and support of this book, its publisher, Randy Stapilus, owner of Ridenbaugh Press. He quickly grasped what I was trying to do and say with this project but turned it into a much better product than I originally envisioned. His advice and counsel along the way has always been spot on. His chief editor, Linda Watkins, was also helpful with her good questions following a careful read of the near final text. Randy too is a master of Idaho political history and that he saw real promise in this project was most gratifying.

I also want to thank Betsie Kimbrough, the chief of the Elections Division in the Office of Secretary of State Ben Ysursa. She patiently fielded all my requests for voting abstracts from various elections referenced in the text and put the results into an Excel spread sheet for easy transfer to Appendix B.

Finally, as always, thanks to my number one supporter and best critic, my dear wife, Marcia. She reads most everything I write and almost always is deadly accurate when she makes a suggestion.

Thanks to all named as well as unnamed, for your assistance in producing a hopefully enjoyable and informative read.

The Author

Chris Carlson has a "checkered past." Born in Kellogg some 66 years ago, the eldest son of two school teachers, the family moved to the Spokane Valley when he was ten.. During teenage summers he held a variety of jobs, from being the town dry cleaner in Salmon to opening old collapsed mine tunnels near Idaho's Big Horn Crags to working in the woods of north Idaho as a choke-setter and tree-faller.

He graduated from Central Valley High School in 1965 and attended Columbia on a scholarship where he received his B.A. in three years by taking the maximum course loads allowed and attending summer school. He majored in English Literature and minored in Comparative Religions. Upon graduation in May of 1968 and facing the prospect of the draft, he took ten education credits at Gonzaga which qualified him for an Idaho provisional teaching certificate. He secured a position teaching 8th and 9th grade classes at Kootenai Junior-Senior High School and also coached the junior varsity basketball team.

In the fall of 1969 he began work on his M. A. in English Literature at Idaho State University where he also taught two sections of Freshman Composition each semester. Planning to marry in June of 1970 and needing more money he secured an additional full-time job as the political and education reporter for Pocatello's daily newspaper, the Idaho State Journal. Completing his M.A. in just one academic year, he decided to pursue a journalism career and worked for six short months for the Spokane Daily Chronicle.

In January of 1970 he became the chief correspondent in Washington, D.C., for the Anchorage Daily News. While there he also began writing a weekly political column carried by five newspapers in his native Idaho. After two years he began a thus far life-long association with Idaho Governor Cecil D. Andrus, and returned to Idaho to become the governor's press secretary. Five years later he returned to Washington, D.C., as the Assistant Secretary of the Interior for Public Affairs when Andrus became Interior Secretary during the presidency of Jimmy Carter.

In January of 1981 Governor John Evans named him to the newly created Northwest Power Planning Council. In November, he resigned to begin his private sector career, first as vice president of The Rockey Company, a Seattle-based public relations firm, where he set up the firm's public affairs division.

In November of 1984 he was lured back to Spokane by the then area's largest private employer, Kaiser Aluminum, which made him the vice president for northwest public affairs. In January of 1989 he left to be the founding partner and open the Spokane office of what would become the region's largest independent public affairs firm, The Gallatin Group, with offices in Boise, Seattle, Portland and Helena as well as Spokane.

Upon leaving the governorship in January of 1995, Cecil Andrus, with whom he remained associated, accepted his offer to join The Gallatin Group as a Senior Of Counsel and operate from the firm's Boise office.

In 1999, Chris was diagnosed with Parkinson's disease which mercifully has moved very slowly and is still confined to his left side. He continued to run the Spokane office and serve on Gallatin's board. In November of 2005, however, he was diagnosed with late Stage IV carcinoid neuroendocrine cancer and given six months to live. The world's premier hospital for this form of cancer, Houston's M.D. Anderson, after looking at his CAT scans and MRI's, refused to see him to give a second opinion. He then turned to the Huntsman Cancer Institute at the University of Utah in Salt Lake City where he underwent a series of chemoembolization procedures including an experimental last one in which radioactive pellets were placed on the remnants of shattered tumors on his liver. He also receives a monthly sandostatin shot. For whatever reason his cancer stabilized and he is still here defying the odds.

He took a medical disability retirement from his firm but has remained active in the public arena. He chaired the 2008 campaign in Washington state against Initiative 1000, the doctor assisted suicide measure. He writes a weekly political column carried by three papers and two blog sites in Idaho. He is the author of Cecil Andrus: Idaho's Greatest Governor and Medimont Reflections, a book of essays on other notable Idahoans and issues he has dealt with over a 40 year career.

He and his wife of 43 years, Marcia, reside at Medimont on Cave Lake. They have four adult children and two grandchildren and attend St. Mary's Catholic Church in St. Maries.

from
RIDENBAUGH PRESS
www.ridenbaughpress.com

A FREE OFFER

Mention your purchase of this book, and we'll send you the next three editions of the Idaho Weekly Briefing for free.

Just send an email to stapilus@ridenbaugh.com

Order more copies of this book

of **Medimont** directly from the publisher. You can also order copies of Chris Carlson's earlier book, Andrus: Idaho's Greatest Governor.

You can order from us on our main page at www.ridenbaugh.com

Or, by e-mail at stapilus@ridenbaugh.com

Reach us by phone at (503) 852-0010; or by paper mail at Ridenbaugh Press, P.O. 852, Carlton OR 97111.

IDAHO WEEKLY BRIEFING Our weekly e-mailed report, every Monday morning, on Idaho and how it is changing. Since 1990.

Name _____

Address _____

City _____ State _____ Zip _____

Email _____